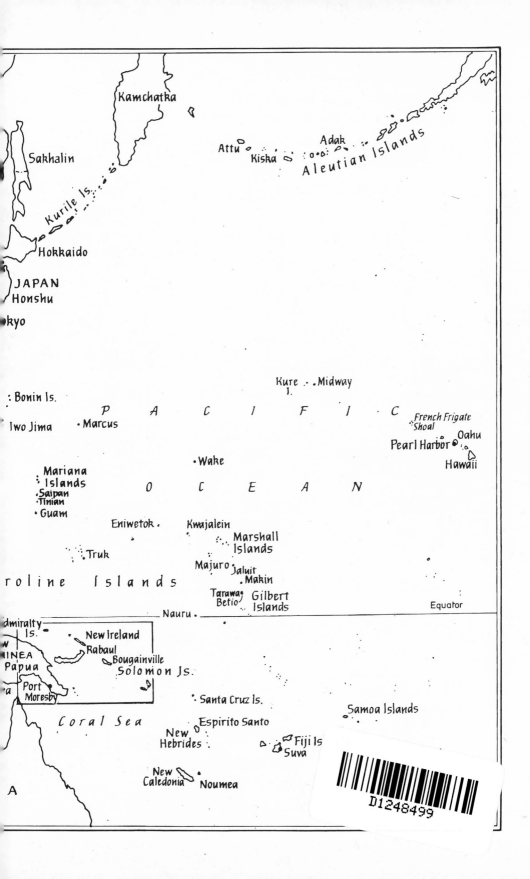

ULTRA IN THE PACIFIC

Other works by John Winton:

FICTION

We Joined The Navy
We Saw The Sea
Down The Hatch
Never Go To Sea
All The Nice Girls
HMS Leviathan
The Fighting Temeraire
One Of Our Warships
Good Enough For Nelson
Aircraft Carrier
The Good Ship Venus
A Drowning War
Polaris Fears and Dreams

NON-FICTION

Freedom's Battle: The War at Sea 1939–1945
The Forgotten Fleet
The Little Wonder: The Story of the Festiniog Railway
Sir Walter Raleigh
Air Power at Sea 1939–1945
Hurrah For the Life Of A Sailor: Life on the Lower Deck of the Victorian
    Navy
The Victoria Cross At Sea
War In The Pacific: Pearl Harbor to Tokyo Bay
Sink The Haguro!
Hands To Action Stations!: Naval Poetry and Verse of WW2
Find, Fix And Strike: The Fleet Air Arm at War 1939–1945
Below The Belt: Novelty, Subterfuge and Surprise in Naval Warfare
Jellicoe
Captains & Kings: The Royal Navy & The Royal Family 1901–1981
Convoy: The Defence of Sea Trade 1890–1980
The Death Of The Scharnhorst
Air Power at Sea: 1945 to Today
Warrior: The First and the Last
The Little Wonder: 150 Years of the Festiniog Railway (Revised edition)
Carrier Glorious: The Life and Death of an Aircraft Carrier
Ultra at Sea
The Naval Heritage of Portsmouth
For Those in Peril: Fifty Years of Royal Navy Search and Rescue

ULTRA IN THE PACIFIC:

How Breaking Japanese Codes & Cyphers Affected Naval Operations Against Japan

1941–45

BY

JOHN WINTON

NAVAL INSTITUTE PRESS

ANNAPOLIS, MARYLAND

Published and distributed in the United States of America
and Canada
by the Naval Institute Press,
118 Maryland Avenue, Annapolis,
Maryland 21402–5035

Library of Congress Catalog Card Number 93–85345
ISBN 1–55750–856–9

Printed in Great Britain

CONTENTS

ACKNOWLEDGEMENTS

A great many people, all over the world, have helped me write this book. I would particularly like to thank: Dr Dean Allard, Chief of Naval History, and the staff in the Navy Yard, Washington DC; Mr John Costello; Mr Hugh Denham, of Cheltenham; Mr Jim Dixon, of Sale; Dr Ed Drea, of Washington, DC; Mr Colin Hanson, of Heretaunga, New Zealand; Vice Admiral Sir Arthur Hezlet, KBE CB DSO★ DSC; Mr Stephen Howarth; Mr Vic Jaynes, of Wellington, New Zealand; Mr David Kahn; Mr Tom Lewis, of Darwin, Australia; Mr Dale Ridder, of Zion, Illinois; Rear Admiral Malcolm Searle CB CBE; Lt Cdr John Somerville, CB CBE RN; Lt Cdr David Stevens RAN, of Fadden, Australia; Mr Alan Stripp, of Cambridge; Mr John E. Taylor and the staff of the Modern Military Reference Branch, Textual Reference Division, National Archives and Records Administration, Washington DC; Captain Mervyn Wingfield, DSO DSC★, and Mr Eddie Yeghiayan, of the University of California, Irvine, CA. Also for their great hospitality in Washington DC, Captain Ray Wallace US Navy, and Martha, and Professor Mario Werner M.D. and Elsbeth.

I

DISASTER IN THE EAST:
PEARL HARBOR AND AFTER

'ADMIRAL Nimitz asked me a question, and I would look over there and see four stars. I would answer that to the best of my ability I was sure of my facts, but stressed that they were only deductions. I could not have blamed him if he had not accepted my estimates. I think, looking back, that it was obvious when Nimitz sent for me that he had already decided on his course of action. His operational orders were set and the matter closed. My appearance at this final staff meeting was to ensure that everyone was thinking alike.'

So said Captain Joseph J. Rochefort, US Navy, recalling, many years after the war, a meeting held at Pearl Harbor on 27 May, 1942. Rochefort was then a Lieutenant Commander, the head of Station HYPO, the US Navy's Combat Intelligence Center, covering the 14th Naval District, based at Pearl Harbor.

Rochefort's audience was a daunting one: Admiral Chester W. Nimitz, Commander-in-Chief, Pacific Fleet, and almost his entire operational staff. The meeting had begun inauspiciously. Rochefort was half an hour late and arrived, dishevelled and bleary-eyed from lack of sleep, to an icy stare from the C-in-C, who did not like being kept waiting. Lieutenant Commander Edwin T. Layton, Nimitz's Intelligence Officer and Joe Rochefort's friend, was looking anxiously at his watch. Several senior staff officers were wearing impatient 'Come on, convince us' expressions.

Rochefort apologized for his lateness, explaining that he had been reviewing last-minute intelligence. Then he began.

What he had to say was nothing less than HYPO's appreciation of the probable Japanese Order of Battle for the major naval operation which everybody knew was now impending in the central Pacific. For weeks past Rochefort and the HYPO staff had been studying decrypts and translation of the Japanese messages which poured in every day from all over the world, analysing traffic patterns, identifying and locating the originators of call signs, weighing up the importance of one message against another.

Joe Rochefort himself had been their guiding spirit and inspiration. He had an amazing memory for names, signals and dates. He never forgot a detail, no matter how unimportant it had seemed at the time. Like Autolycus, he was a snapper-up of unconsidered trifles. He had an eerie knack of putting together seemingly unrelated items of information and revealing their true, unsuspected significance. He could sniff out the enemy's long-term intentions with a brilliant sense of intuition which almost amounted to genius.

Rochefort had already decided that the main Japanese objective was Midway, not Hawaii or the Panama Canal, as Washington believed, nor California, as the US Army thought. Now, he told the meeting that the Japanese carriers would probably attack on the morning of 4 June, from the north-west, on a bearing of 325 degrees from Midway. He could even predict where and when they would launch their aircraft: about 175 miles north-west of Midway, at around 0700 local time.

The outcome was that the United States Navy, with the Marines on Midway Island, won a smashing strategic victory, to rank with Salamis and Lepanto. On Sunday morning, 7 June, Nimitz called another staff meeting, to which he again invited Rochefort. 'This officer deserves a major share of the credit for the victory at Midway,' Nimitz told the meeting. The estimate, Nimitz said with a smile, of where and when the Japanese carriers would launch was 'only five minutes, five degrees and five miles out!' Joe Rochefort and his HYPO team had brought off what was arguably the greatest intelligence *coup* in all naval history.

They also removed for ever any lingering feelings in some quarters of the US Navy's establishment that Communications Intelligence, all this electronic 'spying', was unseemly, where it was not actually a waste of time and effort. 'Gentlemen did not read each other's mail,' and, anyway, 'Who needs all that Comint crap? Much good it did us at Pearl Harbor!'

The Japanese air attack on Pearl Harbor on Sunday 7 December, 1941, was a shocking blow to the self-esteem of the entire American nation. There was an understandable desire to hunt down those who were held to be to blame. Admiral Husband E. Kimmel, C-in-C of the Pacific Fleet, and General Walter C. Short, the Army Commander at Pearl Harbor, were obvious scapegoats and were duly treated as such.

Admiral Kimmel took on his shoulders the main burden of responsibility for Pearl Harbor, just as the captain is ultimately answerable

2

for everything that happens to his ship. 'Immediately after Pearl Harbor,' Kimmel said later, 'I felt that, no matter how hard and how conscientiously I had tried, I had not been smart enough, and to that extent, must accept blame for Pearl Harbor.'

However, Kimmel expected to be given another assignment. He certainly did not expect to be so severely criticized by the Roberts Commission that he would feel compelled to offer his resignation by the end of January, 1942. But, as the several seemingly interminable Pearl Harbor enquiries and investigations dragged on over the years, it began to emerge that Kimmel was much more offended against than offending. When he discovered the truth, he was justifiably angry. 'Since learning that definite information of the Japanese intentions to attack the United States was in the hands of the War and Navy Departments and was not supplied to me,' he said in December, 1944, 'I now refuse to accept any responsibility for the catastrophe.'

The truth was that there had been plenty of intelligence in the months before Pearl Harbor which, with hindsight, can clearly be shown to have revealed Japanese intentions. The failure, if it was a failure, was in evaluating that intelligence and thereafter promulgating it to the operational commanders at Pearl Harbor.

Understandably, the feeling of personal failure after Pearl Harbor was especially keen among the naval intelligence community. Layton, who had been Kimmel's Intelligence Officer, expected to be relieved and sent back to the States. He asked Nimitz if he could go to sea in command of a destroyer, but Nimitz said, 'You can kill more Japs here than you ever could in command of a destroyer flotilla'. Like other officers at Pearl Harbor, Layton was surprised and grateful to find that Nimitz was not going to carry out a witch-hunt against Kimmel's staff.

Rochefort, who had been at Pearl Harbor since June, 1941, also felt personally responsible, believing that it was an intelligence officer's purpose to inform his commander of enemy intentions. 'I took it as my job,' he said, 'my task, my assignment that I was to tell the Commander-in-Chief today what the Japanese were going to do tomorrow.'

Station HYPO, the communications intelligence center on Oahu Island, renamed 'Combat Intelligence Center' at Rochefort's insistence for security reasons, was one of three US Navy Communications Intelligence Centers – the others being Station NEGAT in Washington DC and Station CAST at Cavite in the Philippines. It had begun as a one-man organization in 1936 and grew steadily to become the CIC of the Joint Intelligence Center, Pacific Ocean Area.

'Combat Intelligence' eventually had so many meanings it became virtually meaningless. But the CIC was originally intended to obtain information on, and maintain a plot of, all vessels, Allied as well as German and Japanese, in the Pacific. In time, under Captain Rochefort, it evolved into a complex and subtle organization evaluating and interpreting all forms of Radio Intelligence.

On the morning of 7 December, 1941, CIC became the clearing house for all manner of reports, almost all completely unfounded, of enemy activity. One of the most difficult peacetime problems in training intelligence personnel was the impossibility of simulating a flow of detailed, apparently well-authenticated, *mis*information.

In the first forty-eight hours after Pearl Harbor the CIC had a flood of misinformation which left them ever afterwards with a healthy mistrust of 'eyewitness' accounts, not only from excited civilians but also from experienced Service personnel, both Allied and enemy.

Japanese parachute troops were reported to have landed and to be engaged in a fierce pitched battle with US Marines. The uniforms worn by these mythical Japanese were described in the most minute sartorial detail. Strange vessels were reported arriving offshore, a large enemy fleet had been seen south of the islands and at least one Direction/Finding bearing (later judged to be ambiguous and inconclusive) was obtained. One officer sighted a dirigible over Honolulu, two degrees to the right of the moon and three degrees below it. To make matters more confusing, there were seemingly improbable reports of submarines in Pearl Harbor – but Japanese submarines did indeed take part in the attack.

In the earliest, defensive, stages of the war in the Central Pacific, radio intelligence was not just the most important source of intelligence; it was, for all practical purposes, the only source. There were no photographs of enemy-held positions. There were very few captured enemy documents and even fewer enemy prisoners-of-war. Apart from the Solomons and New Britain, spies and coast-watchers supplied no important intelligence.

Radio Intelligence embraced the interception and exploitation of all enemy radio transmissions which might yield intelligence, including the decryption of coded enemy messages; direction finding (D/F); navigational beacons and aids; enemy radar and infra-red transmissions; traffic analysis, which was the study of communications networks and the procedures, signals, callsigns and plain language messages passing over them; the monitoring of enemy radio broadcasts to the civilian population; and such refinements as the study of the types and peculiarities of particular transmitters and of the idiosyncratic morse characteristics of individual operators.

Fortunately for the Allies, distances in the Pacific were vast – by 1942 the perimeter of the area Japan had conquered was between 3000 and 4000 miles from Tokyo and overland or undersea communications, such as cable, telephones and telex, were scarce or non-existent. Thus the Imperial Japanese Navy routinely generated a huge amount of radio traffic. Again because of the distances involved, much of it was transmitted by High Frequency which was detectable at long ranges by a ring of listening stations down the west coast of the United States, in the Aleutians and Australia and, before the war, at Cavite, Guam, Shanghai and Peking.

The most valuable radio intelligence was obtained from the interception and decryption of encoded or encyphered enemy messages. The Japanese themselves regarded their language as a sacred mystery, not to be vouchsafed to outsiders. Japanese hearing for the first time a Westerner speak their language were known to shake their heads disbelievingly. Such a thing was not possible; they must be dreaming.

Learning to speak or read Japanese was in itself a formidable challenge to western minds. To unravel Japanese *in code* would seem a virtually impossible mental obstacle. In fact, many Allied cryptanalysts found that decyphering Japanese was a matter of persistence, of 'quantity and time rather than difficulty'. It was, if anything, tedious rather than difficult.

That is not to say that the task was easy. Whereas the Germans used versions of the Enigma machine for encyphering virtually all Kriegsmarine, Wehrmacht, Luftwaffe, SS, police and diplomatic signal traffic, the Japanese used many different crypto systems. An operational history of Japanese naval communications from December, 1941–August, 1945, compiled under Allied direction by former Japanese officers who had served during the war, lists three naval code books for strategic and administrative use; six naval code books, a joint Army-Navy code book and a Combined Fleet special code book, for tactical use; for intelligence, an overseas secret telegraph code book, two more naval code books, and five variations of a code distributed to naval officers appointed pre-war as intelligence agents stationed in Europe, the Americas and all over the Far East, and a 'New Code Book' for naval officers stationed on the west coast of the USA; five code books for communications with service branches

5

outside the Japanese Navy, such as merchant ships over 1,000 tons and fishing vessels, and a standard code book used by the Navy, Army and Foreign Ministries, distributed to diplomatic officials stationed in East Asia and principal Navy and Army headquarters. There were also other publications such as books of abbreviations, address codes and call signs, and books of visual signals.

The US Navy's Code and Signal Section was designated OP-20-G (naval communications was OP-20 and the cryptographic unit was listed alphabetically as G). In the early days the US Navy's cryptographic offensive was fragmented. According to Layton, there was a lack of coordination, sometimes amounting to furious acrimony, between the Offices of Naval Communications and Naval Intelligence. This atmosphere of inter-office feuding undoubtedly contributed to the failures in liaison and other mistakes made before Pearl Harbor.

OP-20-G had made considerable progress in breaking Japanese codes between the wars, but on 1 November, 1938, apparently because the Japanese naval commander in China had warned that their high-grade administrative codes were no longer secure, the Japanese introduced a new cypher system, designated 'AD' by OP-20-G.

The task of breaking into this system was given to HYPO at Pearl Harbor. In November, 1940, after a year's painstaking efforts, 'AD' was beginning to yield and produce intelligible text when the Japanese made another major change. The new system, designated 'NL', appeared to be circulated only to flag officers and was thus known as the 'Flag Officers' Code'. It was used very sparingly, few intercepts were obtained, and in fact the 'Flag Officers' Code' was never effectively penetrated.

While HYPO was wrestling in vain with the 'Flag Officers' Code', the US Navy's main cryptanalytical assault was directed against a new 'Operations Code', designated 'AN' by OP-20-G and Naval Code Book (D) by the Japanese, which was first introduced on 1 June, 1939.

This 'AN' code, a numerical system radically different from any other code so far used by the Japanese Navy, was later designated JN-25 (Japanese Navy code No. 25) by OP-20-G. JN-25, with later versions and new additions, was to be widely used by the Japanese Navy throughout the war and carried an estimated 70 per cent of traffic. By mid-1941 it had become the Japanese Navy's principal operational code system.

The first JN-25 decrypts were broken in November, 1940, and the initial 'A' version of the code, which had then been in use for some eighteen months, was solved by the end of the year. But this version was superseded, on 1 December, 1940, by a new 'B' version.

The change in JN-25 was accompanied by other drastic Japanese code changes at the end of 1940. The Japanese, like other navies, made the mistake of giving merchant shipping traffic a low-grade code, so their Naval Code Book (S) for merchantmen was '99 per cent readable'. But otherwise OP-20-G was unable to read anything of the main Japanese naval systems until well into 1941 and was only able partially to read JN-25B before war broke out.

OP-20-G continued to reserve the main attack on JN-25 to themselves, although CAST in the Philippines was permitted to work on it from April, 1941. Meanwhile, HYPO was condemned to go on battering fruitlessly at the brick wall of the 'Flag Officers' Code' during the final critical months before the war began. Thus Rochefort, the US Navy's most able exponent, both linguistically and cryptanalytically, was denied the chance to work on a crucial code which contained many clues to the operational aspects of the attack on Pearl Harbor. Properly handled and promulgated, information from JN-25 intercepts could, in Layton's opinion, have averted the catastrophe.

Information gained from decrypts of high-grade Japanese Navy and Army codes such as JN-25, and from other sources such as traffic analysis and captured enemy documents, was given the name of 'Special Intelligence' and, in mid-1941, the codename ULTRA.

As the war went on, the flow of ULTRA swelled like some great tidal wave, giving accurate and timely information on every aspect of the Japanese war effort, from the strategic to the domestic – not only Japanese war intentions, but individual ships' machinery defects and junior officers' promotions. The number of signals involved was enormous: the National Archives and Research Administration (NARA) in Washington DC has 290,908 decrypts of Japanese Navy signals on file, as well as many more thousands of naval attaché signal decrypts, intelligence summaries and daily digests.

ULTRA provided information broadly in four main categories. There was information of critical operational value, such as convoy sailings, warship movements, impending attacks, tactics and battle orders for on-going operations, which was directly applicable to current operations and provided in time for action to be taken on it. There was information of strategic value, such as intelligence of future operations, supplies, reserves, reinforcements and current strategy; on orders of battle, including the strengths, equipment and disposition of ships, aircraft and troops; and on Japanese intelligence, such as the results of Japanese spy activity, interrogations of Allied prisoners-of-war, captures of Allied documents, and the Japanese' own traffic analysis, reconnaissance, and interceptions and decrypts of Allied signals.

Special arrangements were made for handling ULTRA. It was revealed only to certain Flag and Senior Officers and selected members of their staffs who had been 'indoctrinated' into the secret. When Arleigh ('Thirty-one Knot') Burke was Chief of Staff to Admiral Mitscher in the carrier *Lexington* in 1944, he was at first curious and finally angered by the mysterious behaviour of a junior naval reserve Lt (jg) who, alone of everyone on board, was allowed private and privileged access to the Admiral. Burke would see the two talking in low voices on the wing of the Admiral's bridge, or sometimes withdrawing into the privacy of the Admiral's sea cabin.

The officer was Charles Sims, Mitscher's ULTRA intelligence officer, a Japanese language specialist trained in codebreaking, who gave Mitscher highly classified intelligence available through ULTRA. Burke himself was eventually admitted into the ULTRA secret, despite Sims' protests, but not until special permission had been sought from CincPac.

The US Navy, unlike the Royal Navy, permitted the use of the word ULTRA in the text of signals. They regularly used some phrase such as 'This is ULTRA', but not habitually at the beginning of a signal, which would render it vulnerable to cryptanalytical attack, but always somewhere in the body of the text.

When information from an ULTRA source was passed on in another signal, that signal had to be paraphrased and so worded that, if captured or intercepted by the enemy, any reference to enemy intelligence could not be traced back to ULTRA. Any reference to the name of an enemy ship was to be avoided and any positions taken from an ULTRA signal had to be given in a different way.

ULTRA was so powerful a weapon that it often could not be used. Much of the information it provided could not be acted upon. Too many U-boats sunk at their remote fuelling rendezvous, for instance, would arouse enemy suspicions and imperil the ULTRA secret. Any operation undertaken as a result of ULTRA therefore had to have a 'cover story' – some corroboration from another source, such as naval or air reconnaissance, to account for the presence of Allied forces on the scene and at the time of the action. It was very easy, through an excess of zeal, especially in the Pacific, to make mistakes over this vital requirement.

But, in the early days in the Pacific, the best intelligence in the world could not have stemmed the tide of Japanese victories. Pearl Harbor was quickly followed by more disasters. Guam fell on 10 December, the day General Homma's XIV Army began the conquest of the Philippines with a landing on Batan Island, in the north of the archipelago, and followed with a landing on south Luzon on 12th and a major landing at Lingayen Gulf on 20 December. On Christmas Eve, Homma's army landed at Lamon Bay. General MacArthur's original plan to defeat the Japanese on the beaches had failed and he decided upon a retreat to the Bataan Peninsula and a fight to the last ditch.

Wake Island was attacked on 8 December and an invasion force arrived off the island on the 11th, but the US Marine garrison, never more than 500 strong, put up tremendous resistance, shooting down twenty-one Japanese aircraft and sinking two Japanese destroyers, the first Japanese warships to be sunk in surface action in the war.

When another Japanese invasion force arrived on 22 December, the last defending US Marine fighter was shot down and the garrison's situation was desperate. Help, including the aircraft carrier *Saratoga*, was actually on the way, but Admiral Pye, a very cautious man who commanded the US Pacific Fleet in the interregnum period between 17 December, when Kimmel was relieved of active duty, and Nimitz assuming command on 31st, decided there was no hope of relieving Wake and ordered the relief force to turn back.

That news was received with great bitterness at Pearl Harbor, where the US Navy's morale sank lower than ever. Wake Island surrendered on 23 December, 1941. (The US Marine prisoners-of-war on Wake went on hoping against hope that they would be rescued until they were taken away from the island on 12 January, 1942.)

The Japanese conquest seemed to gain momentum in the New Year of 1942. The priceless strategic position of Rabaul in New Britain was taken on 23 January. The Japanese advanced south-westwards in a rapid succession of amphibious operations, each one an advance of about 400 miles – never further than shore or carrier aircraft could give cover: Sarawak on 23 December, Brunei on 6 January, Tarakan on the 10th, Jesselton on the 11th, Balikpapan on the 24th, Kendari in the Celebes on the 24th, Makassar on 9 February, Timor on the 20th, moving always towards the final objective of Java.

In the Philippines, Homma broke through decisively on 29 December and began to drive the surviving American and Filipino forces back down towards the Bataan peninsula. Station CAST had already moved from the naval base at Cavite to the off-shore island fortress

9

of Corregidor in December, 1941. Now, it was decided by Admiral Ernest J. King, formerly the C-in-C Atlantic Fleet, who had been appointed Commander-in-Chief US Fleet (titled COMINCH from March, 1942) on 20 December, 1941, that all the Station's personnel must be evacuated. If any of them fell into Japanese hands, they would be tortured to reveal information about American code-breaking.

CAST was considered by King to be 'of such importance to the successful prosecution of the war in the Far East' that 'to preserve its continuity' plans had been made in advance for its evacuation by 'any means of transportation'. An evacuation in three stages was planned so that each unit – linguists, cryptanalysts, radiomen and equipment – would be able to continue to operate independently from the others.

The first party, of four officers, thirteen enlisted men and equipment, left Corregidor in the submarine USS *Seadragon* on 5 February, 1942. A second party of thirty-six left for Australia in the submarine USS *Permit* on 15 March. General MacArthur had already left Corregidor on board a PT boat, vowing he would return, on 6 March. *Seadragon* took 34 tons of food to the beleaguered garrison of Corregidor on 6 April (torpedoes and ammunition having to be landed to make room) but had only managed to land seven tons when she was ordered away from the dockside. She stood by until the 8th, when she was told it was not possible to unload anything more. *Seadragon* sailed with the final CAST party of three officers and eighteen men who had worked on in the Malinta Tunnel until the early hours of 8 April when they were ferried out to *Seadragon*. The submarine survived a ferocious depth-charging on the way to Fremantle on the west coast of Australia. The members of Station CAST went to Melbourne, where they became Station BELCONNEN.

Bataan surrendered later that day, 8 April. Corregidor itself held out until 6 May when it too surrendered.

However, amidst all the gloom, there were some hopeful signs. On 17 December, 1941, Rochefort and his HYPO team were finally allowed to abandon work on the 'Flag Officers' Code' and 'commence solution' of current JN-25 intercepts. At last Rochefort's uncanny powers were to be directed in the right direction.

As though to signify that Joe Rochefort meant a change of luck, almost at once Station CAST discovered that the Japanese had made a basic cryptographic error by transmitting the same message both in JN-25 and in plain text. This clarified uncertainties about the changes in JN-25 introduced on 2 December, 1940, and confirmed that the main code book remained the same for JN-25A and 25B.

With this information, with the arrival of a shipment of book recoveries from Washington (which, by bureaucratic mismanagement, had been on their way by sea since November) and with the latest recoveries for the current period transmitted over the secure Copek line from CAST, HYPO went to work on JN-25B and began to make the first fresh breaks into it within three weeks.

Meanwhile, the US Navy was planning the first moves to take the war back to the Japanese. These would involve the Navy's first offensive use of radio intelligence. Admiral King's first directives to Nimitz were that he was, at all costs, to hold the Hawaii-Midway line and to keep the sea route to Australia open by 'covering, securing and holding the Hawaii-Samoa line, which should be extended to include Fiji at the earliest practicable date'.

King ordered Nimitz to carry out raids against Japanese forward bases in the Marshall and Gilbert Islands, and to reinforce Samoa with a division of US Marines from the west coast of America. Using studies previously prepared for Admiral Kimmel, Nimitz's staff quickly produced plans for carrier strikes against the islands, to be coordinated with the troop reinforcements convoys for Samoa.

The US Pacific Fleet had three carriers, *Saratoga*, *Lexington* and *Enterprise*. Task Force 8, with *Enterprise*, wearing Halsey's flag, sailed from Pearl on 11 January, 1942, to rendezvous with the carrier *Yorktown* which had been recalled from the Atlantic to escort the Samoan reinforcements, which were safely landed by 23 January, and then to go north and strike at the Gilberts and Marshalls. However, *Saratoga* was torpedoed by the Japanese submarine *I-6* on 11 January, some 500 miles south-west of Oahu, and so badly damaged she had to return, first to Pearl and then to the States for repair.

Task Force 11, with *Lexington* wearing Vice Admiral Wilson Brown's flag, was to have struck at Wake Island but the force's oiler *Neches* was torpedoed and sunk by the Japanese submarine *I-72* on 23 January. As there was no other oiler, the attack had to be called off. But Nimitz decided to let the Gilberts and Marshalls strikes go ahead.

Nimitz had, of course, based that decision on the intelligence information available to him. With such scarce resources, in carriers as well as in oilers, it was more important than ever to have some idea of Japanese intentions. 'I want you to be the Admiral Nagumo of my staff,' he told Layton. 'I want your every thought, every instinct as you believe Admiral Nagumo might have them. You are to see the war, their operations, their aims, from the Japanese viewpoint and keep me advised what you are thinking about, what you are doing, and what purpose, what strategy, motivates your operations. If you can do this, you will give me the kind of information needed to win this war.'

With HYPO's help, Layton did his best. Rochefort was slowly but steadily chipping pieces – words, then phrases, then complete sentences – out of JN-25B, which, with extensive traffic analysis, showed that there was no likelihood of another attack on Pearl Harbor. The main thrust of the Japanese advance appeared to be swinging away from the east and Pearl Harbor, and more to the south and west, towards New Guinea and Borneo. Rochefort forecast that the main Japanese carrier striking force, the 'Kido Butai', was moving to support operations in the Dutch East Indies. There was a marked increase in radio traffic from the area of Truk in the Carolines, and a decrease in traffic from the Marshalls.

On 18 January Rochefort forecast that the naval ships assembling at Truk were about to support a movement southward towards New Guinea. The vital piece of information was obtained from a message to a Japanese air unit in the Marshalls with a callsign similar to one on a half-burned card among other documents retrieved from a Japanese aircraft which crashed into the seaplane tender *Curtiss* at Pearl Harbor.

At about this time HYPO broke out fragments from three separate messages containing a common code group meaning 'Koryaku butai', 'occupation force'. The same code group had appeared in earlier messages connected with the Japanese occupations of Guam and Wake. This particular code group was prefixed by the letter 'R' – 'R occupation force'.

Rochefort guessed that 'R' stood for Rabaul. On 20 January the Bismarck Archipelago, between New Guinea and New Britain, was attacked by over a hundred Japanese aircraft. The Japanese landed at Rabaul on 23rd.

The Allies could do nothing to prevent the Japanese taking Rabaul, but, not for the last time, Rochefort's inspired hunch had been vindicated. Also, it meant that if the Japanese were preoccupied with Rabaul they would not be able to send forces to respond to carrier aircraft strikes in the Marshalls and Gilberts. The continuing decline in traffic from the Marshalls, evidence that the Japanese had withdrawn their submarines from close surveillance and attack missions in Hawaiian waters, and part-decrypted JN-25 intercepts from CAST revealing that the Japanese carriers were operating off

New Guinea, all tended to show that the main Japanese striking force was now more than 2,000 miles away from the Marshalls. For the first time in the Pacific, radio intelligence had provided a broad but accurate picture of enemy dispositions and intentions.

Furthermore, the Japanese were unaware that *Saratoga* had been sent out from the west coast and, taking at face value *I-6*'s report on 12 January that it had sunk (the similar-looking) *Lexington*, concluded that the US Pacific Fleet now had only one operational carrier, *Enterprise*. Thus, it was now to be the turn of the Japanese to be caught looking in the wrong direction.

Having seen the Samoan reinforcements ashore, Task Force 8 with Halsey in *Enterprise* and Task Force 14, with Rear Admiral Frank J. Fletcher in *Yorktown*, steamed north-west together until the evening of 31 January when they parted company to begin fast runs to the westward, Halsey towards Wotje and Kwajalein in the Marshalls, Fletcher towards Makin in the Gilberts.

Halsey had an additional intelligence aid in the person of Major Bankson T. Holcomb Jr., US Marine Corps, the first radio intelligence officer to be attached to a task force commander's staff in the Pacific, who had been loaned by HYPO after Halsey had asked for a trained Japanese linguist on the chance that he might overhear enemy transmissions.

Holcomb had no intercept unit assigned to him, but was to listen in on any Japanese radio-telephone circuits picked up by *Enterprise* and to serve as Halsey's ULTRA intelligence officer, as well as being available to translate any captured Japanese documents and to interrogate any prisoners.

Holcomb earned his passage on the afternoon of 31 January when he overheard a Japanese pilot from Taroa reporting that he had reached the limit of his patrol sector, had nothing to report, and was heading back to base. Halsey was delighted to be thus reassured that his force was undetected. (When TF 8's aircraft attacked, with the bombs they also dropped mimeographed sheets saying 'Thank you for not spotting us', translated into Japanese by Holcomb.)

By the brilliant light of a full moon, *Enterprise* began to fly off the first aircraft before dawn on 1 February, from a position only 36 miles from the island of Wotje. The strikes went on for some nine hours that day, with Halsey manoeuvring his ships in a tight rectangle of only five miles by twenty, often within sight of Wotje. As the American historian Samuel Eliot Morison wrote, 'Surely some kind angel was guarding them from submarines and air bombers'.

The strikes generated a great deal of radio chatter from the aircrew at the time and large claims of ships sunk and installations damaged afterwards. In fact, little damage was done and no ships were sunk, and Fletcher's TF 14 further south was even less successful.

But that did not mean the operation had achieved nothing. On the contrary, it was a humiliating shock for the Japanese, who realized they had been caught napping. They searched furiously for Halsey's retreating ships who took advantage of a thick weather front and got clear away. Furthermore, the resultant surge of Japanese radio traffic after the raid provided even more cryptographic grist for HYPO's mill.

The effect of the news on the American public was even more dramatic. It was the first American counter-attack. It was good news after so much bad. Some even claimed it was revenge for Pearl Harbor. It was not that, but at least it was a start. Halsey became a war hero and from then on was never to leave the war correspondents short of material.

On 21 February Admiral Wilson Brown led a force including *Lexington* on an even bolder sortie against Rabaul. They were sighted and attacked, but the Japanese aircraft were engaged and repulsed by *Lexington*'s own fighters in a furious series of dog fights which took place in plain view above the fleet, to the cheers of the spectators. Admiral Brown said: 'I even had to remind some members of my staff that this was not a football game'. Few of the Japanese aircraft escaped. Morale in the American carriers soared. '*Lady Lex*' became the best known ship in the Pacific.

Halsey had another radio intelligence officer, Lt G.M. Slonin, and the first intercept unit, consisting of two radio operators, embarked in *Enterprise* when he sailed later in February for strikes against Wake Island on 24 February and against Marcus Island on 4 March. The strike on Marcus, which was only 1,000 miles east of the Japanese home islands, was the deepest penetration yet by an American carrier.

Despite its small size and scanty equipment, the intercept unit provided Halsey with target weather information at Wake and at Marcus by intercepting and decrypting weather reports from both islands, using cryptographic information provided by HYPO.

At Wake, Slonin was able to tell Halsey that the cruiser force bombarding the island had been spotted by Japanese aircraft. At Marcus, Japanese radio circuits revealed that Halsey's ships had achieved complete surprise and that the island's radio station had been bombed and put out of action before it could send out an alarm. Halsey's Task Force was eight hours on its way home before Tokyo learned of the attack from a Maru (merchantman) which reached Marcus that evening and radioed the news to Yokosuka. Once again, the Japanese launched a furious and fruitless chase which became even more confused the following day, after a false report that enemy ships were heading for the coast of Japan.

Admiral Wilson Brown had a radio intelligence officer and an intercept unit on board *Yorktown* when she and *Lexington* combined for an even deeper and more daring venture, through the Coral Sea and into the Gulf of Papua, only some forty-five miles off the southern shores of the island. On 10 March 100 carrier planes crossed the 7,500-ft Owen Stanley range of mountains and, concealed by a tropical rain storm, attacked the Japanese occupation at Lae and Salamaua, sinking four ships and damaging thirteen.

These were the Imperial Japanese Navy's heaviest losses of the war so far, and they caused the first postponement in Japan's so far overwhelmingly triumphant progress of conquest in the east. The intended invasion of Port Moresby was put back from early April to early in May. In the radio intelligence war this was to prove a crucial delay. The Japanese had pulled off a stunning shock at Pearl Harbor. They were never to achieve such surprise again.

II

DISASTER IN THE EAST: SINGAPORE AND AFTER

WHILST Admiral Nagumo's aircraft were attacking Pearl Harbor, General Yamashita's XXV Army landed at Singora and Patani, on the Kra Isthmus of Thailand, and at Kota Bharu in Malaya. The Japanese quickly captured the local airfields and began to advance southwards, driving increasingly exhausted and demoralized British and Indian forces before them.

Warnings of an approaching war against Japan had been broadcast from many quarters in the months beforehand. The British Military Attaché in Chungking, for instance, sent a message to Hong Kong on 24 October, 1941: 'Following from Chinese General Staff: Japanese fleet fully mobilized and now at Sasebo'. On 28 October the Admiralty sent a signal to a worldwide range of addressees: 'It has been decided to replace the appointment of C-in-C China [Admiral Sir Geoffrey Layton] by a new appointment styled C-in-C Eastern Fleet [Admiral Sir Tom Phillips]'.

After defining the duties of the new C-in-C, the signal continued with a frank forecast of the future: 'On outbreak of war with Japan, or when directed by Admiralty, C-in-C Eastern Fleet will, in addition to above duties, assume strategic control of all British and Dutch Naval Forces.'

On 6 December the Admiralty received a signal from Singapore: 'At 0300 today two Jap forces were sighted off Cambodia Point course 270. First group 25 transports 4 CA, 2 CL, 10 Destroyers. Second group 10 transports, 2 cruisers, 10 destroyers'.

Force Z – the battleship *Prince of Wales* (wearing Phillips' flag), the battle-cruiser *Repulse* and four destroyers – sailed from Singapore to disrupt the Japanese landings. Instead, the ships were themselves attacked on 10 December in the South China Sea, east of Malaya, by Japanese bombers and torpedo-bombers of the 22nd Air

Flotilla operating from bases near Saigon in southern Indo-China.

On 10 December ALUSNA Chungking (the US Navy Liaison Officer in China) sent a signal to Cavite: 'Tokyo Local time Dec. 10. 60 bombers left Formosa southward at 0610. 1220 Reconnaissance plane giving position only as Celebes Sea reported Quote Main Navy Force seen off Kwaneang steaming 75° Speed 17 (?) knots. At 1220 (?) stated two ships sinking after Jap bombing southeast of Philippines near PW (?) and naming KING GEORGE and AEPPVSE (Repulse). Ten minutes later reported one ship heeling badly then sinking bow first. Source of above not available until break of war but past circumstantial evidence lends credence. Urgently request evaluation for further use of direct intercept claimed.'

The main gist of the intercept was true enough. *Prince of Wales* and *Repulse*, lacking fighter cover, had both been sunk by repeated bomb and torpedo hits, with the loss of 840 officers and men, including the captain of *Prince of Wales* and Admiral Sir Tom Phillips.

This appalling calamity was the end result of a train of unfortunate circumstances: of decisions taken in London, after prolonged disagreement between the Prime Minister, Mr Churchill, and the Admiralty; the grounding, in Kingston, Jamaica, of the aircraft carrier *Indomitable* which had been intended to provide air cover for Force Z; underestimates, in London and Singapore, of the offensive skill of the Japanese pilots and the operational ranges of their aircraft; the false report, received in *Prince of Wales* late on 9 December, of a Japanese landing at Kuantan on the east coast of Malaya which caused Phillips to divert his ships to investigate and thus delayed their progress to the south; the unlucky chance which led a returning Japanese striking force directly over the British ships; and last, Phillips' own insistence on keeping radio silence and his evident belief that there were in Singapore staff officers with the almost psychic powers of insight needed to divine, without being asked, that Force Z would require air cover off Kuantan from dawn onwards on 10 December.

It was a double blow felt more deeply in Britain than any other loss, even of HMS *Hood*, that the country had suffered at sea. Schoolboys at home in England went down to breakfast that morning and knew by their parents' faces that something terrible had happened. Churchill himself said that on hearing the news he never in all the war received a more direct shock. It was a disaster which was at once a severe strategic set-back for the Allies, a shocking tactical defeat for the Royal Navy and a personal tragedy for the officers and men of Force Z and their families.

It was also to be the first time for hundreds of years that the Royal Navy lost its supremacy in any theatre of war at sea and failed eventually to regain it. The US Navy assumed the mantle in the Far East on that day. When the Royal Navy eventually reappeared in strength it was to be as a junior partner.

The combat performance of the latest Japanese aircraft appeared to be unremarked by Allied intelligence (as was the very existence of the formidable Type 93 oxygen-powered 'Long Lance' torpedo, which had the phenomenal running range of 44,000 yards at 36 knots). When one of *Prince of Wales'* lookouts reported the approach of a Japanese torpedo-bomber, Admiral Phillips is reported to have remarked, 'Don't be silly, they don't have any'.

Phillips was, of course, notorious for his 'wall of steel' theory, believing that a modern capital ship could quite adequately defend herself against air attack with her own fire power. But there may have been a further reason for his ignorance of Japanese aircraft. Before being appointed to command the Eastern Fleet, he had been on the Board of Admiralty as Vice Chief of the Naval Staff, and, as such, received intelligence reports from all over the world.

But it is possible that Phillips did not receive every report from the Far Eastern Combined Bureau (FECB: the British equivalent of HYPO) at Singapore. The FECB had first been set up in Hong Kong in the mid-1930s, with offices in the naval dockyard and a powerful intercept station, capable of picking up any transmission from Japan, on Stonecutter's Island in the harbour.

At the time of the Japanese attack, the Chief of Intelligence Staff (COIS) and administrative head of FECB was Captain Kenneth Harkness, a gunnery officer by specialization. When Harkness returned to the United Kingdom late in 1942 and visited the Admiralty, he had the strong impression that he was being held to blame for the lack of intelligence warnings from the Far East.

In fact, Harkness had sent home regular intelligence appreciations of Japanese intentions and capabilities. To the day of his death in 1990, Harkness insisted that, on enquiry, he discovered that his reports had been held up at a junior level, on the desk of a certain Commander, and had never reached the Vice Chief of Naval Staff.

By the outbreak of war FECB had considerable experience of monitoring the Japanese Navy's operational behaviour and could keep track of their main naval movements by traffic analysis, direction-finding and identification of callsigns. In July, 1937, for instance, the FECB was able to give a reasonably accurate summary of the Japanese Navy's total strength in aircraft and the numbers and types embarked in the three carriers, *Ryujo*, *Hosho* and *Kaga*. But the information, like Harkness' reports, aroused very little interest in London where, until as late as 1943, it seemed that intelligence about the Far East was inclined to be regarded as mainly the concern of the United States.

Late in 1939 the British radio intelligence facilities in the Far East consisted of three High Frequency Direction Finding Stations (later increased to 17) at Hong Kong, Kranji (Singapore) and Kuching in Borneo, a 'Y' intercept station at Kranji, for D/F fixes, callsign identification and traffic analysis of Japanese naval W/T and air traffic, and a naval and military crypto section at Seletar Bahru in Singapore.

FECB's counterpart to Rochefort was Captain Eric Nave of the Royal Australian Navy, a trained Japanese linguist and as inspired a cryptanalyst as Rochefort. By September, 1939, when FECB had been moved to Singapore, Nave had made some progress in breaking into JN-25, which he found 'tedious rather than difficult'. The Government Code & Cypher School (GC&CS) had also broken into JN-25, much of which was thus being read at Singapore by the end of 1939. By March, 1941, FECB was able to pass their recoveries in JN-25 to the US Asiatic Fleet, delivering their keys to the code to CAST at Cavite on the 5th.

JN-25 was the code in which most of the operational (as opposed to the diplomatic) signals about the attack on Pearl Harbor were transmitted. The knowledge, imperfect though it was, both OP-20-G and FECB had of JN-25, and the cryptographic cooperation and exchange of information between the two, makes the surprise the Japanese achieved all the more remarkable – and reprehensible.

Admiral Sir Geoffrey Layton, who had not relished being relieved by Phillips, had been on board a ship just about to sail for home when the news of the disaster to Force Z arrived. He came ashore at once to take up the reins again in a steadily deteriorating situation.

By Christmas Eve Layton was considering moving 'Y' Section of FECB to Colombo, 'in view of the irreplaceable nature of its personnel and material'. At that time, Harkness had under him a secretary, a deputy and an assistant chief of staff, seven intelligence officers dealing with such matters as Warships, W/T and D/F, Merchant Shipping and security, and a cypher staff of six Paymaster Lieutenants RNVR.

Hong Kong fell on Christmas Day, 1941, and this seems to have made up the Admiralty's mind about evacuating FECB. On the 27th the Admiralty signalled: 'Intend to transfer to Ceylon the naval section of F.E.C.B. (including Captain on Staff, Y and Special intelligence) by transport returning from Singapore about 5th January.'

FECB's personnel and equipment embarked in the troopship *Devonshire* which left Singapore bound for Colombo on 5 January, 1942. Layton and his Chief of Staff, Admiral Palliser, went to Batavia, Layton in the cruiser *Dragon*, Palliser in *Durban*.

In Malaya Yamashita won a decisive battle at the Slim River on 7 January, 1942, and entered Kuala Lumpur on the 11th. On the 20th the Japanese began a major offensive northwards into Burma and within weeks had inflicted defeats, amounting to disasters, upon British and Indian troops at the Binin and Sittang rivers.

The Japanese had allowed a hundred days for the conquest of Malaya and their programme ran well ahead of schedule. The last British and Indian troops crossed the causeway from Johore on to Singapore Island on 31 January. The Japanese began their assault on the island on 8 February. General Percival, the army commander, surrendered Singapore on Sunday, 15 February, after seventy days of one of the least competent campaigns ever fought by any British general.

The Japanese had begun their conquest of the Dutch East Indies on 11 January, 1942, when Lt-General Imamura's 16th Army landed at Tarakan in Borneo, and Manado in the Celebes. In Sumatra, Japanese airborne troops dropped on the important oil refineries at Palembang on 14 February and the main invasion force landed the next day. On the 19th the Japanese landed on Bali, thus isolating Java from the east and west, and the same day launched a heavy, punishing air strike against Darwin in northern Australia.

The Darwin raid was the first time carrier and shore-based aircraft co-operated in a major strike. Admiral Nagumo, with a strong force of four carriers, two battleships and three cruisers, had entered the Banda Sea undetected and unmolested. In two raids, the first of 188 carrier aircraft and the second of 54 from Kendari in the Celebes, the Japanese brushed aside the slight fighter and anti-aircraft defences of Darwin and sank ten ships in the harbour, as well as destroying ten aircraft. The Darwin strike, with another at Broome further along the coast on 4 March, when sixteen flying boats and seven other aircraft were destroyed, were designed to prevent Allied interference with the forthcoming Japanese invasion of Java.

By February, 1942, the only effective force left to the Allies was the Combined Striking Force of American, Dutch, British and Australian warships commanded first by Admiral Hart, US Navy, and then from 25 February by the Dutch Admiral Helfrich. The ships did their best but bad luck, lack of air support and the Japanese Navy took a steady toll.

On 4 February the Dutch Admiral Karel Doorman led the Dutch cruiser *De Ruyter* (wearing his flag), the American cruisers *Houston* and *Marblehead*, the small Dutch cruiser *Tromp*, four Dutch and three American destroyers to attack a Japanese invasion convoy assembling at Balikpapan on the east coast of Borneo. Their route was long and exposed to air attack and they were duly attacked: *De Ruyter, Houston* and *Marblehead* were all damaged – *Marblehead* so badly she had to go back to America for repairs.

On 18 February Doorman, an unlucky admiral, led another sortie against the Japanese invasion convoy heading for Bali. Although Doorman had for once superior strength, the attempt to stop the Japanese landing failed. The Dutch destroyer *Kortenaer* grounded and had to be left behind. In a night battle in the Lombok Strait, the Dutch destroyer *Piet Hein* was sunk and *Tromp* so badly damaged she had to be sent to Australia for repairs. One Japanese destroyer and a transport were damaged.

The Japanese were now ready to invade Java. From 'Y' intelligence and from JN-25 decrypts, FECB were able to give some prior warning. On 24 February 'Captain on Staff Colombo' (the cover title for COIS) sent a signal to a worldwide range of addressees: 'From Y Intelligence 23rd February. Wireless telegraphy traffic indications. Possibility of large operation pending in unknown area under direction of C. in C. 2nd Fleet. Units involved include C. in C. 3rd Fleet, at least one aircraft carrier and air tender, 7th Cruiser Squadron, destroyer and submarine units, units of Combined Air Force and 1st Air Fleet and Jap. Cruiser NATORI possibly with Chief of Staff 16th Army on board.'

Two days later, 'Captain on Staff, Colombo' sent a signal to the Senior Officer China Force, repeated to the Admiralty for D.N.I. and the British Admiralty Delegation in Washington: 'ZYMOTIC [code name for special intelligence derived from some high-grade Japanese cyphers and codes such as JN-25]. Naval Special Intelligence dated 25th. 10 transports for operation T for Tommy will leave Muntok vicinity 1200 Japanese time 26th. Further convoy of 10 ships will leave Palembang and an unknown place on 28th. Comment. Call signs believed to belong to Fourth Destroyer Squadron and an air unit are included in address.'

D-Day for the Japanese invasion of Java was 28 February. As forecast by FECB, the Supreme Commander of the Invasion Force was the commanding general of 16th Army, General Imamura, with the C-in-C 2nd Fleet, Vice Admiral Kondo, as the Naval Commander and the C-in-C 3rd Fleet, Vice Admiral Takahashi, commanding the Attack Forces. Kondo also commanded the Southern Striking Force of four battleships in the Surface Group and Nagumo's four carriers in the Carrier Group.

The accuracy of the information FECB obtained from studying enemy radio traffic was shown by the composition of the main Western Attack Group which sailed with 56 transports and freighters from Camranh Bay, Indo-China, on 18 February. It was commanded by Rear Admiral Kurita, who also commanded the Seventh Cruiser Squadron. The covering force did include one carrier, *Ryujo*, and a seaplane tender, and one of its cruisers was indeed *Natori*. The Eastern Attack Group, commanded by Rear Admiral Nishimura, sailed with 41 transports from Jolo in the Sulu Archipelago on the 19th.

The Eastern Attack Group was reported on 26 February some 190 miles north-east of Surabaya. Once more Doorman led his ships to sea. With five cruisers – *De Ruyter*, the Dutch *Java*, *Houston*, whose after turret was still out of action from the 18th, the Australian *Perth* and the British *Exeter* – and nine destroyers, Doorman was only slightly inferior numerically to his Japanese opponents. But the Japanese made deadly use of the hitherto unknown 'Long Lance' torpedo and in a battle in the Java Sea on 27 February sank *De Ruyter* and *Java*, the British destroyers *Electra* and *Jupiter*, and *Kortenaer*. Admiral Doorman went down in *De Ruyter*. On the same day the American aircraft tender *Langley* was badly damaged by shore-based bombers and was scuttled.

Houston and *Perth* reached Batavia on 28 February, refuelled and sailed that evening for Tjilatjap. They encountered part of a Japanese convoy at Bantam Bay, east of the Sunda Strait, and sank four transports but were then themselves sunk by the Japanese covering force of three cruisers and nine destroyers. The Dutch destroyer *Evertsen* was so badly damaged she had to be beached. The next day, 1 March, *Exeter*, which had been badly damaged on the 27th, and the destroyers *Encounter* and *Pope* sailed from Surabaya and were also sunk.

The Allied ships had been led by a fatally unlucky admiral, had been bedevilled by communications difficulties, had had little opportunity to exercise together, lacked air cover, and were faced by an enemy who possessed the devastating 'Long Lance' and ample numbers of strike and reconnaissance aircraft. Their forlorn battles, as Churchill described them, delayed the Japanese invasion by barely twenty-four hours. The Japanese came ashore in western and eastern Java during the night of 28 February/1 March. The Dutch East Indies Government surrendered unconditionally on 9 March. Thus, in a total campaign of sixty days (compared with the Japanese estimate of 150 days) the Japanese had captured Makassar, Timor, Sumatra and Java. In Burma, Rangoon fell on the 8th.

The chief problem facing naval intelligence in the war in the Far East was to guess Japan's next move. Unlike the Germans in the west, whose main objective was always the Atlantic convoys, or the Italians in the land-locked Mediterranean, where the land and sea campaigns were closely linked, the Japanese had a wide choice of objectives – at least while they were still winning – all thousands of miles apart.

After Java, the Japanese could have struck again at Hawaii, or even at the west coast of the United States, which was still only sketchily defended. But the Royal Navy, though it had suffered some hard knocks, still had a 'fleet in being' in the Indian Ocean, with naval bases in Ceylon, and as such represented a threat on the flank of the Japanese campaign in Burma. Therefore, whilst still having designs upon an advance on Australia, the Japanese chose next to strike westwards, into the Indian Ocean, with a raid on Ceylon. It was only a raid, albeit in great strength, and not an intended invasion, but this was not realized until much later, long after the raiding forces had withdrawn.

Once again, FECB (who had, incidentally, just learned from a JN-25 intercept that the Japanese knew that they had all moved to Colombo from Singapore) were able to provide some warning. They had succeeded in deciphering the Japanese code letters for various places in the theatre: DG was Ceylon, DGP was Trincomalee, DS Sydney and DP Darwin. On 21 March FECB were able to read a JN-25 intercept about an attack '31 March against DG. Evidence for India/Ceylon departing Staring Bay 21 March'. A second intercept a day later gave the date of the attack on DG as 1 April. On 22 March the Admiralty signalled to the US Chief of Naval Operations: 'British Special Intelligence, reporting on seven messages from 13-17 March, Japanese carrier force at Staring Bay, attack DG about 1 April'.

Confirmation that a Japanese attack was impending came from CincPac's Fleet Intelligence Summaries. On 26 March, for instance: 'All evidence points to very definite plans for offensive action in the Indian Ocean in the immediate future, which will include action against the Andaman Islands and possibly followed by action against Ceylon.'

On 26 March Admiral Sir James Somerville, who had come out from the United Kingdom in the carrier *Formidable*, landed at Colombo airport, having flown the last ninety miles in a Fairey Fulmar. Next day he hoisted his flag as Commander-in-Chief, Eastern Fleet in the battleship *Warspite* in Trincomalee harbour, while the vigorous personality of Admiral Sir Geoffrey Layton became Commander-in-Chief, Ceylon.

James Somerville had a bright war record, having commanded Force H with great success. He was a bold, witty, outspoken man, an admiral with the common touch and, at times, a somewhat Rabelaisian sense of humour. The sailors loved him.

On first seeing his fleet at sea, Sir James signalled: 'So this is the Eastern Fleet. Well never mind. There's many a good tune played on an old fiddle.' That somewhat rueful signal had some justification. The Eastern Fleet was the largest yet assembled by the Royal Navy in the war and it contained every ship a hard-pressed Admiralty could spare.

On paper the fleet looked convincing enough: five battleships, three aircraft carriers, two heavy and five light cruisers (including the Dutch *Heemskerck*), sixteen destroyers and seven submarines. But, of the battleships, only *Warspite* (recently repaired in America after damage off Crete in 1941) was modernized and capable of more than 20 knots. The other four were antique 'R' Class ships, *Resolution*, *Ramillies*, *Royal Sovereign* and *Revenge*, built for First World War action in the North Sea; they were slow, with a top speed of 18 knots, and had a short endurance, both in fuel and fresh water.

Of the carriers, *Hermes* was old, slow and small. As for the two larger, faster and more modern carriers, *Formidable* had just been repaired in the States, *Indomitable* had been employed ferrying aircraft to Singapore and Java while they remained in Allied hands, and both ship's companies and air groups lacked training and battle experience; between them the three carriers had a total of 57 Swordfish or Albacore torpedo-bombers and 36 Fulmar fighters. Many of the cruisers were old and unmodernized and some of the destroyers urgently needed refitting.

Outwardly radiating a breezy confidence he certainly did not feel, Somerville set about preparing his variegated fleet for battle. In fact, there was no time to lose. OP-20-G had already signalled that: 'Lack of recent telegraphese on carriers may indicate they are in service with Task Force believed schedule (?) to operate offensively Bengal

Bay area'. FECB obtained further confirmation from a JN-25 intercept on 28 March. The following day CNO in Washington was informed 'Colombo reports Operation "CX" to be carried out. Attack on shipping in vicinity of "DC".'

On 31 March the message from OP-20-G was 'First Air Attack force scheduled 1 April against ships as primary objectives. Time and area unknown but believed Bengal Bay. Translation available relative message later. Colombo unit informed'. A day later, with increasing urgency, the signal read: 'Unknown UMO3 [callsign], using highest priority requests weather Indian Ocean Coastal regions. Believe this all adds up to launching air offensive Bay of Bengal region today 1 April'.

Somerville had taken his fleet to sea on 30 March, flying his flag in *Warspite*. He faced an unusually difficult situation. He still had no idea of the exact strength of his enemy, but it was likely to be greater than his own and he was determined at all costs to avoid a direct confrontation. 'The loss of Ceylon would be a most serious matter,' he wrote to Admiral Sir Dudley Pound, the First Sea Lord, on his way out to the East, 'but if the Japanese attempted the capture with practically the whole of their Fleet we should obviously be unable to deal with this scale of attack.

'Providing the Americans adopt a more forward policy – even if it is for the moment confined to feinting or quite light scales of attack – we feel it is unlikely the Japanese would denude their lines of communication of protection in the Pacific.

'If they attempt a lesser scale of attack on Ceylon, the best deterrent, and the best counter too, is to keep our Eastern Fleet "in being" and avoid losses by attrition. This can best be achieved by keeping the Fleet at sea as much as possible with feints east of Ceylon from time to time.

'I feel that we must avoid having our Fleet destroyed in penny numbers by undertaking operations which do not give reasonable prospects of success.'

Above all, it was vital to keep the fleet 'in being'. 'If the Japanese get Ceylon,' he wrote, 'it will be extremely difficult but not necessarily impossible to maintain our communications to the Middle East. But if the Japanese capture Ceylon *and* destroy the greater part of the Eastern Fleet, then I admit the situation becomes really desperate.'

Somerville and Layton decided that Colombo and Trincomalee were not satisfactory as bases for the fleet, and ships using them would be in constant danger of attack. Therefore, it was decided to use a secret base, unknown to the Japanese and in fact never discovered by them, at Addu Atoll, the southernmost of the Maldive Islands, some 600 miles south-west of Ceylon.

From intelligence and his own summing up of the prospects, Somerville expected the Japanese attack on Colombo and Trincomalee to be made from the south-east at dawn on or about 1 April. He had his ships rendezvous on the evening of 31 March, in a waiting position, eighty miles south of Dondra Head, the most southerly point of Ceylon. He still had no clear information on his enemy's strength, but he intended at all costs to avoid being attacked by enemy carrier aircraft and any direct fleet action. Instead, he hoped to be able to launch a night torpedo-bomber strike by the light of the full moon.

In daylight Somerville withdrew his ships to the west, out of the likely range of searching enemy reconnaissance aircraft. He found himself constantly hamstrung by the slowness of the 'R' Class battleships, so he divided his fleet into a fast Force 'A', of *Warspite*, *Indomitable*, *Formidable* and the cruisers *Cornwall*, *Emerald* and *Enterprise*, and a slow Force 'B', of the 'R' Class battleships and the remaining cruisers, under his Flag Officer Second-in-Command, Vice Admiral Algernon Willis, flying his flag in *Resolution*. The destroyers were divided about equally between the two forces.

On 1 April the cruiser *Dorsetshire*, which had abruptly stopped her refit in Colombo, joined Somerville's fleet, but there was no sign of the enemy. It seemed that either the Japanese had learned of his fleet putting to sea and had postponed their attack, or the previous intelligence had got the timing wrong, and there was no fresh intelligence.

By 2 April Somerville's battleships 'confessed with salt tears running down their sides, that they must return to harbour quickly as they were running out of water'. *Dorsetshire* was ordered back to Colombo to resume her refit, accompanied by *Cornwall* who was to provide onward escort for an Australian troop convoy due to arrive on 8 April. *Hermes*, with her attendant 'plane guard' destroyer *Vampire*, was ordered to go to Trincomalee to prepare for her part in the attack on Madagascar projected to take place in May.

Having thus dispersed some units of his fleet, so that they risked being destroyed in the very penny numbers he had referred to, Somerville decided that a return to Colombo, with its weak air defences, might be to invite another 'Pearl Harbor' and instead headed his fleet for Addu Atoll, six hundred miles away.

Clearly Somerville was convinced that the Japanese must have abandoned their plan to attack Ceylon. 'I fear they have taken fright, which is a pity,' he wrote, 'because if I could have given them a good crack now it would have been timely.'

In fact, the 'R' Class battleships' shortage of water was providential. It was extremely fortunate that no encounter with the Japanese fleet took place. Barring a miracle, the outcome would have been another shattering disaster to the Eastern Fleet, for, as Somerville's ships turned towards Addu Atoll, Admiral Nagumo's formidable Striking Force was rounding the southern tip of Sumatra, with five of the carriers which attacked Pearl Harbor, with more than 300 aircraft embarked, four fast battleships, three cruisers and eight destroyers.

The intelligence of a forthcoming Japanese attack was correct. Only the timing was wrong. Nagumo planned to attack Ceylon on 5 April, actually Easter Sunday. Meanwhile, Admiral Ozawa's Malaya Force, of one light carrier, six cruisers and four destroyers, which had sailed from Mergui on 1 April, was also on its way, unremarked by intelligence, to carry out a sweep against shipping in the Bay of Bengal.

Force 'A' reached Addu Atoll at noon on 4 April, followed at 3 pm by Force 'B'. Force 'A' had barely begun to refuel when the news arrived that a Catalina flying boat from Ceylon had sighted a large enemy force, in position 155° Dondra Head 360 miles, just after ten that morning. The Catalina had been shot down before it could give any more information about the composition of the enemy force.

The signal, though long awaited, still caused a shock, especially as the first version shown to Somerville, soon corrected, read 'south-east of *Addu Atoll*'. But even with the correction, the Eastern Fleet had been caught hopelessly out of position, 600 miles from the enemy, with empty fuel and water tanks.

Force 'A' could sail that afternoon, except for the cruisers *Enterprise* and *Emerald*, which would not be ready until midnight. Force 'B' could not sail until the following day. It was still vital for Somerville to keep his fleet in being. He considered his old battleships to be more of a liability than an asset, but if *Warspite* and the carriers operated away from the support of the battle squadron, his fleet risked being defeated in detail. Somerville therefore ordered Force 'A' to sail as soon as *Enterprise* and *Emerald* were ready and Force 'B' to follow as soon as possible the next day.

Meanwhile in Ceylon Layton was making such preparations as he could. Colombo harbour was cleared of all ships that could sail. *Dorsetshire* and *Cornwall* were ordered to make for a rendezvous with Force 'A' some 380 miles east-north-east of Addu Atoll. *Hermes* and

Vampire were sailed from Trincomalee, with orders to steer clear to the north-east.

Force 'A' sailed just after midnight on 5 April and Force 'B' followed at 7 am. The JN-25 revealed on 5 April that Naval Intelligence in Tokyo had been given intelligence information on Indian airfields, but nothing further on Nagumo's ships, which, however, were by now within actual spotting distance. The Catalinas had stayed in touch through the night and one was shot down, but soon after daybreak, at 6.48 am on the 5th, a Catalina sighted and reported two battleships and three cruisers steering north-west, only 100 miles south-south-west of Ceylon.

At 8 am Nagumo's aircraft – 36 fighters and 91 bombers including some 70 dive-bombers – arrived over Colombo. They were opposed by three RAF squadrons of Hurricanes, two at Colombo and one at Trincomalee, and two squadrons of naval Fairey Fulmars, 42 fighters in all. Seven Japanese aircraft were shot down, for the loss of 19 British. Six unfortunate Fairey Swordfish from Trincomalee, intended to form a torpedo striking force, arrived in Colombo at the height of the fighting and were all shot down.

In the harbour, the destroyer *Tenedos* and the armed merchant cruiser *Hector* were sunk, and the submarine depot ship *Lucia* and a merchant ship were damaged. But the damage was nothing like as bad as at Darwin and the port of Colombo remained open.

At 6.17 pm on the 5th Somerville received another aircraft report, of two carriers and five unknown ships, sighted at 4 pm in a position some 300 miles to the north-east of him, and not far to the east of the track of *Dorsetshire* and *Cornwall* who were still on their way to rendezvous with him. He concluded that the carriers were no danger to his two cruisers who were estimated to be then some 150 miles further to the southward and opening their distance from the enemy all the time.

The truth was that *Dorsetshire* and *Cornwall* had both been sunk hours earlier. They were sighted by Japanese reconnaissance aircraft that morning. At 1 pm, when the cruisers were only some 90 miles from the rendezvous and had themselves sighted Japanese aircraft, Captain Agar in *Dorsetshire* thought he should warn his C-in-C. But his message was received in *Warspite* in mutilated form and it was not until 2 pm that it was identified as coming from *Dorsetshire*.

By then it was in any case too late. At 1.45 pm *Warspite*'s radar picked up aircraft echoes 84 miles away to the north-east. They came no closer and soon faded. In fact, they were more than 50 Japanese bombers attacking *Dorsetshire* and *Cornwall*. Both ships were hit many times and both had sunk by 1.55 pm. Once again, Nagumo's aircraft had demonstrated how devastatingly efficient they were against ships with no fighter cover.

At 3.30 pm Somerville received a report that the enemy squadron was now 100 miles to the northward and steering south-west, as though heading for Addu Atoll. Somerville was by now in no doubt of the peril his Fleet was in, being opposed by a very powerful and dangerous enemy fleet. He had to appear to his own Fleet to be cheerfully eager for action and actively seeking out the enemy, being optimistic about the outcome, whilst in reality he was carefully avoiding any contact. He now turned south to keep his distance until nightfall when he hoped to launch a torpedo attack. But when he received the aircraft report of 6.17 pm, he altered to the north-west.

Air searches were flown through the night but nothing was seen. The fast and slow forces met at dawn on 6th and turned to the south-east, to maintain a distance from where Somerville hoped to be able to launch night torpedo strikes against the enemy during their return passage from Addu Atoll. Somerville thought it still possible Nagumo was about to attack Addu Atoll, or was lying in wait near it to attack the Eastern Fleet.

Late on the afternoon of the 6th *Enterprise* and two destroyers were detached to look for survivors of *Dorsetshire* and *Cornwall*. They picked up 1,122 officers and men, but 424 lives had been lost, to the enemy or to sharks.

After a signal from Layton, estimating that a strong enemy force was now between Ceylon and Addu Atoll, Somerville decided he must keep clear. Flying constant air searches and taking a wide circuitous route around to the west, Somerville finally reached Addu Atoll at 11 am on 8 April and refuelled.

It was quite clear to Somerville that his fleet could never stand to fight the enemy who now confronted him. He must concentrate upon keeping his fleet in being. In the early hours of 7 April the Admiralty signalled to him that they now realized that their hope that his fleet and American pressure would discourage the Japanese from sending a powerful task force into the Indian Ocean had been a vain one. 'If the Japanese cared to concentrate they could produce a fleet which is superior in aircraft carriers and superior in capital ships in speed, gun range and possibly numbers.

'It is possible you are finding the "R" Class battleships more of a liability than an asset. You have full discretion to withdraw them

29

possibly to Aden or Zanzibar. We fully appreciate the very difficult game you are called upon to play.'

To add to the gloom, there was news of Ozawa's Malaya Force, which had unchallenged mastery of the Bay of Bengal and was attacking shipping at will, completely disrupting sea communications along the east coast of India. Between 4 and 9 April Ozawa's force sank 23 merchantmen of 112,312 tons.

Meanwhile Nagumo had been making strenuous efforts to find Somerville's ships. His reconnaissance aircraft searched a wide circle to the south-east of Ceylon, but Somerville was well to the west and, by what now seems a merciful providence, his ships were never found.

After fuelling, Nagumo's Striking Force approached Ceylon again for an attack on Trincomalee. Early on 8 April 'Y' Intelligence picked up a D/F bearing, callsign 'MEHU' which was the aircraft carrier *Akagi*. At 3.17 pm on the 8th a Catalina reported three battleships and one carrier four hundred miles east of Ceylon, steering towards the island. Trincomalee harbour was cleared of shipping. *Hermes*, *Vampire* and several merchantmen and fleet auxiliaries sailed southwards that night, with orders to hug the coastline and to be at least 40 miles from Trincomalee by dawn on the 9th.

The Japanese attacked Trincomalee with about 90 aircraft at 7.25 am on 9 April. Several dockyard buildings were hit and the monitor *Erebus* was damaged. Nine RAF Blenheims of No. 11 Squadron – the only bombers on the island – took off to find the enemy, but they scored no hits and five of them were shot down.

But there was still a further price to pay for failing to give Ceylon adequate air defences, and still more agony for the Eastern Fleet. The ships which had cleared from Trincomalee were about 65 miles down the coast when the Japanese attack took place. At about 9 am they were sighted by a Japanese reconnaissance aircraft whose report was intercepted in Colombo and interpreted as a sighting report of *Hermes*.

The ships were ordered to return to Trincomalee forthwith and by 10.25 were off the port off Batticaloa. Ten minutes later about 50 Japanese aircraft were sighted diving out of the sun from ten thousand feet. Shore-based fighters could not reach the scene in time. *Hermes* was overwhelmed and sunk by forty bomb hits in ten minutes. *Vampire*, the corvette *Hollyhock*, and the tankers *Athelstane* and *British Sergeant* were all sunk. The hospital ship *Vita* picked up some 600 survivors (among them Petty Officer Eric Monaghan, a survivor of *Hermes* who had also been a survivor of *Repulse* and of the aircraft carrier *Courageous*, sunk in September 1939).

Somerville decided that both Ceylon and Addu Atoll were too dangerous as bases. He sent the slow Force 'B' to Kilindini, Mombasa, to guard the WS convoy route up the east coast of Africa, and took Force 'A' to Bombay. 'I shall have to lie low in one sense but be pretty active in another,' he said, 'keep the old tarts out of the picture and roar about with the others.'

Ironically, Somerville's ships withdrew from Ceylon as Nagumo and Ozawa were withdrawing. The Japanese Navy was never again to enter the Indian Ocean in strength. But this was not known to Somerville or to the British Government for some time.

On 6 May Corregidor, the last Allied stronghold in the Philippines, surrendered. In the north, the British and Indian troops of the Eastern Army in Burma were approaching the Assam frontier, after a retreat of 1,000 miles – the longest in British military history.

In six months the Japanese had established their Greater Asia Co-Prosperity Sphere, an empire of 90,000,000 people stretching from Rabaul to Rangoon and containing 88 per cent of the world's rubber, 54 per cent of its tin, 30 per cent of its rice, 20 per cent of its tungsten, and the rich oilfields of the East Indies. All this they had done at the cost of some 15,000 men, about 400 aircraft and a couple of dozen warships, none of them larger than a destroyer.

It was at this point, when the Far Eastern world rang with their victories, when they really did seem invincible at sea, in the air and in the jungle, that the Japanese overreached themselves. Nagumo's aircrews returned to Japan on 22 April, 1942, like the conquering heroes they were, most of them suffering from what the Japanese themselves called *shoribyo*, 'Victory Disease', a very human affliction which the Greeks knew as *hubris*. For the Greeks it was almost always followed by *nemesis*. The Americans had just as expressive a term: Japan was very shortly to receive her 'come-uppance'.

III

THE BATTLE OF THE CORAL SEA

THE carrier raids on Japanese-held islands early in 1942 were excellent for American morale but, as one officer said, 'The Japs didn't mind them any more than a dog minds a flea'. In April, however, a raid took place which the Japanese minded very much indeed.

On the 18th, about 800 miles east of Japan, sixteen B-25 Mitchell bombers of the US Army led by General James Doolittle took off from the aircraft carrier *Hornet*. The B-25s were so big that they prevented *Hornet* operating her own aircraft while they were on board, and she had been escorted to the launch point by *Enterprise*, wearing Halsey's flag, cruisers and destroyers.

Halsey had been briefed that US submarines on their way to patrols off Japan had met a ring of picket boats some 600 miles out from the Japanese coastline. But at 3 am on 18 April and again at 4.30, when Halsey's ships were still 800 miles from Japan, radar echoes were detected ahead, and the first search plane launched from *Enterprise* at dawn reported a picket boat only twenty miles ahead. Shortly afterwards the cruiser *Nashville* sighted an unidentified vessel and opened fire.

Enterprise had on board Lt. G. M. Slonin, the same radio intelligence officer who had been embarked for the Wake and Marcus strikes of February and March, and three operators, who picked up the Japanese radio traffic which revealed that Halsey's force had been sighted.

At 6.30 am local time, an originator with the call sign 'AKU5', tentatively identified at the time as a merchant Maru but actually one of the picket boats, transmitted a contact report: 'HITEHITE.3.6SINRO6 TOO630(AKU5)'. This was broadcast by Tokyo Radio at 8.15, repeated to Commander-in-Chief Fifth Fleet, and was translated as '3 enemy planes on course S.W. at 0630'.

Meanwhile, at 6.45 am, AKU5 transmitted another signal which was assumed to be reporting contact with two aircraft carriers and three of another type of ship. At first these contact reports seemed to be regarded with disbelief in Tokyo, which was very slow to react to the possibility that there could actually be an attack on Japan itself, and took no action for about two hours.

But once the penny had dropped, there was a storm of frantic high precedence radio traffic (all in due course providing fresh grist for HYPO's cryptanalytical mill) addressed to the C-in-Cs Combined, First, Second, Fourth and Fifth Fleets, Commanders First and Eleventh Air Fleets, Commander Submarine Force, Commanders Fourth and Sixth Air Attack Corps and a host of other participants including Tokyo Intelligence, local naval commanders from Sasebo to Yokosuka to Chichi Jima, and individual squadrons and ships at sea.

Amongst this clamour of radio traffic, Slonin's staff in *Enterprise* intercepted a message in JN-25 from Radio Tokyo which they could not decipher. But it had a long list of addressees, one of whose callsigns Slonin did recognize – the Kido Butai, Nagumo's Carrier Striking Force. This suggested that Nagumo's carriers had returned from the Indian Ocean and might be taking part in the search. (In fact they were about to return to Japan that very day and were indeed ordered to steer east for a time to search for Halsey's ships.) The inference was that *Hornet* might be heading towards a hornet's nest.

But the strike was already on its way. Halsey had decided that he would launch at once, even though it was further from Japan than planned, as soon as it was clear that surprise had been lost. Slonin's deductions made it now more urgent than ever for Halsey to launch and get away before he was caught.

The first B-25, piloted by Doolittle himself, took off at 7.25 am and the last of the sixteen was airborne by 8.24. A minute later one of Halsey's staff was writing in the flag log: 'Changed fleet course and axis to 90°, commencing retirement from the area at 25 knots'.

Thirteen B-25s bombed Tokyo and the other three dropped incendiaries on Nagoya, Osaka and Kobe. The aircraft then flew on and landed where they could, one of them in the sea off Ningpo, and four crash-landed. Of the 80 aircrew on the raid, 71 survived; one was killed in his parachute descent, four were drowned, three were executed by the Japanese and one died in prison.

Yamamoto himself signalled the Combined Fleet: 'Enemy task force containing three aircraft carriers as main strength sighted 0630 this morning 730 miles east of Tokyo . . . Operate against American fleet'.

By the next day virtually every warship in the Japanese Navy which could put to sea, from the home islands to the Marianas and the Marshalls, was hunting for Halsey. But it was all to no avail. Halsey had got clean away. At dusk on 20 April Yamamoto called off the hunt.

Later examination of the signals ordering the searches showed that the Japanese realized that American intelligence as to the location of their forces was very good. The signals also showed that the Japanese soon knew that the attacking aircraft must be from aircraft carriers, although they were puzzled by the type of aircraft used, calculating that a strike by normal carrier-borne aircraft could not have been launched until the following morning.

'Doolittle's Raid', as it was called, was a case of *'C'est magnifique, mais est-ce que la guerre?'* It was an enormous publicity success for the United States, but there were some who questioned whether it had been worth the risk of two of the US Navy's precious four carriers.

However, though news of the raid was kept from the Japanese people at large, it both shocked and alarmed the Japanese military who, like the citizens of Berlin, had believed they were immune from air attack. 'Even though there wasn't much damage,' Yamamoto wrote, 'it's a disgrace that the skies over the imperial capital should have been defiled without a single enemy plane shot down. It provides a regrettably graphic illustration of the saying that a bungling attack is better than the most skilful defense.'

Thus, those sixteen aircraft which, as Roosevelt sardonically said, for all the Japanese knew, might have taken off from 'Shangri La', had an effect on the progress of the war out of all proportion to the minor amount of physical damage they actually did. Above all, they served to concentrate sharply the Japanese debate on future strategy.

The Japanese had achieved their war objectives, especially the supply of oil, so quickly and so completely that the Imperial General Staff had given little thought to the future. Japan now had a choice of offensive strategies. She could strike west, with invasions of Ceylon and southern India, aiming for an eventual link with the forces of the Wehrmacht in the Middle East, or she could move south and invade Australia.

Both these alternatives were favoured by the Naval General Staff, but not by the Army, whose thoughts were on China and particularly on a possible offensive against the old enemy, Russia, and who were in any case always reluctant to assign any troops to any theatre of war likely to be under the control of the Navy.

A third choice was to strike east, at Midway and Hawaii, and in the process provoke a major fleet action in which the main US Pacific Fleet, with its carriers, would be utterly and finally destroyed, leading then to the possibility of a negotiated peace.

The destruction of the American fleet was a consummation very dear to the hearts of Admiral Yamamoto Isoruku, the C-in-C Combined Fleet, and his staff. The Naval General Staff preferred a modified plan: if not an actual invasion of Australia, then at least a drive to isolate her from her Allies by seizing the chains of islands running south-east from the tip of New Guinea, through the Solomons, the New Hebrides and the Fijis to Samoa. It was to begin to put this plan into effect that the landings at Lae and Salamaua in New Guinea had been made in March, 1942.

Yamamoto himself was always conscious that time was running out for Japan. The sooner the US fleet was 'taken out' the better. The longer the delay, the stronger the Americans would be. The Doolittle Raid therefore served to strengthen Yamamoto's argument for an attack on Midway. The cheek of it, the sheer unbelievable audacity of a bombing attack on sacred Japanese soil and the unthinkable possibility of a menace to the Emperor's sacred person, made it all the more imperative that the American fleet be destroyed. The capture of Midway would give the Japanese a vital strategic outpost (though Yamamoto's staff conceded that it might be difficult to defend) and would inevitably bring on a conflict with the US Pacific Fleet. Nimitz simply could not stand by and watch Midway invaded.

In the event, the Japanese Naval General Staff compromised: they agreed to continue with the advance towards the Solomons, *and* to attack Midway. The first part of the plan was to begin in May with landings at Tulagi in the Solomons and at Port Moresby on the south-eastern coast of Papua. The second part, the landing at Midway, was to follow in June.

The way to the crucial battles of the Coral Sea and Midway was now open. So, also, was the path to Japan's defeat, for as the American war effort gathered momentum and strength Japan would have been hard-pressed to keep what she had already won. These two new offensives, with the continuing campaigns in China and Burma, proved to be more than Japan could sustain.

The Japanese could have assembled an invasion force, given it the strongest available escort, and simply sent it to occupy Port Moresby.

But that was not their way. Whenever possible, the Japanese liked to elaborate, splitting their forces into separate groups with separate objectives, inviting defeat in detail. They laid intricate traps, with complicated diversions, sacrificial decoys and optimistic pincer movements. Japanese plans demanded a degree of co-operation between their own ships and commanders which no navy in history has ever achieved. They made few allowances for the contingencies of war. Most dangerous of all, they often relied upon the enemy doing what was expected of him.

The plan to capture Port Moresby, codenamed MO, was a typically complicated Japanese undertaking. A Port Moresby Invasion Group of six destroyers, eleven transports and miscellaneous minesweepers and oilers, under Rear Admiral Sadamichi Kajioka in the cruiser *Yubari*, was to sail from Rabaul on 4 May, 1942. A smaller group of minelayers, transports and two destroyers was to invade Tulagi in the Solomons and set up a seaplane base there. A support group of two cruisers and four gunboats and including the seaplane carrier *Kamikawa Maru* was to establish a similar base in the Louisiades Islands.

The main covering group, under Rear Admiral Aritomo Goto in the heavy cruiser *Aoba* with three other heavy cruisers and the light carrier *Shoho* (incorrectly called *Ryukaku* by American intelligence, due to misinterpretation of Japanese ideographs for *Shoho*), left Truk on 30 April to support first the Tulagi and then the Port Moresby landing. A striking force of two heavy cruisers, the carriers *Shokaku* and *Zuikaku*, destroyers and an oiler, under Vice Admiral Takeo Takagi, sailed from Truk on 1 May, to steam round the eastern end of the Solomons and enter the Coral Sea from the east.

The C-in-C Fourth Fleet, Vice Admiral Shigeyoshi Inouye, also sailed from Truk on 1 May in the cruiser *Kashima* for Rabaul from where he would command the whole operation and where he would also have the (not always easily biddable) support of the 25th Air Flotilla.

The intention was that any Allied force attempting to molest the Port Moresby landing would be caught between the pincers of Goto's force to the west and Takagi's carriers to the east. Once this Allied force had been destroyed, Japan would control the Coral Sea and be able to neutralize air bases in Queensland before going on to invade the Ocean and Nauru islands, whose phosphates would be valuable for Japanese agriculture.

It was an ambitious, ingenious and indeed feasible plan; but for tricks of weather and inexplicable errors by the Japanese air groups, it might have worked.

The MO plan might also have worked had it not been for meticulous and imaginative use of radio intelligence, in which method and inspiration were brilliantly combined. The listeners in Washington, Melbourne and Pearl Harbor could analyse only a fraction of the many thousands of messages transmitted by the Imperial Japanese Navy on any one day. Even by May, 1942, they were copying only about 60 per cent of Japanese naval transmissions and analysing only about 40 per cent of these, because of lack of time and shortages of qualified personnel.

Nevertheless, they could recognize associations between units and commands, identify callsigns and by inspired extrapolation and leaps of imagination made shrewd guesses at the meanings of signals. Meanwhile the work of recovering Japanese code values went on gradually but remorselessly; by 8 January, 1942, for instance, 3000 had been recovered out of 5366.

The Japanese had their own difficulties, caused largely by their successes. The security of any code or cypher diminishes in direct ratio to the numbers and lengths of times it is used. The rapidity with which the Japanese Empire had expanded made it physically difficult to distribute new code books to its furthest-flung parts. This not only increased the chances of basic encrypting errors, such as an operator transmitting text in a new code which had already been passed in the old, but could delay the actual introduction of a new code.

JN-25b, for instance, first introduced on 4 December, 1941, was to have been changed on 1 April, 1942. This was postponed to 1 May and not actually carried out until 28 May – a delay which was to have a crucially important effect on the outcome of the Battle of Midway.

There had been speculation about an imminent offensive against Port Moresby as early as 5 March, 1942, when intelligence staff in Australia estimated that there were two or three aircraft carriers and an army division in the Rabaul area ready for an operation. But the first real indication of a campaign specifically against Port Moresby, apart from the usual regular air attacks, emerged in a decyphered Japanese dispatch on 25 March, 1942.

It was an Air Force Operation Order issued by the Commander South Sea Air Force at Rabaul, ordering: 'No. 2 Attack Force continue to support main task and using fighters assist No. 5 Attack Force in the RZP campaign, and with scouts carry out patrol of your assigned area. No. 5 Attack Force continue attacks on RZP'.

At that time 'RZP' was tentatively identified as being in the Port Moresby area. Further messages definitely fixed RZP as Port Moresby and RZQ as Port Moresby Seaplane Base. On 3 April HYPO issued a general warning of 'Numerous indications which point to impending offensive from Rabaul bases are augmentation and reorganization of air in area, numerous movements of air tenders from Truk to Rabaul, and transfer of air strength from the west to Rabaul'.

Early in April HYPO discovered the name of one of the ships earmarked for the forthcoming MO operation. The fleet carrier *Kaga* had run aground, causing herself moderate damage, during operations in the East Indies and was under repair at Sasebo naval base, on the southern Japanese island of Kyushu. On 5 April she was assigned to Vice Admiral Inouye's South Seas Force for the MO operation. Her callsign began to appear an an addressee in messages between Combined Fleet and South Seas Force.

Confirmation came when a message dated about 7 April was decrypted, asking for a 'report on progress of repairs to KAGA. As she is scheduled to participate in RZP Campaign, desire repairs to be completed as soon as possible'.

Although Layton noted in the Pacific Fleet war diary on 9 April that *Kaga* was expected to reach the New Britain area by the end of April, in fact she did not take part in the MO operation, possibly because repairs were not finished in time. But the allocation of such a large fleet carrier, normally part of the Kido Butai, showed the importance of the impending operation and provided another definite indication that the Japanese were planning some offensive in the South Pacific.

There was further evidence of enemy interest in the Coral Sea when a message of 4 April, from the Commander of the Air Group at Rabaul to the Commander of an Air Group in the Truk-New Guinea area, was decrypted and circulated by OP-20-G on the 7th. It included the report that 'also from RTM the sector 150 degrees to 200 degrees was searched a distance of 500 miles'. OP-20-G commented: 'RTM is new but the sector definitely extends into the Coral Sea'.

From 10–24 April many more messages were decrypted concerning Japanese air strength in the Rabaul and Mandates area, especially the types of aircraft carried, state of training and movements of *Ryukaku* (*Shoho*) from Yokosuka to Truk, and then on to the Rabaul area. On 15 April it was learned that two more carriers were scheduled to take part in operations south of Truk. A message on the 13th from

Rear Admiral Tadaichi Hara, Takagi's carrier admiral, to Inouye – intercepted and recovered almost in full by HYPO – stated that the 5th Carrier Division, *Shokaku* and *Zuikaku*, would proceed to Formosa on the 18th, arriving Truk ten days later. An intercept of 25 April revealed the presence of yet another carrier, the converted *Kasuga Maru*, which 'was scheduled to arrive in Yokosuka 20 April from Rabaul and return planes and supplies to Rabaul leaving the 23rd. This is apparently in accordance with previous schedule'.

On 15 April Nimitz's Grey Book recorded 'an offensive in the South-West Pacific is shaping up'. What shape that offensive was likely to take was becoming clearer from callsign identification. For instance, a message from Fourth Fleet Communications Section at Truk on 24 April was addressed to MO Fleet, MO Occupation Force, MO Attack Force, RZP Occupation Force, RXB (Tulagi) Occupation Force and RY (probably Gilbert Islands) Occupation Force.

The 14th Naval District Radio Intelligence unit (HYPO) updated their estimates of enemy strength virtually every day. A stream of signals on 27 April, for instance, indicated the future concentration of Japanese Air Attack Forces: '4th, 5th and 6th in Rabaul, 2nd continues in Indies, 3rd in Malaya; and 1st between Wake and Rabaul. Operations of these major air corps in Rabaul may be supplemented by Cardiv 5, Crudiv 5, and possibly RYUKAKU and Crudiv 8'.

Submarines were also observed: 'Commander Submarine Force is placed in the Caroline Islands, and Subron 8 is believed to be with him. Subron 7 not definitely placed, but has recently been associated with Subron 8, and both have been associated with Rabaul.' As for the aircraft carriers, 'Comcardiv 5 with the ZUIKAKU and SHOKAKU found using Truk radio as a concealed origin, confirming the presence of Cardiv 5 there.'

On 27 April there was a change of Japanese code callsigns, which the watchers had learned was an almost infallible indication that an operation was about to begin. The next day HYPO broadcast a message that 'CinC 4th Fleet originated urgent dispatch believed may represent operation order for offensive operations in southeast theater, addresses 4th Fleet, Crudiv 5, Cardiv 5, RYUKAKU, KAMIGAWA MARU (?), 2 to 3 Desdiv Plane Guards, Comsubfor, 4th and 5th Air Attack Corps, Genzan and Yokohama Air'.

That day, 28 April, the Japanese made their first move in what was to be the Battle of the Coral Sea, when the auxiliary *Nikkai Maru* arrived at Shortland in the Solomons and began to construct a seaplane base. Five large four-engine flying boats flew there from Rabaul to begin long-range patrols the next day.

Several important Japanese orders to the Occupation Forces were intercepted and decoded. One, on 29 April, was from the Chief of Staff, Combined Fleet, to the Chief of Staff 4th Fleet, 11th Air Fleet, Comcrudiv 5, Comcardiv 5, exhorting the Task Force, on the eve of operations, to do its utmost to achieve the basic objectives: 'SECRET: With Reference to the Mandates Force Operation Order No. 13, the objective of the MO will be, first, to restrict the enemy fleet's movements and will be accomplished by means of attacks on outlying units and various areas along the north coast of Australia. The Imperial Navy will operate to its utmost until this is accomplished. Further, we will continue to operate against all bases used by enemy aircraft.'

Although, in an effort to improve security, the Japanese tried to disguise their radio calls in the approach to the Battle of the Coral Sea, traffic analysis produced an enormous amount of valuable information. Enough warning of enemy intentions in the Coral Sea could have been given through traffic analysis alone, but decrypted Japanese messages were always an important check on the accuracy of traffic analysis.

With such full and timely information from decrypts and traffic analysis, Nimitz was able to make his preparations. He had decided he would oppose any Japanese attempt on Port Moresby. The town and harbour, with the airstrip, were vital and had to be defended (although General MacArthur, who assumed formal command of the South-West Pacific Area on 18 April, did not reinforce the Port Moresby garrison until 14 May, long after the battle was over). Port Moresby was not only the key-point for the protection of Australia, but would be an essential launching stage for any future Allied land offensive in New Guinea.

However, it was one thing to know Japanese intentions, but quite another to defeat them. There were some 300 U.S.A.A.F. and R.A.A.F. aircraft based in Australia available for long-range search and attack missions, but their crews lacked experience in identifying and attacking shipping (as the coming battle would demonstrate) and in any case the aircraft were in MacArthur's South-West Pacific Command. The Combined Chiefs of Staff had already approved strict rules of demarcation between the two Commands. Nimitz would just have to hope for whatever co-operation he could get from MacArthur.

Clearly, the main effort would have to come from Nimitz's own carriers. He sent Task Force 11, with *Lexington*, two heavy cruisers and six destroyers, under Rear Admiral Aubrey W. Fitch, south from Pearl Harbor to rendezvous with Task Force 17, commanded by Fletcher in *Yorktown*, with three heavy cruisers, six destroyers and two oilers, in the Coral Sea approaches west of the New Hebrides on 1 May. A support group, Task Force 44 or the ANZAC squadron, of two Australian heavy cruisers, *Australia* and *Hobart*, the US cruiser *Chicago* and two US destroyers, was commanded by the British Rear Admiral J.C. Crace RN. *Chicago* and one destroyer were to join Fletcher on 1 May, the rest by the 4th.

Nimitz gave Fletcher overall command, instructed him to 'destroy enemy ships, shipping and aircraft at favourable opportunities in order to assist in checking further advance by enemy in the New Guinea–Solomons Area' and, with marvellous reliance on the man on the spot, left the rest up to him.

Fletcher's carriers mustered between them 42 Grumman F4F Wildcat fighters, 74 Douglas SBD Dauntless dive-bombers and 25 Douglas TBD Devastator torpedo-bombers. Both these bomber types were by then obsolescent, but *Yorktown* herself was relatively new, having been completed in 1938. *Lexington* was a veteran, completed in 1927 but recently modernized and, of course, with previous success under their belts, her air group was probably the most confident in the US Navy.

For the Japanese, Hara had 37 'Zeke' fighters (five under the authorized strength), 41 'Val' dive-bombers and 42 'Kate' torpedo-bombers, these aircraft being fairly evenly divided between *Shokaku* and *Zuikaku*. *Shoho* had twelve 'Zekes' and nine 'Kates'. Most of the aircrew were veterans, but there was already a slight but ominous dilution of skill; Japan was already having some difficulty replacing experienced aircrews.

On 1 May HYPO broadcast the warning: 'MO campaign now underway; involves south-east New Guinea and Louisiade Archipelago; suggest Moresby for MO. Forces engaged will consist of Cardiv 5; Crudiv 5 less *Nachi*; Crudiv 18 if available [it was]; Desron 6 available; Gunboat Div 8 (now called 19th Division); new Britain Air which is known as No. 5 Attack Force and consisting of Tainan Air Group; 4th Air Corps, and Yokohama Air Group'. (The message also mentioned that various Japanese radio intelligence stations had recently shown an interest in the Aleutians.)

Fletcher and Fitch met on 1 May some 350 miles north-west of New Caledonia and at once began to fuel. As usual in Fletcher's forces, fuelling was rather leisurely. Fitch was still fuelling until 4 May. Fletcher reorganized his ships into an enlarged Task Force 17 and announced his operational plan, that his force 'will operate generally about seven hundred miles south of Rabaul. Upon receiving intelligence of enemy surface forces advancing to the southward, this force will move into a favorable position for intercepting and destroying the enemy.'

In short, Fletcher intended to remain out of enemy air search radius, wait for the Japanese to make the first move, and then counter-attack. Nevertheless, when Fitch had not finished fuelling on 2 May, Fletcher set off westward in *Yorktown* alone to look for the Japanese, so splitting his force in the likely presence of the enemy.

The MO operation went smoothly for the Japanese until 2 May, when there was a snag, revealed in the decrypt of a message that day from No 5 Attack Force at Rabaul to MO Striking Force, 'Tomorrow the 3rd we will have 10 fighters for use, judging from present expenditures, we will require replenishment 9 type Zero fighters which are scheduled to be supplied by —— for MO operations. Please accomplish ferrying of these planes to Rabaul tomorrow.'

On the morning of 2 May the MO Striking Force was some 240 miles north-east of Rabaul. The fighters were flown off but the weather was so bad that they had to return to the carriers, as reported in another decrypt the same day of a message from MO Striking Force: 'Because of bad weather, the ferrying of 10 aircraft to RR has been postponed to 3rd'.

On 3 May Rear Admiral Kiyohide Shima's Tulagi Invasion Group, assisted by strikes from *Shoho*, accomplished the invasion of Tulagi without opposition, as the Australians had already evacuated the place.

Fletcher, still steaming north-west throughout 3 May, heard of the Tulagi invasion late that afternoon and determined to attack, noting, 'This was the kind of report we had been waiting two months to receive'. He detached his oiler *Neosho* and attendant destroyer *Sims* to rendezvous with Fitch while he increased speed to 27 knots so as to close Guadalcanal and launch the first of three strikes on Tulagi at dawn the next day.

Yorktown's SBDs and TBDs expended 22 torpedoes, 76 1,000-lb bombs and 83,000 rounds of machine-gun bullets to damage the destroyer *Kikuzuki* so badly she was beached and abandoned the next day, and sink three small auxiliaries, a result which Nimitz later called 'disappointing in terms of ammunition expended to results obtained'. However, *Yorktown*'s aircrews believed, and claimed, much greater results at the time, and Task Force 17 returned in very good spirits to

42

meet Fitch and Crace the next day, 5 May, and, once again, refuel.

These strikes on Tulagi came as a rude shock to Admiral Inouye, who had not suspected that American carriers were so close. Because of the delay in ferrying the nine fighters to Rabaul – a delay which Inouye himself had approved – the MO Striking Force with *Shokaku* and *Zuikaku* was still about 340 miles north of Tulagi, well out of supporting distance, instead of only 120 miles north of Tulagi at dawn on the 4th, as originally intended. Traffic analysis was showing that, for the first time, the Japanese were beginning to realize that the MO Operation was not such a surprise to the Allies as they had hoped and expected.

Fletcher rejoined the rest of his ships on 5 May and spent the day refuelling. Meanwhile, Inouye did not know whether the American aircraft had struck Tulagi from the north or the south, so the Striking Force aircraft searched both sides of the island and ahead of the force's line of advance on the afternoon of 4 May and the morning of the 5th. Fletcher received news of this on 5 May in a partial decrypt from CincPac of a message sent by Inouye to Takagi, noting that the Japanese carriers 'will proceed north-north-east of Bougainville, thence southward' if the Japanese decided that the American carriers were in the Coral Sea; if not, then the MO Striking Force was to go to Tulagi.

Fletcher also received from CincPac a second decrypted message on 5 May, giving vital information on the direction and timing of future Japanese attacks. It had been sent the day before, by C-in-C 4th Fleet over Rabaul Radio, to Comcrudiv 5 and Comcardiv 5: 'In order to wipe out enemy air bases in the RZP area, the MO Striking Force will launch attacks from a south-easterly direction [this direction not certain, but looks like easterly or southerly in other traffic] on bases in Moresby area on X-3 Day and X-2 Day. This order is in effect until its successful completion. Commence preparations.' To this, HYPO added the comment: 'Best estimate here of X-day is 10 May, based on previous message saying that Division 19 was leaving Marshalls X-7 day and going to Deboyne X-5.'

Takagi's force entered the Coral Sea from the north on 5 May and early on the 6th *Shokaku* and *Zuikaku* were only some 70 miles north of *Yorktown* and *Lexington* who were then, with the rest of Fletcher's ships, refuelling in the open, under a clear, brilliant sky. Inexplicably, Hara had ordered no air searches to the south-east that morning, while Fletcher's searches stopped short of Hara's ships, which were then hidden under thick cloud overcast. So, an excellent chance for a carrier battle, on terms favourable to them, passed Takagi and Hara by.

After fuelling, *Neosho* and *Sims* were detached to steam southwards to the next fuelling rendezvous. In so doing they unwittingly provided the perfect decoy. They were sighted on 7 May by one of Hara's reconnaissance aircraft, which reported them as 'a carrier and a cruiser'.

Delighted and relieved to have found his enemy at last, Hara launched a bomb and torpedo strike at maximum strength of 78 aircraft, thus committing his main force to a very minor target. *Sims* was sunk and *Neosho* was disabled and, because of a wrongly reported navigational position, drifted helplessly for four days before being sighted and sunk by a torpedo from a US destroyer.

Meanwhile, Fletcher dispatched Crace's force westwards to attack the Port Moresby Invasion Group which had been reported nearing the Jomard Passage, about 100 miles off the eastern tip of New Guinea. By so doing Fletcher weakened his own anti-aircraft screen and, of course, deprived Crace's ships of air cover.

Crace's force were duly attacked by aircraft from Rabaul and also, incidentally, in error by U.S.A.A.F. B-17s from Australia. After undergoing and surviving unscathed air attacks equally as intense as those which had sunk *Prince of Wales* and *Repulse*, Crace's force disengaged to the south when, some time later, the invasion group was reported to have retired.

Crace's force, too, had been an ideal decoy. Just as *Neosho* and *Sims* had drawn off Hara's main assault, so Crace had diverted the attack by land-based aircraft from Rabaul.

The watchers at the plotting tables in Pearl Harbor could now see a perfect situation developing for Fletcher – both threats temporarily removed, allowing him to get at the Port Moresby Invasion Group unmolested.

One of *Yorktown*'s dawn search aircraft on 7 May reported sighting 'two carriers and four heavy cruisers'. Fletcher understandably assumed this must be Takagi's striking force and, without further verification, launched a full strike of 93 aircraft. But when the search aircraft returned, it was found that there had been a decoding error: the message should have read 'two heavy cruisers and two destroyers' (the aircraft had actually sighted two light cruisers and two gunboats of a support force intended to build advance seaplane bases in the Solomons). So Fletcher had also committed his maximum force to attack a subsidiary target.

Bravely, Fletcher allowed the strike to go on. Once more, his incredible luck held. The strike was passing off the Louisiades, flying through cloud and mist at 15,000 feet when, by the greatest good luck, *Lexington*'s air group commander and one of her most experienced pilots, Commander William B. Ault, sighted a carrier and other ships almost thirty miles away in clearer weather to starboard.

This was Goto's force and the carrier was *Shoho*. Despite opposition from *Shoho*'s Zekes, the two air groups smothered *Shoho* with thirteen bomb and seven torpedo hits. She sank at 11.33 am and the listeners in the operations rooms in *Lexington* and *Yorktown* heard the exultant voice of Lt Cdr Robert E. Dixon, leading one of *Lexington*'s Dauntless squadrons, calling out loud and clear: 'Scratch one flat-top! Dixon to carrier, scratch one flat-top!' It was Japan's first carrier loss of the war, and a great moment for the Allies.

Lexington and *Yorktown* were ready to launch another strike that afternoon, but Fletcher wisely decided against it. He did not know where Takagi's carriers were, and with the weather worsening there was hardly time to launch and recover in daylight, even if the enemy was found. Fletcher headed westwards, hoping to catch the Port Moresby Invasion Group the next morning, 8 May.

But it was by no means too late for Takagi. He now had a good idea of Fletcher's whereabouts, and his aircrews were itching to attack, after a very frustrating period for them. Hara so far had nothing but blunders and omissions to show for his part.

At 4.30 pm a strike of twelve bombers and fifteen torpedo-bombers was launched, but in squally weather they missed their targets and, ironically, had jettisoned their bombs and torpedoes when they inadvertently found Fletcher's ships by flying right over them. Nine Japanese aircraft were shot down in dog-fights with Wildcats. Three actually tried to land on *Yorktown*, apparently mistaking her for *Shokaku*. More were lost while trying to find and land on their carriers. Eventually, only six of the 27 aircraft of that strike survived.

This contact produced a burst of radio traffic, as recorded by HYPO in a message timed late on 7 May: 'Intense activity, with large number of plain text despatches. Contact report tactical system begun at 0558 (-9), decreased after 1730 (-9). This heavy traffic is all connected with sighting US Operating forces in general New Britain-Solomon Islands area. One productive channel was 31.6 megacycles, using plain language between planes and surface ships. Although identification of surface units is not definite, SHOKAKU appeared likely as one of them. Aircraft homing channel used by carrier SISO was 7035 kilocycles.'

Both fleet commanders considered, and rejected, plans for a surface action that night. The main battle therefore took place the next day, 8 May, with carrier strike and counter-strike.

Fletcher's ships were now well on into the Coral Sea, in exactly the position the Japanese had hoped to catch them. But by now one arm of the pincer, *Shoho*, was gone, and Hara's air groups had suffered losses. Both sides could muster about 120 aircraft, although the balance of combat experience still rested with the Japanese.

Inouye had already ordered the invasion force to withdraw, after he had heard of *Shoho*'s loss and the presence of Crace's ships, but it was still possible for the invasion to proceed again if Hara's aircrews could pull it off.

Both sides flew searches before dawn and sighted each other at about the same time. Hara tried to gain time by launching his strike without waiting for an exact sighting report, but the Americans were the first actually to attack, arriving over Takagi's force just before 11 am.

Zuikaku happened to be hidden under cloud and the main attack fell upon *Shokaku*. More than twenty of the bombers failed to find the enemy at all and the torpedo-bombers released their torpedoes at too great a range, so that they were easily evaded. But *Yorktown*'s dive-bombers scored two hits, and *Lexington*'s one, on *Shokaku* setting her on fire forward so that she could land on but not launch aircraft. Many of *Shokaku*'s aircraft were transferred to *Zuikaku* and Takagi ordered her to break off and head for home shortly after 1 pm.

Takagi had let *Shokaku* go because by that time he thought that both American carriers had been sunk. Hara's strike, of 18 Zekes, 33 Vals and 18 torpedo Kates, found *Yorktown* and *Lexington* in bright sunshine, with visibility almost unlimited.

Now, at last, the Japanese pilots had the targets they longed for. *Yorktown* was hit by one bomb forward, which did no serious damage, and managed to dodge several torpedoes. *Lexington* was hit by two torpedoes and two bombs. But the fires were put out, the list corrected by counter-flooding, and the ship seemed safe.

Japanese aircrew were as prone to exaggeration as the Americans, and Hara's pilots returned claiming to have sunk two American carriers. Later that day Tokyo Radio broadcast the good news in plain language: '6th Division and an enemy Striking Force are now fighting. In addition to sinking one carrier, we are sure that there were 3 hits on one other, 0920 (-9) position 14° 08' South, 155° 50' approximate speed 16; originated by Commander Striking Force.'

But Hara's pilots were only half-right. Often in the Pacific, a carrier survived the initial damage only to succumb to later fires and explosions. So it was with *Lexington*. At 12.47 pm there was an explosion caused by an electrical spark igniting petrol vapour. This was followed by a second explosion and more fierce fires. At 5.10 *Lexington* had to be abandoned, to be sunk at 8 pm by a torpedo from a destroyer.

Yamamoto ordered Takagi to return to the battle, but Fletcher had withdrawn. Curiously, the Port Moresby Invasion Group could now have turned round and made their landing with every chance of success. Their only opposition would have been land-based aircraft, which had already shown their fallibility in attacking ships. But the Invasion Group also retired. The battle was over.

At Pearl Harbor HYPO monitored enemy reactions and reported on 9 May: 'Lack of plain language contact reports from Coral Sea Area believed to be an indication of at least temporary cessation from active operations. Rabaul Radio was used as cover-up for majority of units involved in south-eastern area, with SHOKAKU, appearing under Truk radio call, originating a series of dispatches which may mean her imminent return to Truk Area en route to Empire?

'SHOKAKU is believed to be en route north with destroyer escort. No traffic to or from RYUKAKU (*Shoho*). Last reported operating in the Solomon Island area.'

The next day an official order was issued by Combined Fleet to 'postpone' the occupation. A decrypted message from Rabaul read: 'Request urgent dispatch approval of my action in postponing the occupation of RZP (Moresby) because of the necessity of eliminating the enemy forces.'

Another decrypted message of Rabaul Radio gave precise details of enemy losses: 'Our losses: RYUKAKU, sunk (hit by 7 torpedoes and 13 bombs), 22 aviation personnel made forced landings; eighty of these were injured, 16 seriously, 64 minor; others went down with the ship.

'SHOKAKU —— hits, 3 and 8; damage to gasoline storage, engine room, etcetera; (some blanks here); 94 killed, including 4 officers, 96 seriously injured, —— number of minor injuries.'

Shokaku had reached Truk and was indeed on her way home to Japan. A message giving her route was decrypted, but the coordinates of points along the route were in an unsolved secret grid, so only the points of departure and arrival were known. There were several US submarines on patrol within range of the likely route between Truk and the Bungo Suido, the entrance to the Inland Sea. Four of them searched for *Shokaku* and one, *Triton*, actually sighted her, making 16 knots but just outside torpedo range. *Shokaku* eventually reached Japan after an exciting passage in which she nearly capsized.

So ended the Battle of the Coral Sea. It was the first in naval history in which no ship on either side ever caught sight of an enemy ship, the whole action being fought by aircraft. Tactically, it could be said the Japanese had gained yet another victory. *Shoho* was a fair exchange for *Sims*, *Neosho* and *Lexington*. However, *Shokaku* was badly damaged and *Zuikaku*'s air group had suffered serious losses, so that neither took part at Midway, where their presence might well have been decisive.

At Pearl Harbor there was grief over the loss of '*Lady Lex*', but Coral Sea was very soon perceived as the strategic victory it was, and one in which radio intelligence had played a crucial part. For the first time in the war Japan's invasion plans had been thoroughly upset and her invasion forces had been made to turn back. The effect on Allied morale was enormous. The Japanese were not invincible after all.

IV

'SHOW-DOWN' AT MIDWAY

IF there had been any remaining post-Pearl Harbor doubts about 'all that Comint crap', then the Coral Sea removed them once and for all. It was quite clear that, had it not been for radio intelligence, the first the Americans would have known about the Japanese invasion of Port Moresby would very likely have been a triumphant communiqué from the Tokyo *Domei* news agency announcing the victory. As a secret assessment of the role of radio intelligence carried out in September, 1942, commented: 'It takes nothing from the achievements of the fleets of the US Navy at Coral Sea to say that they had been brought to the right spot at exactly the right time by the work of radio intelligence'.

In fact it was possible that the deployment of American forces before the Coral Sea had been too successful. Was there no Japanese staff officer anywhere sceptical and suspicious enough to wonder how it had come about that in the vast wastes of the Pacific Ocean those American aircraft carriers had appeared just where and when they were least expected and could be most effective? But the Japanese were as reluctant as the Germans to entertain the thought that their high-grade codes and cyphers might have been compromised.

The Coral Sea was an undoubted set-back for the Japanese, but was not too dismaying for the Japanese High Command. It was merely a temporary back-eddy in the irresistible tide of victory. On 5 May, 1942, while the battle was still in progress, Imperial Japanese Headquarters gave Yamamoto a directive to carry out Operation MI, the invasion and occupation of Midway Island and the western Aleutians, and they did not see fit to cancel the directive when the results of the Coral Sea were known. The date set for the invasion of Midway was the night of 5/6 June.

Midway would give the Japanese an advanced warning and defence post at the western end of the Hawaiian chain, while the Aleutians would pin down the northern end of the Japanese defence line. More important to Yamamoto, a move against Midway would surely bring about a confrontation with the US fleet.

Yamamoto's desire for one great decisive, 'show-down' battle with the US fleet was strategically sound. If the American fleet were decisively defeated, Hawaii would fall and the Japanese would be able to roll back the war to the shores of America, which were very inadequately defended. In such circumstances the American people would hardly have agreed to concentrate upon the defeat of Germany first – not with a treacherous enemy of their own off their western coast. A Second Front could not then have been mounted until the United States had settled with Japan, by which time Russia might have defeated Germany on her own, with such assistance as Great Britain and the United States could afford. The Iron Curtain would not then have dropped at the Elbe, but at the Rhine, possibly even at Calais.

Other quiet victors of the Coral Sea were Joe Rochefort and the staff of HYPO. From now on Nimitz tended to trust their judgement rather than the often conflicting advice of OP-20-G. Rochefort and HYPO had done brilliantly before the Coral Sea. They were now about to surpass themselves.

For some time even before the Battle of the Coral Sea Rochefort had suspected that the Japanese were planning to achieve another major objective, through some offensive much greater and more ambitious than Operation RY, Admiral Inouye's known plan to capture the Ocean and Nauru Islands.

As before, Rochefort built up his concept of the enemy's plans with uncanny insight through an accumulation of small, seemingly unrelated details. As early as February, 1942, it had been established that the prefix 'A' in coded Japanese signals referred to American Pacific possessions. Thus 'AA' was Wake and 'AK' Pearl Harbor. In one signal there was a reference to a 'pending offensive', designated 'K', scheduled for 5 March.

On 3 March Station CAST provided a garbled intercept of a Tokyo signal which was readable enough to be understood as referring to forces in 'AH, AFH and AF areas' involved in the 5 March operation. It seemed that 'AH' was Hawaii and 'AFH' stood for islands in the Hawaiian group. On the 4th 'AF' was identified as possibly being Midway, HYPO commenting that day upon a Japanese message: 'This dispatch seems to indicate that areas AF and AFH are in the vicinity of Hawaiian Islands'.

But Rochefort and Layton both missed the clue, that the 'K' operation was derived from the designator 'AK' for Pearl Harbor, i.e. that it was an attack on Pearl Harbor. A few Japanese flying boats did make an unexpected and unintercepted but ineffectual bombing attack on Oahu in the early hours of 5 March.

It was realized that the Japanese had no aircraft capable of making the round trip from Wake, their nearest base, to Oahu. Layton suggested that they had flown from Wotje in the Marshalls and landed to refuel from submarines at French Frigate Shoals, towards the western end of the Hawaiian chain. Recent direction-finding fixes had indicated Japanese submarines operating around the shoals. Nimitz had a warship sent to patrol there and later had a defensive minefield laid.

The search for 'AF' went on. When a message of 9 March from Tokyo to air group commanders in the Mandates was decrypted, it was found to be a two-day forecast of wind force and direction at 'AF'. The local submarine commander was not an addressee of this message, as he had been in previous ones, so Rochefort guessed that the forecast was for the weather over target American island bases which were within range of Japanese air attacks from the Marshalls. This, as Layton said, 'was our very first inkling that "AF" could be Midway'.

Rochefort also detected a growing Japanese interest in the Aleutians. On 9 March decrypt intelligence revealed that '1st Air Attack Force in discussing air operations with 5th Fleet gives impression these two units arranging as yet unknown operations northern sector involving close coordination sea and air activities. Same forces involved in Bali-Java attack. Appear to be replenishments and upkeep schedules 9 to 19 March staying at Kendari and Makassar City areas'. The Radio Intelligence comment was: 'If this impression is correct it may indicate possible operations against Aleutian Islands with air and sea forces'.

On 27 April Rochefort noted the CinC 2nd Fleet's request for charts of the Gulf of Alaska, the Aleutian Islands and the Bering Sea, and in a message of 1 May he commented that 'Various Radio Intelligence stations have recently exhibited interest in Aleutians. Best indicator of future operations is Tokyo Office which assigns place name designators. Last January this office listed places in Aleutians indicating they were areas of forthcoming operations. Therefore second choice for operations of available forces is raid on Aleutians. This is considered unlikely at this time, but is certainly probable at a later date. CinC 2nd Fleet will command available forces'.

51

There were other pointers. On 4 May a partially translated decrypt revealed that an (unnamed) battleship had signalled to the CinC 1st Fleet and Combatdiv 3: 'This ship will be undergoing repairs during the time of the said campaign. Work has already been started on ——. The date of completion being (near 21 May), will be unable to accompany you in the campaign'.

The next day a decrypted message originated by Imperial Headquarters but sent by CinC Combined Fleet (Yamamoto, who had evidently just received the directive to carry out Operation MI) to Tokyo read: 'For current scheduled operations, expedite delivery of fueling hose as follows:

For	4½ meter lengths	12 meter lengths
Crudiv 4	0	5
Crudiv 7	0	5
Desron 4	8	5
Desron or Desdiv 8	8	5.'

Some indication of the forces to be employed in the operations appeared in a decrypted message of 6 May, from 1st Air Fleet to five addressees, two of them identified as Cardiv 5 and Iwakuni Air Station (on the Inland Sea in southern Honshu): 'Because of the necessity for completing preparations for —— operations, transfer replacement personnel for this fleet direct to indicated bases at once:
'For AKAGI and SHOKAKU to Kagoshima Base
'For KAGA, ZUIKAKU, and SORYU, to ——Base
'For RYUJO, HIRYU,——
'For RYUKAKU, as ordered by her commanding officer.'
A raid on the Aleutians would certainly involve extensive fuelling at sea, which would account for the demand for more hoses. But the appearance of so many carriers of the Kido Butai in decrypts and in traffic analysis led Rochefort to suspect that the main Japanese objective was not the Aleutians but in the mid-Pacific, in the Hawaiian area. There was also a change in the pattern of radio traffic, with increasing traffic between ships and Saipan, suggesting that a great many ships were assembling in ports in the Marianas to take part in some operation in the Central Pacific unconnected with the drive on Port Moresby.

Another, seemingly trivial, signal of 6 May had a deeper significance. It was from 4th Air Attack Force Headquarters on Kwajalein:

'Request we be supplied 10 crystals for frequencies 4990 and 8990 for use in aircraft in the second 'K' campaign. Above to reach this headquarters prior to 17th.'

4th Air Attack Force followed with another signal of 10 May: 'Request that the crystals for use in the K operations be forwarded via plane leaving Yokosuka Air on 12th (delivery to be made at Imieji).'

The crystal frequencies were unusual for aircraft. But it was the mention of 'the second "K" campaign' and 'the K operations' which attracted Rochefort's special attention. It seemed the Japanese were about to carry out another flight over Oahu.

That had indeed been Yamamoto's intention. The unexpected appearances of American carriers in the Coral Sea convinced him that he must have the latest accurate information of the whereabouts of the American fleet before MI. But the projected reconnaissance was thwarted by the presence of the warship at French Frigate Shoals. In a sense, this was the first thing to go wrong for Yamamoto in the sequence of events known as the Battle of Midway.

When Yamamoto came to plan MI (for Midway) in detail, the Navy's previous successes led him to neglect some basic rules of warfare. At the very time when he could have brought about the decisive battle he longed for, he chose to disperse his ships to pursue different objectives. He could have drawn up his immense armada, of eight carriers with their 400 aircraft, eleven battleships, thirteen heavy cruisers, eleven light cruisers and 65 destroyers, and advanced upon Midway. Nimitz would have had to give battle with what ships he had, as indeed he did, and Yamamoto's fleet should have been more than strong enough to win.

But, once again, that was neither the Japanese nor Yamamoto's way. Instead, Yamamoto and his staff prepared a characteristically labyrinthine Japanese plan, including a diversionary decoy and a pincer movement, involving no less than five major forces, some of which were themselves further divided into two, three or even four subdivisions.

An advance expeditionary force of submarines was to spread out in a line to report the movements of the American fleet when, as Yamamoto expected, it sallied forth from Pearl Harbor after receiving the news that Midway was under attack. The Carrier Striking Force, once again under Nagumo flying his flag in *Akagi*, with *Kaga*, *Hiryu* and *Soryu*, would strike first at Midway and then at the American fleet when it arrived. The Midway Occupation Force, commanded by Vice Admiral Nobutake Kondo, was to consist of a covering group, with battleships and cruisers, a close support group of cruisers and destroyers, a transport group under Rear Admiral Raizo Tanaka, of transports and freighters screened by destroyers, a seaplane group to set up a base at Kure Island, and a minesweeping group.

Yamamoto himself was to command the Main Body, with three battleships, one of them his flagship, the 70,000-ton 18-inch-gunned monster super-battleship *Yamato*, and the light carrier *Hosho*. Four of the Main Body's battleships were to be detached to cover the Northern Area Force, under Vice Admiral Boshiro Hosogaya, with its own carriers and cruisers, to invade the Aleutian Islands of Adak, Attu and Kiska. The Aleutian attack was the diversionary decoy which would, Yamamoto hoped and expected, at least distract attention and at best divert powerful American forces northwards, away from the main action.

The plan was for Nagumo's carriers to strike at Midway. When the American fleet came out, Yamamoto's battleships would close them. The American ships would then be crushed by the triple pincers of Nagumo's carriers, Yamamoto's battleships and Kondo's battleships from the Midway Occupational Force. It was curious that Yamamoto, the most enlightened advocate of carrier warfare, should still place such emphasis on destroying his enemy with heavy guns. The battleships would have been much better employed in close support of the carriers. The two light carriers *Ryujo* and *Junyo*, far north off the Aleutians, would have been better employed under Nagumo.

The other major weakness in Yamamoto's planning was more excusable. Unaware that so much of JN-25 was being read, and so many of his ships' movements were being revealed by traffic analysis, he was sure that the American fleet would not sail from Pearl Harbor until the first news that Midway was threatened. Japanese aircrew reports from the Coral Sea indicated that both American carriers had either been sunk or so badly damaged that they could not take part, even if the American fleet did put to sea. In short, Yamamoto proceeded with his plans in the firm belief that it was virtually impossible for American carriers to be anywhere near Midway when he attacked it.

The MI plan was so complicated that the admirals and captains who were to carry it out met on 1 May for a four-day conference in *Yamato*'s wardroom, presided over by Yamamoto himself, when they studied in war games the possible courses the battle might take.

Ironically, one game produced a situation in which American carriers appeared on Nagumo's flank while he was striking at Midway – exactly as it happened in the battle. In that game Midway was not captured before the American carriers arrived. As a result, two Japanese carriers were sunk and a third so badly damaged it had to retire, while a division of destroyers was lost for lack of fuel and Midway itself was not captured for another week. But Rear Admiral Matome Ugaki, Yamamoto's chief of staff, who had already somewhat arbitrarily weighted the games in the carriers' favour, brushed these mishaps aside, while the umpires, evidently also suffering from *shoribyo*, permitted all three carriers to be miraculously resurrected, two of them from the ocean floor, to take part in the next stage of operations.

Some officers present were brave enough to express their worries about the plan. But Yamamoto would brook no alterations nor any delay. He had every confidence in his own design. In any case, the Imperial General Staff had set a rigid timetable for the invasion. Also there were meteorological limitations. Midway had to be invaded in the first days of the month, when high water slack after dawn would allow assault craft to cross the atoll's reef. The Aleutians were forecast to be clagged in by fog in July. MI therefore had to be in the first week of June.

Meanwhile, Rochefort and the HYPO staff were day by day winkling out more information about MI. On 7 May it was a signal from the CinC 1st Air Fleet giving an amended agenda and the list of speakers for a conference of Japanese air commanders at Kagoshima on 16 May. The subjects to be discussed, from (1) 'the battle for air superiority' to (10) 'strategy in general' and including (6) 'organization of air fleet aviation and fleet air units ashore and their training', indicated a forthcoming operation of immense complexity and the greatest importance.

In the next four days there were signals giving the departure dates of major units, including carriers of the Kido Butai escorted by destroyers, leaving Japan for the Saipan-Guam area. A signal of 12 May from the CinC Combined Fleet to the CinCs 2nd and 4th Fleets said, 'We are now arranging for the military equipment, shells, and bombs which you will require at Truk during the forthcoming campaign.' There were hints that the new campaign was to begin about 21 May.

The general tone of the Japanese signals was always one of sublime confidence. It would not be whether but *when* Midway was captured. Fresh evidence flooded in every day. A signal of 13 May from an unknown ship requested charts of Hawaii, Oahu and Pearl Harbor, '500 copies of northern ——' and Hawaiian Area publications to be flown to Saipan. Another the same day, from 4th Air Attack Force, positively linked 'base equipment and ground crews and advance to AF ground crews' with 'everything in the way of base equipment and military supplies which will be needed in the K campaign.' On the 16th a long four-part signal gave details of a full-scale Japanese rehearsal of their occupation manoeuvres.

The first definite mention by the Japanese of the objective of the forthcoming campaign was in another message of 13 May, but not decrypted until the 20th, from an unidentified sender to the Chiefs of Staff of the Combined, 2nd and 4th Fleets and 11th Air Fleet: 'Says the PS (Saipan) —— Force which is concerned in the occupation of MI [later identified as Midway] is scheduled to hold an operation conference on the 26th and to depart on the 27th'.

Saipan was 2,191 miles from Midway, or five days' steaming at 20 knots. Thus ships leaving Saipan on 27 May would reach Midway on 2 or 3 June – that, Rochefort calculated, was 'N' Day, the date of the attack. A day earlier, on 19 May, Rochefort had partially decrypted a message of the 16th from the 1st Air Fleet staff: ' . . .As we plan to make attacks from a general northwesterly direction from N-2 days to N-day inclusive, please send weather three hours prior to take-off on the said day', and giving an undecipherable map reference '50 miles north-west of AF'.

Rochefort was now sure that 'AF' was Midway, and it would be attacked by the Kido Butai on or about 3 June, 1942. Washington did not agree, and went so far as to suggest that Rochefort was being duped by an elaborate Japanese deception. Admiral King and NEGAT believed that the real target of the Japanese was the west coast of the States and the date of the attack a fortnight later than Rochefort's forecast.

Rochefort and a colleague, Lt Cdr Jasper Holmes, devised a scheme to prove Washington wrong. Holmes knew that Midway got all its fresh water supply from an evaporator plant. Supposing, he suggested, Midway was to report some mishap in its evaporator, leading to an emergency cry for fresh water, transmitted so that the Japanese could overhear it?

Nimitz approved the plan. On 19 May Admiral Bloch, Commander Hawaiian Sea Frontier, passed a message on the secure submarine cable to Midway instructing the garrison commander to transmit immediately, in plain language, a report that there had been an explosion in the distilling plant and urgently requesting an emergency supply of fresh water. To add conviction, the report was also made by one of the strip-cypher systems the Japanese were known to have captured on Wake Island. When he received Midway's signal, Bloch replied, also in plain language, that a fresh water barge would be sent at once.

The Japanese took the bait, as Holmes said, 'like hungry barracuda'. On the 20th Station Belconnen in Melbourne signalled to Washington the decrypt of the Japanese version of Midway's urgent signal: 'AF air unit sent following radio message to commandant 14th Naval district. AK (Pearl Harbor) of 20th. With reference to this unit's report dated 19th. At present time we have only enough water for two weeks. Please supply us immediately'. Belconnen added: 'This will confirm identity of AF'. Rochefort himself waited a tactful further three days before signalling Washington: 'As stated previously AF confirmed here as Midway'.

Between 18 and 25 May decrypts revealed that something tremendous was underway and gave an astoundingly detailed picture of how it was to be done; that the positions to be taken up by Japanese submarines before the attack on Midway were to be 150 miles westward of Oahu; land-based fighters were to be used as part of the Midway Striking Force; the Occupation Force was to have its own independent air arm; a list of letter symbols to be used as designators for certain places and areas; important Japanese warship movements to appointed rendezvous; the arrival of more supply and fuel vessels, with new personnel, at Saipan; from the number of Special Landing Troops and other units which were being added to the Occupation Force, it appeared that the capture of Midway was only the first step in a programme of Japanese conquest and evidently the seizure of Hawaii, including Pearl Harbor, was to follow; the callsigns of the Japanese forces which were to operate at Midway; an important Japanese conference of naval staff members had taken place to discuss the coming operations; more Japanese callsigns had been recovered and several more ships had arrived at Saipan; aircraft and pilot replacements were being sent to *Akagi*, *Hiryu*, *Kaga*, *Soryu* and a new unidentified carrier; another convoy of supply ships had arrived at Saipan; reserve pilots were being brought in for the Striking Force; another destroyer group had been added to the 2nd Fleet which was to attack Midway; and an intimation that the Japanese were soon to change their code.

On 22 May a British intelligence source (deleted from American records, but almost certainly FECB Colombo) sent a message to the US Navy showing that they too had been monitoring Japanese signals, although they had not confirmed the Japanese objective nor seen the indications of Japanese interest in the Aleutians.

The message gave details of the forces under CinC 2nd Fleet, as 'Crudiv 7, Cardiv 7, Desron 2, Special Base establishing units of Naval Landing Party, and Transports are concentrating at Saipan in near future, date unknown', listed other ships in the 'fleet anchorage Kyushu', and concluded this 'is possibly the force ordered to carry out invasion of AF (thought to be Midway but not confirmed). No evidence to show of any other objective or that of Northern Force.'

A final flurry of decrypts from 26 May revealed the schedules and locations of Japanese convoys en route to seize Midway; more callsigns for the operation areas; additional units attached to the Midway forces; an urgent request from Saipan for seaplane replacements by 3 June; and the rendezvous of Occupation Forces at 27° North, 170° East. At 0000 on 28 May, the long-delayed code change took place and very little further information could be gathered from Japanese messages.

But, so far as Japan was concerned, the harm had already been done. Rochefort was at last able to strip out the date-time group of operation MI and reveal that N-Day was 4 June. By the time he came to make his celebrated contribution to Nimitz' staff conference on 27 May, Joe Rochefort had almost all of MI at his fingertips – dates, times, places, ships, rendezvous, plans and intentions. He and Layton predicted that the Japanese carriers would probably attack on the morning of 4 June, from the north-west on a bearing of 325 degrees. They could be sighted at about 175 miles from Midway at around 0700 local time. That forecast was the most stunning intelligence *coup* in all naval history.

Nimitz himself was always unshakeably convinced that Yamamoto's objective was Midway. With so much accurate prior intelligence, Nimitz was able to beat Yamamoto to every conclusion. For example, when the Japanese submarines formed their patrol line on 3 June, the American ships were already well past them. The submarines saw nothing throughout the whole battle.

The US fleet had sailed in two task forces on 28 and 30 May and included *Yorktown* whose Coral Sea bomb damage had been repaired by the dockyard at Pearl in three days (the original estimate was three months). Nimitz also had *Enterprise*, his most experienced carrier, and *Hornet*, who was still comparatively new to Pacific battle, with a total of some 230 aircraft, thirteen cruisers and about 30 destroyers.

On Midway Island itself, where the ground defences had been strengthened as much as possible in the previous few weeks, there was a heterogeneous collection of about 150 aircraft, from B-17 Flying Fortresses to ancient Brewster Buffalo fighters, and including six of the new Grumman Avenger TBRs, which would replace the Devastator in the Fleet.

As he had done in the Coral Sea, Nimitz divided his ships into two groups. TF 16, with *Enterprise* and *Hornet*, was to have been commanded by Halsey, but he had already had an energetic war and was suffering from a debilitating skin disease. He was replaced for the operation by Rear Admiral Raymond Spruance, who could not have been a greater contrast to Halsey: quiet where Halsey was forthright, shunning personal publicity where Halsey was a war correspondent's dream, a shy, thoughtful ascetic man who ate and drank frugally. Bold yet wary in action, he was capable of thinking clearly under the greatest stress, and in time he emerged as the greatest sea-captain in the Pacific, who went on winning battles for his country.

TF 17, with *Yorktown*, was commanded by Fletcher, who was senior to Spruance and had overall command. Nimitz still had some old battleships but they were too slow to keep up with the carriers and would themselves need air cover, so he kept them off the west coast of America, as he had done at the time of the Coral Sea action.

After fuelling, Spruance and Fletcher met on 2 June about 325 miles north-east of Midway, a carefully-chosen position where the carriers could lie undetected, whilst long-range 700-mile searches from Midway looked for the Japanese fleet.

Nimitz had also sent five cruisers and thirteen destroyers north to engage Hosogaya's Aleutian Attack Force. He had now done all he could: he had his maximum strength in the optimum position for its use. Events must now wait on the Japanese.

The component parts of Yamamoto's complicated scheme sailed from various ports in Japan and the Marianas at the end of May and by 1 June they were all steaming eastwards through fog, rain and high winds. On 3 and 4 June aircraft from *Ryujo* and *Junyo* attacked Dutch Harbor in the Aleutians. The islands were lightly defended and the Japanese were eventually able to land and occupy Attu and Kiska islands, after some minor naval engagements and strenuous counter-attacks by the USAAF.

To some Americans the loss of these admittedly insignificant islands slightly tarnished the great victory to come. But Nimitz was not to be drawn into what he knew was only a sideshow. The vital battle would be fought around Midway and it opened shortly before 9 am on 3 June when the pilot of a Catalina at the end of his patrol 'leg', some 700 miles out from Midway, sighted what he took to be the main Japanese fleet, about thirty miles ahead. 'Do you see what I see?' he asked his co-pilot. 'You're damned right I do!' was the reply. They tracked the ships, actually part of the Midway

Occupation Force, until 11 am, when they reported 'eleven enemy ships, steering east, at 19 knots'.

A strike of nine B-17 bombers from Midway found the ships at about 4.30 that afternoon and made three high-level bombing attacks. They claimed to have damaged 'two battleships or heavy cruisers' but actually they obtained no hits. Four Catalinas armed with torpedoes had slightly better luck in a moonlight attack by radar at about 1.30 am the next morning. They hit one tanker and caused some damage and casualties, although the ship was able to steam on. This was the only success by any shore-based aircraft in the battle, although they were to have an important diversionary effect at a crucial time.

Nimitz and Fletcher knew from previous decrypted information that this force could not be their main opponent. Nagumo's carriers had to be much closer, probably not more than 400 miles west of Midway.

At 7.50 in the evening of 3 June Fletcher altered course to steer south-west, aiming to be about 200 miles north of Midway by dawn on the 4th, in position to fly off strikes against Nagumo as soon as he was found. At the same time Nagumo was steering south-east at 25 knots through the night, so as to be in position to strike at Midway soon after dawn. So the two carrier forces were converging upon each other for a confrontation on 4 June. The difference was that Fletcher could guess where his enemy was, while Nagumo did not suspect that his opponent was even at sea.

Thursday, 4 June, 1942, dawned bright and clear, with visibility up to 40 miles and a light south-easterly trade wind blowing, which dropped away as the sun came up at 4.30. *Yorktown* launched search planes to cover a northern semi-circle up to 100 miles in radius, just at the time Nagumo, about 215 miles to the west, was launching his first strike against Midway.

Nagumo's ships were still shrouded in the cloud cover of the cold front which had hidden them for some days, but they were sighted and the eagerly expected message was intercepted from a Catalina transmitting to Midway. Nine minutes later the Catalina reported, 'Many enemy planes heading Midway bearing 320° distant 160'.

Shortly after 6 am the same aircraft reported 'two carriers and battleships bearing 320°, 180 miles from Midway, course 135° speed 25'. This position, about 200 miles west-south-west of TF 16, was the first firm news about Nagumo's carriers. Fletcher chose to recover his search aircraft and await more intelligence before launching *Yorktown*'s strike. He ordered Spruance to 'proceed southwesterly and attack enemy carriers when definitely located' and said he would follow himself as soon as his aircraft had been recovered.

Meanwhile Nagumo's strike of 36 Kates and 36 Vals, escorted by 36 Zekes and led by Lt Tomonaga of *Hiryu*, were on their way to Midway, where they arrived at about 6.30. They bombed buildings, hangars, oil storage tanks and the hospital, but they did not put the runways out of action and killed very few people on the ground. The Marine fighters did their best but the antique Buffaloes and the Wildcats were outclassed, and seventeen were shot down. However, they and the Midway gunners shot down about a third of the strike, which was very good going indeed. More important, Midway survived the attack.

Midway also tried to strike back. Warned by radar, six Avengers and four B-26 Marauders of the USAAF took off at 6.15 and reached the Japanese fleet at about 7.10. Unescorted by fighters of their own, the bombers were severely handled by the carriers' Zekes; only two Marauders and one of the Avengers, and that badly shot up, returned to Midway. None of them scored any hits on any Japanese ship.

However, their attack was most fortunate in the end. Tomonaga had come back from Midway, reporting that another strike was needed. These attacks by Midway bombers proved him right. It was at this point, when Nagumo had to make a series of crucial decisions, that things began to go wrong, for him and for Japan.

The Japanese had begun to fly off searches by seaplanes from the cruisers at 4.35 that morning. Nagumo had kept back a full strike of 93 aircraft, armed with torpedoes and bombs, to deal with any enemy ships sighted. Three float-planes took off smartly, but the fourth, from the cruiser *Tone*, was delayed until 5 am.

By 7 am, when Nagumo learned from Tomonaga that Midway needed another strike, he had still heard nothing from any of the searching float-planes. So, at 7.15, he ordered the ranks of waiting aircraft to be broken up and the aircraft to be struck down into the hangars below, while the Midway strike landed on. He also ordered the Kates that had been armed with torpedoes – for use against ships – to be rearmed with bombs – for bombing Midway. This was an evolution which would take at least an hour.

It was unlucky for the Japanese that the US fleet should happen to be in the search sector covered by the delayed float-plane from *Tone*. At 7.28 the first message arrived from this aircraft: 'Ten enemy surface ships, in position 10° Midway, distance 240 miles, course 150°, speed over 20 knots.' There was no mention of carriers, but this was the first inkling Nagumo had that he might have opposition. But ten ships 240 miles away did not worry him, and he did not cancel his order to break up the strike. Also, he had to keep decks clear for the returning Midway strike.

But something must have snagged in Nagumo's cautious mind, or perhaps it was the advice of one of his staff, for at 7.45 he changed his mind. He gave the orders: 'Prepare to attack enemy fleet units' and 'leave torpedoes on those aircraft not yet changed to bombs'.

At 7.47 Nagumo signalled to *Tone*'s maddeningly deliberate pilot to 'Ascertain ship types and maintain contact'. At 8.09 the pilot replied: 'Five cruisers and five destroyers'. But, at 8.20, there came the addition which changed the whole picture of the battle for Nagumo: 'Enemy is accompanied by what appears to be a carrier'.

This message could not have come at a worse time for Nagumo. Some of his aircraft were still on deck, some struck down below in the hangars, some still armed with torpedoes, some with bombs, while the incoming Midway strike still had to be landed on.

Rear Admiral Yamaguchi in *Hiryu*, a most able officer, suggested that at least his ship's strike should be flown off to attack the American ships. Nagumo rejected the suggestion, which was a good one, and might well have caught Spruance still closing his target. He ordered all aircraft to be struck down and the returning aircraft landed on.

It was difficult for Nagumo to make the right decision because he was being harried at every turn. His fighters were at that moment beating off another attack from Midway, and if he had launched a strike it would have had no escort. The Marines and the USAAF on Midway had attacked with Devastators, Flying Fortresses (which had taken off before dawn) and Vindicators. Several aircraft were lost, for near-misses on *Hiryu* and *Akagi*, but they did serve to keep Nagumo preoccupied at a critical time. The US submarine *Nautilus* added to the confusion by attacking a battleship and evading the subsequent depth-charge attack.

The Midway strike had been recovered by 9.18 and all four Japanese carriers at once began furiously to refuel, rearm and range up a full strike against the American carrier, or carriers.

Spruance by now had the information that his opponent was some 200 miles west-north-west of Midway and he coolly calculated that the best time to attack would be when Nagumo was just recovering his Midway strike and his decks were hampered with landing aircraft.

Spruance also decided that his would be an 'all-out' effort using every available aircraft except those needed for protecting his own ships, even if that meant that the first aircraft off had to orbit for an hour while the second group was ranged up and launched.

The first aircraft of TF 16's strike of 67 Dauntless dive-bombers, 29 Devastator torpedo-bombers and 20 Wildcat fighters took off at 7.02. But the strike was not the heavy combined blow Spruance had intended. A Japanese reconnaissance plane was seen circling on the horizon. TF 16 had been sighted and so *Enterprise*'s Dauntlesses, led by Lt Cdr McClusky, were ordered to go on at once without waiting for the rest, and they took departure at 7.52.

The rest formed up in some confusion, *Enterprise*'s fighters mistakenly taking station above *Hornet*'s Devastators, leaving their own Devastators unescorted. *Hornet*'s fighters lost their Devastators and flew with their Dauntlesses instead. Thus the strike flew in four separate groups: *Enterprise*'s dive-bombers, *Hornet*'s dive-bombers and the fighters, followed by two Devastator torpedo-bomber squadrons.

Nagumo had steamed north-east to close the distance while ranging up his next strike, so that when the first of TF 16's aircraft arrived at his reported position, the sea was empty. *Hornet*'s dive-bombers and fighters turned south-east to search and found nothing. The dive-bombers returned to their ship or to Midway, while the fighters ran out of fuel and ditched. The two torpedo-bomber squadrons turned north and, just after 9.30, sighted the Japanese fleet.

The two Devastator squadron commanders, Waldron of *Hornet* and Lindsey of *Enterprise*, knew very well how vulnerable their aircraft would be without close fighter support. Waldron had written before the battle: 'My greatest hope is that we encounter a favorable tactical situation, but if we don't, and the worst comes to the worst, I want each of us to do his utmost to destroy our enemies. If there is only one plane left to make a final run in, I want that man to go in and get a hit. May God be with us all.'

In the event the tactical situation could not have been less favourable, and the worst did come to the worst. Skimming low and slow over the sea, with no fighter escort, the Devastators were sitting ducks for the attacking Zekes. All Waldron's squadron were shot down. Only one man, Ensign Gay, survived by clinging to a rubber seat cushion and ducking underwater whenever strafing Zekes passed overhead. Ten of Lindsey's were shot down, and no hit was scored on any Japanese ship.

However, the Devastators' sacrifice was not in vain. They provided the perfect decoy. While the Zekes had been drawn down to sea-level to attack them, the dive-bombers from *Enterprise* and *Yorktown*, which had flown off an hour later, met over the Japanese fleet. Finding nothing where he had expected to see the enemy, McClusky had turned north and soon sighted the destroyer *Arashi*, steaming to rejoin the main fleet. *Arashi* obligingly led the dive-bombers to the carriers.

The timing was perfect. The Japanese aircraft had been rearmed and ranged up. All four carriers had evaded the torpedo attacks and were racing up into wind to launch their aircraft, their flight decks crowded, when the dive-bombers struck.

From 15,000 feet above, the Japanese carriers appeared as long, bright yellow rectangles, each with a fifty-foot red disc painted forward. McClusky's two squadrons began their dives at about 10.25. As one pilot, Lt Dickinson, said, 'The target was utterly satisfying. The squadron's dive was perfect. This was the absolute. After this, I felt, anything would be just anti-climax.'

Akagi was hit by three bombs, the second of which penetrated to the hangar and exploded, setting off explosions in the torpedoes stored there. Great fires broke out, fed by petrol and spread by more bomb and torpedo explosions. Nagumo and his staff were soon forced to transfer to a cruiser. They left *Akagi* in a state, as Nagumo's chief of staff said, 'Just like hell!' Her crew abandoned her at 7.15 that evening, but she floated until just before dawn, when she was dispatched by a Japanese destroyer's torpedo.

Kaga was hit four times, one bomb demolishing the bridge, killing the captain and everybody on it, with the same fatal sequence of fires and explosions. She too was abandoned and broke in two after an enormous internal explosion at about 7.30 that evening. *Yorktown*'s dive-bombers dived on *Soryu* and scored three hits. Within twenty minutes fires and explosions forced her to be abandoned and she sank, on fire from end to end, after three torpedo hits by *Nautilus*, about the same time as *Kaga*.

Hiryu, some way ahead of the others, alone escaped and launched two strikes of eighteen Vals, ten Kates and twelve Zekes. Some of them were shot down, but shortly before noon the first of them reached *Yorktown* and hit her with three bombs and two torpedoes. The ship was crippled and came to a standstill. Her crew abandoned her that afternoon just as ten of her Dauntlesses, transferred to *Enterprise*, were getting revenge for her by taking part in a strike on *Hiryu* which obtained four hits. *Hiryu* went the way of her three sisters, although she survived for some time. Her crew abandoned her at 3.30 the next morning, and Japanese destroyers torpedoed her.

But it was 9 am before she finally sank, taking with her Rear Admiral Yamaguchi.

Yamamoto was slow to realize the disaster that had overtaken the Kido Butai. That evening he was steaming up in *Yamato* from the west, still anticipating a major gun action. But Spruance was cautious when caution was needed and although he had no intelligence information of Yamamoto's ships, Spruance feared a trap, which indeed Yamamoto had set for him. He refused to be drawn within range of battleship guns or land-based aircraft and cannily withdrew to the east.

In the early hours of 5 June Yamamoto finally awoke to the catastrophe which had befallen the Japanese Navy and ordered a general retreat. Aircraft did search for the retreating Japanese ships on 5 and 6 June but without that razor-sharp intelligence information they had become used to they had little success, although the heavy cruiser *Mikuma* was sunk by *Enterprise*'s aircraft on the 6th.

Yorktown stayed afloat, and men were put back on board her, she was taken in tow, and there seemed a good chance of saving her. But in the early afternoon of 6 June, the Japanese submarine *I.168* found her, and put two torpedoes into her and one into the destroyer *Hammann* alongside her. *Yorktown* finally rolled over and sank at 6 am on 7 June.

That was the final act in the Battle of Midway. The Americans had lost *Yorktown* and *Hammann*, 147 aircraft and 307 dead. The Japanese had lost four fleet carriers from the Kido Butai, a heavy cruiser, 322 aircraft and 3,500 dead, including many irreplaceable experienced aircrew. But, like Waterloo, it had been a 'damned close run thing'. One signal misplaced, one float-plane taking off on time, one more observant pilot, one accident of timing favourable to Japan, and, above all, one code change a month earlier, might have made all the difference.

Nimitz called another staff conference on Sunday morning, 7 June, to which he again invited Rochefort and said, 'This officer deserves a major share of the credit for the victory at Midway'. The Layton–Rochefort forecast of where the Japanese striking force would be found, Nimitz said, 'was only five minutes, five degrees and five miles out'.

Radio intelligence had given Spruance his chance and he had seized it. He had struck at the right time, with the right weapon in the right place. With the help of radio intelligence, the US Navy and the men on Midway had together won a strategic victory to rank with Salamis, Lepanto and Trafalgar.

V

GUADALCANAL: SAVO ISLAND
TO THE EASTERN SOLOMONS

THE victory at Midway, coming as it did like a flash of light and hope for the Allies at a very gloomy time, prompted consideration of some kind of defensive counter-attack in the Coral Sea area. But the debate was complicated by the fact that this area was in General MacArthur's South-West Pacific Command, while the troops, war-ships and transports needed for such a campaign were administered by Admiral Nimitz's Pacific Ocean Area.

MacArthur proposed a direct frontal assault upon Rabaul. Nimitz demurred. He was reluctant to commit his ships, and especially his few and precious remaining carriers, to such a venture. A compromise was eventually reached. Vice Admiral R.L. Ghormley, C-in-C South Pacific Area under Nimitz, would command an assault upon the Santa Cruz Islands and the seaplane base at Tulagi. When a satisfactory base had been established, command would be transferred to MacArthur, who would direct a dual advance through Papua and the Solomons, to converge finally upon Rabaul. The demarcation line between Nimitz's and MacArthur's areas was shifted one degree west to admit the targets to Nimitz's command.

Plans were well advanced for Operation WATCHTOWER, as it was called, when there was disturbing evidence from traffic analysis, reconnaissance aircraft and coast-watchers that the Japanese were building an airstrip on a grassy plain on the north coast of an island in the Solomons called Guadalcanal.

The Japanese had first inspected the possibilities of an airstrip on Guadalcanal on 27 May. After Midway the Imperial Navy General Staff authorized Operation 'SN', to strengthen Japan's outer perimeter by building airfields on the Papuan peninsula, and in the Louisiades and the Solomons. The first Japanese actually reached Guadalcanal on 8 June and it was decided to place an air base there on 13th.

On 19 June a high-ranking party, led by Admiral Inouye himself, toured the area around the Lunga Plain. On 20 June coast-watchers saw clouds of smoke as the Japanese began burning grass on the plain. A convoy of ships carrying men and equipment for airfield construction arrived on 6 July.

It had been noticed, as early as 1 July, 1942, that the hitherto obscure Solomon Islands had become a centre of Japanese activity. The strategic implications of that were clear; if the Japanese secured the Solomons, their land-based aircraft would be able to disrupt the supply line from America to Australia, and the islands themselves could be used as stepping-stones for an invasion of the Australian mainland.

Guadalcanal was, in fact, one of the only places suitable for an air base in the whole of the mountainous, jungle-clad Solomon Island chain. As such, it was strategically priceless. Previous planning was abandoned and everything was concentrated upon Guadalcanal.

The cryptanalytical situation had utterly changed since Midway. On 26 May, just before Midway, it was estimated that 60 per cent of Imperial Navy traffic was being intercepted and 40 per cent read, although the content recovered from the typical message averaged only about 10-15 per cent. But the change from JN-25b to JN-25c on 28 May plunged the US cryptanalytic effort into an almost total eclipse which lasted for much of the Guadalcanal campaign.

The only enlightenment came from occasional and fragmentary reading of individual messages, and from a few lower grade codes which were still being read. The most informative of these was used by the Emperor's Harbourmaster at Truk, who regularly reported to Tokyo – and thus to HYPO, NEGAT, Belconnen and FECB Colombo – warship arrivals at and departures from Truk atoll.

The possibility of a cryptanalytical black-out had been foreseen and preparations had been made to use refined methods of traffic analysis instead. This involved techniques such as direction finding; plotting the density of radio transmissions throughout the Japanese Empire; monitoring the patterns and rhythms of Japanese radio activity; charting Japanese radio frequency selection; identification of individual Japanese radiomen by their own idiosyncratic 'fist', or keying style, which was as distinctive as their fingerprints; and studying the external characteristics, such as originators, addresses and routing instructions, of encrypted messages.

Traffic analysis was not as glamorous or dramatic, or as accurate, as decrypting enemy messages. It was painstaking day-by-day drudgery. An American summary, dated June, 1943, said of radio intelligence in the Guadalcanal campaign that, 'There were no brilliant cryptanalytical solutions . . . though the work involved was no less difficult; there were no statements concerning the enemy's intention which could be made as confidently as was done at Midway; in fine, the period was one of much confusion and obscurity, lightened somewhat by hypotheses of the traffic analysis, which could be proved or disproved only by the passage of time.'

In July, 1942, traffic analysis provided early and unmistakable evidence of logistic preparations in progress for a Japanese campaign in the South Pacific. Heavy air reinforcements were being flown into the area – a sure sign of coming operations, for no important enemy movement had ever been made during the war without heavy air protection. Japanese army units at Rabaul were constantly communicating with other Army units at Davao and Palau, suggesting they were expecting reinforcements from the Philippines.

In the Marshalls increased aircraft radio traffic indicated future operations, and the presence of several Japanese submarines suggested they had taken up preliminary scouting positions. There was much convoy activity in the New Britain area and the Eighth Base Force, the Fifth Air Attack Corps and the Sasebo Landing Force had all been identified at Rabaul, where fifteen Japanese warships and a dozen transports were also noticed. Cruiser Divisions 6 and 18, as well as some Army and Air Group commanders, were indicated in the Rabaul area.

Documents captured from the enemy in New Guinea confirmed that the Japanese were planning operations in the New Guinea, Bismarck Archipelago and Solomon Islands areas. A report on 13 July confirmed that the Japanese were building an airfield on Guadalcanal and, two days later, that it was now operational (in fact, it was not).

On 22 July enemy documents recovered from a canvas bag thrown from a Japanese naval bomber shot down at Gaille in New Guinea confirmed known information about the enemy's weather reporting code and methods of reporting contacts with Allied forces.

Throughout July there was more traffic evidence: of the arrival of many new warships, supply ships and Japanese army engineering units at Rabaul; of enemy air strength moving from Rabaul to Lae in New Guinea; of enemy submarines concentrating along the Truk-Rabaul supply lines; and that eight heavy and two light cruisers had been assigned to the Rabaul area, including Cruiser Divisions 6 and 18, plus *Chokai*, *Suzuya* and possibly *Maya*.

68

On 24 July a long-expected change in Japanese Navy, shore radio and high command callsigns took place – a sure sign of increased Japanese concern about communications security before an impending operation. At the same time it was clear that the Japanese radio intelligence units were constantly on the alert and were stepping up their efforts to locate US forces prior to launching an attack. Often Japanese D/F bearings of US aircraft operating from Port Moresby were intercepted.

So far the ferrying movements of Japanese aircraft down to Rabaul had been from land base to land base, and traffic had been anxiously studied for information on the carriers. On 28 July there was an indication of their whereabouts: exercising off southern Japan, after carrying out a major reorganization of their divisions and air groups after the losses suffered at Midway.

Japanese naval command in the South Pacific Area was divided. The C-in-C of a new 8th Fleet would command the Solomons-New Guinea-New Britain area, while the C-in-C 4th Fleet would command the Truk area. The C-in-C 8th Fleet, Vice Admiral Gunichi Mikawa, arrived at Rabaul on 29 July to take over command, flying his flag in the heavy cruiser *Chokai*.

Every day traffic analysis revealed new Marus and transport units arriving in Rabaul, with more destroyers and submarines on their way to the South Pacific. By the end of July, 1942, the Commander, Fifth Air Attack Force, in command of the Tulagi-Guadalcanal area, had received massive aircraft reinforcements. New air units were being discovered at many strategic points in the Solomons, as well as in New Britain and New Guinea. Heavy radio traffic between Yokosuka and aircraft factories and assembly plants in the western Mandates showed that more aircraft reinforcements were on their way to Rabaul. The route taken by aircraft flying from the 'Empire' (as mainland Japan was always called in American radio intelligence) would be Chichi Jima, Saipan, Truk and Rabaul.

Meanwhile, the Guadalcanal landing was proving to be a planners' nightmare. There were no proper maps or charts and little detailed knowledge of the gradients and textures of the beaches. Irrevocable decisions had to be made on incomplete data. The Allied command structure was clumsily improvised. General Vandegrift, whose 1st US Marine Division was to make the landing, asked for a postponement. Admiral King would only agree to put the date back seven days, from 1 to 7 August. Amphibious training continued, using beaches in the Fijis.

A sudden burst of radio activity in the Bungo Strait on 3 August suggested that the carriers which had been operating off Kyushu were returning to the Empire. Analysis disclosed that the carrier divisions had been reorganized, with *Zuikaku, Shokaku* and *Zuiho* in Cardiv One, and *Ryujo, Hayataka* and *Hitaka*, with three air groups, from *Akagi, Soryu* and an unidentified ship, in Cardiv Two.

A summary of Japanese warship dispositions on 4 August – significant in view of what was to come – noted that 'Cruiser Division 6 was believed to be in the Solomons area, as was the TENRYU and TATSUTA of Cruiser Division 18'. This was confirmed and amplified in the daily bulletin, derived directly from radio intelligence and classified 'Top Secret ULTRA', which CinCPac issued to all his subordinate task force commanders. That for 4 August stated in part: 'Crudiv 6, Crudiv 18 and Desron 6 remained in the New Britain-Solomons area.'

At 0000 on 5 August the Japanese carried out another communications security measure by changing all their major command and shore radio callsigns. Later that day it was announced that *Chokai* and *Aoba* were at sea in the Rabaul area. Again, on 6 August, there was a warning that *Chokai*, flagship of the C-in-C 8th Fleet, and Cruiser Division 6 were at sea in the Rabaul area.

The CinCPac ULTRA bulletin (given in full as a typical example) was No. 143, of 060245, August 1942, and it read:

'FROM: CinCPac. TO: Opnav, Cominch, Comnaveu, Comsopacfor, Comsouwespacfor, All Task for Comds Under Your Command, Com Norwest Seafron, Com Wesseafron, Com Panseafron, Com Hawseafron.

'KAMOI in Marshalls. Estimated location of Cruisers. Crudiv four, five and eight in home waters. *Crudiv six in Rabaul area*. Crudiv seven (part) Bay of Tengali. One unit now at Truk probably leaving shortly for Japan in company with repair ship AKASHI. *Crudiv eighteen Solomon Islands*. KASHIMA at Kure . . . CHOKAI *in New Britain area*.'

Thus ULTRA gave several prior warnings that the Japanese had considerable cruiser strength in the area which could operate as a striking force.

Mikawa and his staff, being newcomers to the South Pacific, were able to take a fresh look at the situation. It seemed to them that an Allied attack on Guadalcanal was not at all unlikely. Reports from the Special Duty Group (Radio Intelligence) at Imperial Headquarters in Tokyo of increased Allied radio activity, which might point to an Allied operation in the South Pacific, and from the 8th Fleet's own radio intelligence staff, who had noted changes in the patterns of Allied radio traffic, suggested that something was in the wind. One 8th Fleet staff officer later claimed that he had studied the intercepts and concluded that Guadalcanal must be the target. But when Mikawa and his staff voiced their opinions, they were pooh-poohed by the 'old-timers' on the 4th Fleet staff, who scoffed at the idea of an Allied attack on Guadalcanal, saying it was absolutely out of the question.

Preceded by B-17 'softening-up' bombing raids and cruiser and destroyer bombardments from Fire Support Groups, and covered by aircraft from *Saratoga*, *Enterprise* and *Wasp* (newly arrived from the Atlantic) in Admiral Fletcher's task force east of Guadalcanal, the Marines went ashore on Tulagi and Guadalcanal on 7 August, 1942, making the first landings by US troops on enemy soil since 1898.

The Japanese were taken utterly by surprise. Although the Tulagi assault met fanatical resistance (an ominous foretaste of other landings to come), the Guadalcanal landing, on the north coast, east of Lunga Point, was unopposed, which was as well, for the manner and organization of the landing left much room for improvement.

In thirty-six hours the Marines had taken the airstrip and named it Henderson Field, after Major Lofton R. Henderson, US Marine Corps, who had died leading a bombing attack from Midway on *Hiryu* on 4 June. In the next six months the struggle for Guadalcanal was virtually to mean the battle for Henderson.

The Japanese might have been taken unawares, but their naval reaction was swift and savage. At 8 am on 7 August Mikawa signalled that at 1300 that day *Chokai*, Cruiser Division 18 and another unidentified unit would sail from Rabaul and rendezvous with Cruiser Division 6 in the vicinity of Bougainville, and would then proceed to Guadalcanal where subsequent operations against an enemy convoy would be based on reconnaissance reports. Had the ULTRA situation been as it was up to 28 May, the disaster off Savo Island would most likely have been averted. Unfortunately, Mikawa's crucial signal was not decrypted until 23 August.

Mikawa sailed that day in *Chokai*, with four heavy cruisers, *Aoba*, *Kako*, *Kinugasa* and *Furutaka* of Crudiv 6 who had joined him from Kavieng, two light cruisers, *Tenryu* and *Yubari*, of Crudiv 18, and one destroyer, *Yunagi*.

This Striking Force was sighted twice by aircraft the following day and reported, but the messages were delayed and then relayed in such a way as to cause no alarm at Guadalcanal. Mikawa handled his ships so as to minimize the risks of being sighted from the air and there were in any case gaps in the air patrol coverage.

That evening, the 8th, Belconnen Station in Melbourne passed a message giving the position at 1127 that day of three cruisers, three destroyers and two seaplane tenders or gunboats, course 120°, speed 15. When the position was plotted it was decided that these ships were too far away to be an immediate threat to Guadalcanal.

Mikawa's cruisers had flown off reconnaissance float-planes during the day which had told him what he wanted to know: fifteen transports off Guadalcanal, three off Tulagi, escorted by cruisers and destroyers and, one report said, a battleship. Mikawa estimated that there were no carriers within 100 miles of Guadalcanal and, in spite of the battleship, decided to attack on the night of 8/9th. His Striking Force would enter the south channel between Guadalcanal and the small, hump-backed jungly island of Savo, torpedo enemy ships off Guadalcanal, sweep towards Tulagi to attack ships there with gunfire and torpedoes and withdraw through the passage north of Savo so as to be beyond the range of carrier aircraft by dawn.

It was a bold plan (actually bolder than Mikawa knew, for it would bring his ships within range of Fletcher's three carriers) but his ships were trained for night action. They had no radar, but they did have abnormally gifted night look-outs with superb binoculars. They had the Long Lance torpedo and searchlight batteries whose controls were linked to the main gun armament. By night, Mikawa was confident of the outcome.

Meanwhile, on the Allied side, everything was peaceful. Nobody suspected an imminent attack. A Southern Group, of the cruisers HMAS *Australia* (flagship of Rear Admiral V.A.C. Crutchley VC RN), HMAS *Canberra*, and USS *Chicago* with the US destroyers *Patterson* and *Bagley*, patrolled the South Savo channel. A Northern Group of the US cruisers *Vincennes*, *Quincy* and *Astoria*, with the US destroyers *Helm* and *Wilson*, patrolled the channel north and east of Savo. Two radar-equipped US destroyers watched the approaches west of Savo, *Blue* to the south and *Ralph Talbot* to the north.

On the evening of 8 August Admiral Crutchley was summoned urgently to a conference with General Vandegrift and Rear Admiral Kelly Turner, commander of the amphibious force, in Turner's flagship *McCawley* lying among the transports in Lunga Roads. The three commanders had to debate a most alarming development: Fletcher had been complaining that his ships were short of fuel and his fighter strength was dwindling dangerously. He had announced that he was taking his carriers away forthwith.

Crutchley had left no particular instructions with his ships in his absence. When the conference broke up just after midnight and he rejoined *Australia*, such was the false confidence the Allies had been lulled into that Crutchley decided not to search for his ships off Savo in the darkness but to remain on patrol off the troop anchorage.

At 0054 on 9 August, a few minutes after Crutchley rejoined his ship, *Chokai*'s lookouts sighted *Blue*, fine on their starboard bow. *Chokai* was making 26 knots and her bow wave was showing a great white 'bone in her teeth', but, incredibly, *Blue*'s lookouts saw nothing and her radar screen was blank. Mikawa's ships slipped by unchallenged.

At 1.30 *Chokai* led through the southern channel and sighted another destroyer, *Jarvis*, damaged in an air attack the previous day and now returning to Sydney for repairs. Once again, Mikawa was unchallenged, and soon the black shapes of *Canberra* and *Chicago* could be seen in line ahead, silhouetted against the clear horizon behind them. Mikawa gave the order to attack, ships to fire independently, and they launched torpedoes at 1.38.

About five minutes later the Japanese ships were at last sighted, by *Canberra*, *Patterson* and *Bagley* together, and the alarm was raised. But it was too late. *Canberra*'s turrets were still trained fore and aft. Illuminated by flares from Mikawa's aircraft overhead, overwhelmed by shells and one torpedo hit on the port bow, *Canberra* was crippled and came to a dead stop in the water. *Bagley* managed to get off one salvo of torpedoes, but *Chicago* sighting a light to seaward, steamed out towards it and took no further part.

Having demolished the Southern Group, Mikawa now stalked the northern ships. His force had split into two columns steaming northeast, with *Furutaka* and the two light cruisers passing closer to Savo. *Vincennes* could be seen ahead with *Quincy* and *Astoria* as the Japanese closed them from either quarter, *Chokai* to starboard, *Furutaka* to port.

At 1.50 *Chokai*'s searchlights caught and held *Astoria*. One salvo set her aircraft alight, making a perfect aiming mark. *Astoria* got one hit on *Chokai* before she was smashed into a wreck by successive salvoes and, on fire from end to end, fell out of line. Ahead of *Astoria*, *Aoba*'s searchlights revealed *Quincy* with her turrets still trained fore and aft. Her upperdeck a shambles, and her port side amidships blown open by a torpedo, *Quincy* capsized and sank at 2.35 with her captain and 370 of her people.

Captain Riefkohl, commanding *Vincennes*, did not know that Crutchley was absent. *Chicago* had not raised the alarm. The thunder from the south Riefkohl put down to the southern ships firing at aircraft. Even when *Vincennes* was lit up by a Japanese searchlight Riefkohl was convinced it was friendly and ordered it to be extinguished. *Vincennes* possibly got one hit on *Kinugasa* before she too was smothered under a hail of shells and torpedo hits. Most of her crew managed to abandon her before she rolled over and sank at about 3 am, but more than 300 died in her. *Canberra* was dispatched by an American torpedo at 8 am. *Astoria* lasted until noon, when she sank after one final magazine explosion.

At 2.20 Mikawa collected his ships together and retired to the west, giving *Ralph Talbot* a severe hammering in passing. In a brisk action lasting some fifty minutes he had inflicted a defeat on the Allied navies (four cruisers sunk) comparable to that inflicted on the Italian navy in the night action off Cape Matapan (three cruisers and two destroyers sunk) in March, 1941.

But it could have been worse. Mikawa did not go through and attack the transports which had been his primary target, because he feared attacks by Fletcher's aircraft at first light. Later, Yamamoto somewhat unjustly criticized Mikawa for retiring. Mikawa was not to know, and could never have guessed, that Fletcher had actually carried out his intention of withdrawing the carriers, and the troopship anchorage lay at Mikawa's mercy.

Deprived of air cover, Turner hauled his ships out of the anchorage at sunset on 9 August and departed to New Caledonia, taking half the stores and food with him, and leaving the Marines on their own on Guadalcanal. The Marines, convinced they had been left to die in another Bataan, set about fortifying their position round the airstrip and getting the strip ready for service.

The runway was only 2,600 feet long and had no drainage or steel matting for taxiing, but on 20 August twelve Marine Dauntlesses and nineteen Wildcats flew in from the converted light carrier *Long Island*. These few, almost symbolic, aircraft flying into Henderson Field properly began the Allied counter-offensive in the East. These wings, multiplied by the thousand, would carry the Allies to Tokyo Bay.

However, this was not so apparent at the time. The Japanese High Command, still preoccupied with their campaign to capture Port Moresby overland through New Guinea, were somewhat slow to realize Allied intentions on Guadalcanal. The sharp repulse, at the Tenaru River, of an overconfident and unsupported attempt to take Henderson on 21 August awoke them.

The Japanese then began to reinforce their troops by what became known as the 'Tokyo Express' under Rear Admiral Raizo Tanaka, who led swift convoys of warships and troopships by night down from Rabaul through the 'Slot', the passage between the twin chains of the Solomon Islands.

By the time the battle off Savo Island took place, some progress had been made in deciphering JN-25c. For example, dispatches originated by the CinC 8th Fleet on 7 August were deciphered on the 9th, revealing some of the moves by Japanese Special Landing Force troops and by two Marus which had set out to counter-attack the American landings on Guadalcanal. Better still, a complete copy of JN-25c and its additive books was recovered from a cache of Japanese documents found by the Marines after they landed on Guadalcanal.

However, on 10 August Tokyo broadcast a message to all major commands which was suspected of referring to a future change in Japanese codes or ciphers. The suspicion proved to be true enough. The Japanese changed their main operational code again, from JN-25c to 25d, on 14 August. This was not because the Japanese suspected that their current code had been compromised in the field. The last JN-25c messages to be decoded had been from local Japanese commanders on Guadalcanal informing Rabaul that all confidential material had been destroyed.

The reason for the Japanese code change of 14 August, 1942, was undoubtedly certain press and political indiscretions in the United States which had revealed that the US Navy had known through code-breaking of Japanese intentions before Midway. Thus, the main weight of R.I. in the Guadalcanal campaign had to be borne once again by traffic analysis.

Once again, there were unmistakable signs that the Japanese were preparing for another offensive in the Solomons, possibly towards the end of August. CincPac's ULTRA Bulletin of 10 August, 1942, warned all major commands that heavy Japanese reinforcements of surface, submarine and air fleets were being poured into the Solomons. Every day traffic analysis and air reconnaissance showed the movements of large numbers of Marus carrying supplies, and especially replacement aircraft, along the enemy's supply lines from the Empire to Rabaul.

At the same time the Japanese were intensifying their efforts to make their radio communications more secure – always a sure sign of an impending operation. On 11 August the C-in-C Combined Fleet originated a huge volume of radio dispatches from his flagship, the battleship *Yamato*, which was in the Empire area, using a special cypher evidently held by some of his subordinate commanders. On the same day traffic analysis revealed that the Japanese were attempting radio deception by trying to disguise the source of important messages.

There was more indication of possible future movements on 12 August when the Japanese used a special type of code, believed to be employed in the South Pacific only when prospective operations required the utmost radio security. On the 15th, a day of comparatively low enemy radio traffic volume, a special five-figure cypher system, used by the Japanese in the southern area during the previous few days, was thereafter used for general purposes in all areas, making it more difficult to identify enemy units. The task became even harder at midnight on 17 August, when the Japanese changed all their callsigns.

The main task was to locate the Japanese carriers. An enemy document captured on 12 August showed the organization of the Japanese Eleventh Air Fleet at Rabaul and traffic analysis the same day revealed the location of several air commanders and their units, and indicated that the Japanese carriers were reorganizing and that training of new carrier groups was taking place off Sasebo.

But for some days there was no definite evidence that the carriers were leaving the Empire and moving south, although on the 13th much radio activity and the many reinforcements being sent to them at Kure suggested that *Shokaku*, *Zuikaku* and *Ryujo* were being prepared for operations outside Empire waters. However, CincPac's ULTRA Bulletin for that day stated that *Shokaku*, *Hayataka*, *Ryujo*, *Zuiho* and *Hitaka* were all in southern Japan. D/F bearings on the 14th placed *Shokaku* and *Zuikaku* in Empire waters.

A message from Carrier Division Two, intercepted on 12 August and more fully deciphered on the 14th, revealed that the enemy was planning to strike at an Allied task force. This was the first hard evidence of a coming Japanese offensive. On the 15th single bearings placed *Shokaku*, *Hitaka* and *Hosho* in Empire waters but the other carriers were silent. There was still no indication of carriers in the South Pacific, but the summaries did point out that the possibility should not be overlooked.

On 16 August all Japanese carriers were keeping radio silence. Two Japanese destroyer divisions were known to be en route from Truk to

Rabaul, arriving on the 16th, and it was considered possible that the destroyers' movements were connected with the carriers. However, it still appeared that all Japanese carriers were in home waters at this time. That day's US Pacific Fleet intelligence summary stated that reinforcements were being shipped by the Japanese to the Rabaul area; the carriers *Hitaka*, *Hayataka* and *Zuiho* were believed to be operating near Marcus Island (as a result of USS *Boise*'s diversionary attack a few days earlier); the locations of *Shokaku*, *Zuikaku* and *Ryujo* were not known exactly but were thought to be in southern Japan although it was possible that some or all had left for the south.

By 17 August the Japanese carriers had been silent for some time. The day's CincPac intelligence summary stated that *Hiyo*, *Hayataka* and *Zuiho* were remaining in Empire waters but *Zuikaku*, *Shokaku* and *Ryujo*, though still apparently in Empire waters, would definitely go south if they were not already under way. Tactical exercises by four carriers in Empire waters on the 20th were believed to be covering an actual movement southward.

On 21 August the intelligence picture came a little more sharply into focus. CincPac's ULTRA bulletin emphasized the conclusions drawn from traffic analysis: there was a striking force, of *Shokaku*, *Zuikaku* and *Ryujo*, with Crudiv Eight, one unit of Crudiv Four, plus the battleships *Kirishima* and *Hiei*, but its destination was unknown and there were still no indications that Japanese carriers had left Empire waters. Belconnen in Melbourne suggested that day that the Japanese carrier task force was already at Truk, but Pearl Harbor remained sceptical.

The next day, 22 August, routeing of messages from Cardiv One to Truk inclined Layton at last to the view that a carrier task force was en route to Truk or actually at Truk. But CincPac's summary was non-committal. Although it stated that the possibility that Japanese carriers had departed home waters undetected before 16 August 'should not be disregarded', there was no definite evidence to confirm it.

In fact, Rear Admiral Raizo Tanaka, flying his flag in the light cruiser *Jintsu*, had sailed from Truk on 16 August with the first 'Tokyo Express', of three Marus, carrying 1500 Japanese troops, with a destroyer escort.

This convoy was supported by two powerful fleets north of the Solomons. The Third Fleet, or Main Body, was commanded by Nagumo, flying his flag in *Shokaku*, with *Zuikaku* and the light carrier *Ryujo*, the battleships *Hiei* and *Kirishima*, cruisers and destroyers. The Second Fleet (Advanced Body) was commanded by Vice Admiral

Nobutake Kondo, flying his flag in the heavy cruiser *Atago*, with the carrier *Junyo*, the seaplane carrier *Chitose*, the battleship *Mutsu*, cruisers and destroyers. Yamamoto himself, flying his flag in *Yamato*, was directing affairs from Truk.

The two fleets rendezvoused at sea early on 21 August and then split again to steam southwards separately. Nagumo and Kondo and their staffs had not had a chance to confer, because Kondo had inexplicably taken his Advanced Force to sea from Truk before Nagumo arrived there, but the main objective was clear to everybody: to find and destroy the American carriers. Defence of Tanaka's convoy was a second priority.

The American Task Force 61 was also at sea, commanded by Vice Admiral Frank J. Fletcher, flying his flag in *Saratoga*, with *Enterprise* and *Wasp*, the new battleship *North Carolina*, cruisers and destroyers. Fletcher kept his ships south-east of the Solomons out of range of Japanese search aircraft from Rabaul.

The US Pacific Fleet intelligence summary of 22 August suggested that a major thrust by the Japanese would occur in the Rabaul area shortly. The CincPac ULTRA Bulletin of the same day reported three carriers in the Empire but warned of the possibility of them moving to the south shortly. Three other carriers were stated to be either in the Truk area or en route there.

Task Force 61 flew search patrols twice daily and on 23 August they sighted part of Kondo's fleet. Fletcher dispatched a strike of dive-bombers and torpedo aircraft but Nagumo had reversed course to the north so as to keep his carriers out of sight, Kondo had followed suit, and their ships remained hidden under low cloud and rain storms. Tanaka's convoy was also sighted 250 miles north of Guadalcanal. The Japanese submarine *I-17* was attacked by three aircraft south-east of Guadalcanal.

Japanese warships, a troop convoy and a submarine, all sighted at sea, might have suggested to Fletcher that Japanese carriers were also at sea. But now ULTRA caused him to make an error of judgement. CincPac's ULTRA summary of 23 August read: 'Disposition of Carriers. SHOKAKU, ZUIKAKU enroute Japan to Truk. Possible HITAKA, HAYATAKA, ZUIHO may depart Empire for Truk shortly. Estimate RYUJO in home yard. HOSHO in Honsu waters. KASUGA MARU enroute Truk. Detachment Kisaratsu Air Group at Kavieng. CHIKUMA in Truk area. Possibly 2 battleships BATDIV 3 also in vicinity of Truk.' The US Pacific Fleet intelligence summary of the same day said that Carrier Division One and *Ryujo* were scheduled to enter Truk, but gave no indication that Carrier Division Two would move from the Empire. It also stated that heavy enemy landings were expected in the Guadalcanal area in the next twelve hours.

Therefore Fletcher was given no indication that any Japanese carriers were south of Truk. His own aircraft had sighted no carriers. Fletcher's staff reminded him of the convoy and submarine sightings and suggested that carriers might also be at sea but Fletcher decided to detach Task Force 18 with *Wasp* to refuel that evening. Task Force 61 outnumbered the Japanese Third Fleet in heavy carriers and in aircraft. As it turned out, with *Wasp* went the last chance for that year of a carrier action in which the US Navy would have had the advantage of numbers.

The next day, 24 August, the Japanese pushed forward a sacrificial decoy, the small carrier *Ryujo*, which was duly sighted and attacked. Thus Fletcher, as at the Coral Sea, had unwittingly sent his main blow against a minor target, for scouts soon discovered the big carriers. Fletcher tried to divert his strike but bad communications only complicated an already confused situation. *Ryujo* was sunk, by bombs and one torpedo hit. *Enterprise*'s aircraft found *Shokaku* and did some damage to her.

Fletcher had sent off his strike with no fighter escort. He had fifty-three fighters 'stacked' in three layers overhead, waiting for the attack he knew must come. All remaining dive-bombers and torpedo aircraft had taken off, with orders to counter-attack the Japanese fleet. Meanwhile, *Saratoga* and *Enterprise* waited, with every gun manned and loaded, all fuel lines drained and filled with inert gas, battened down as though against a tropical typhoon.

It was not long in coming. The radar screens showed swarms of incoming hostile aircraft. The fighters rose to meet them. Fighter direction had not been refined to anything like the standard it achieved later and there was a time of wild activity, a hubbub of shouting over the R/T, when it was impossible to tell friend from foe.

All the torpedo-Kates were beaten off, but some thirty Val dive-bombers arrived undetected at 18,000 feet over *Enterprise*. The fleet's anti-aircraft barrage had been reinforced by *North Carolina* who mounted a massive battery of anti-aircraft guns (a sign of the times), but nevertheless enough Vals survived to hit *Enterprise* with three bombs, two of them penetrating deep into the ship before exploding.

Damage control had improved since Midway and *Enterprise* was soon able to steam at 24 knots and recover her aircraft. But her steering gear broke down and for an agonizing time she lay immobile, while the Japanese searched frantically for her just over the horizon, before being able to get under way again and escape. *Saratoga*, who had not been attacked at all, mounted a strike which badly damaged the seaplane carrier *Chitose*. At sunset both sides retired, thus ending this inconclusive Battle of the Eastern Solomons.

However, the most serious reverse for the Japanese happened the next day, when Marine dive-bombers from Henderson attacked and set on fire *Jintsu* and a troop transport, *Kenryu* Maru, and both had to turn back. Flying Fortresses from Espiritu Santo sank the destroyer *Mutsuki* and finished off *Kenryu* Maru.

As both sides steadily raised their stakes on Guadalcanal it was some time before the American people awoke to the fact that their boys were fighting a major campaign on this island nobody had ever heard of. As more details became known of the Marines' ordeal on this loathsome, lethal island, where the malarial mosquito became as great a danger as the machine gun or the mortar, the question increasingly asked, in the Chiefs of Staffs' meetings as well as in public, was not 'Can we win?' but 'Can we hold on?'

The answer to that lay with the respective navies, as both sides sought to bring in reinforcements and choke off the other's reinforcements arriving by sea. The Guadalcanal campaign came to involve every kind of warship from battleships to PT boats. There were carrier engagements and submarine attacks, surface ship actions by day and by night, shore bombardments by heavy naval guns, and bombing by land-based aircraft. On land, the scale of the engagements ranged from frontal attacks in regimental strength to individual patrol activity, where murderous groping in the jungle often ended in hand-to-hand combat. Guadalcanal was to be a whole war on its own.

VI

GUADALCANAL: 'TORPEDO JUNCTION' AND 'IRONBOTTOM SOUND'

In September, 1942, every chance was taken to fly more aircraft into Henderson Field, to reinforce the 'Cactus Air Force' as it was dubbed (CACTUS being the codename for Guadalcanal), while 'Tenacious' Tanaka, as he became known, took every opportunity to run the 'Tokyo Express'. Eventually, over the weeks, a curious balance of power was struck. By day Allied aircraft from the carriers and Henderson ruled. By night the initiative returned to Tanaka and the Japanese.

Although one 'Tokyo Express' was derailed by aircraft from Henderson on 28 August, when the destroyer *Asagiri* was sunk and two others badly damaged, the Japanese succeeded in getting enough reinforcements into Guadalcanal to launch another attempt on Henderson in mid-September, D-Day for the attack being 12 September.

Due warning was given through CincPac's ULTRA bulletins. On the 11th: 'Four auxiliaries departed Truk 9th. Ultimate destination through Guadalcanal by way of Shortland harbour. Desron 3 and Crudiv 6 probably associated with this outfit'. The next day the warning was more specific: 'Enemy contemplating early attack Guadalcanal area'.

Yamamoto had assembled another task force of carriers, battleships and cruisers at sea, to support the forces expected to recapture Henderson or, if necessary, to accept battle with the American fleet. This too was revealed in the ULTRA bulletin of 14 September: 'Cdrs Desrons 3, 7, 9, 17 and 19 believed Solomons. Serious attempt to retake Guadalcanal area expected by above units plus cruisers, carriers supported possible HIEI, KIRISHIMA, ZUIKAKU and SHOKAKU believed in striking force, perhaps ZUIHO also'.

This 'serious attempt' to retake Guadalcanal was indeed launched against Henderson on the forecast D-Day and was defeated by the Marines at the aptly-named Bloody Ridge on 12/13 September. Yamamoto's striking force returned to harbour.

But the Japanese continued to have success at sea, where Allied ships tended to linger too long and carelessly in areas where Japanese submarines were known to be operating. *Saratoga* was torpedoed by *I-26* on 31 August and put out of action for three months. On 7 September *I-11* near-missed *Hornet* and *North Carolina*, and on the 15th one salvo from *I-19* struck a major blow: three torpedoes hit *Wasp*, who later sank, and the others sank the destroyer *O'Brien* and damaged *North Carolina*. It was no wonder that the waters between San Cristobal and Espiritu Santo became known as 'Torpedo Junction'.

Likewise, the waters off Savo Island were nicknamed 'Ironbottom Sound'. The action of 8/9 August had demonstrated that the Japanese were not a short-legged, short-sighted race with poor night vision and an imitative view of tactics. The US Navy were learning off Guadalcanal, as the US Army were to learn against Rommel at the Kasserine Pass in Tunisia, that superior technology and an ever-improving logistical supply of weaponry were not enough against a skilful, well-trained and determined enemy. But lessons were rapidly learned. Groups of ships exercised together, with particular attention to night-fighting. Improved radar was fitted and combat information centres developed in command ships.

The Japanese continued for some time to give their land campaign against Port Moresby the higher priority. But by the end of September, 1942, they were at last beginning to realize the true importance of what was happening on Guadalcanal. The ULTRA bulletin of the 26th noted the 'Interest of C-in-C Combined Fleet in Solomon operations is shown by one or more staff officers that command being aboard SENDAI flagship Desron 3'.

On 28 September HYPO's estimate of enemy capabilities noted that 'The enemy is copying our communications methods with good success. As a result we continue to be unable to read his mail (i.e. by cryptanalysis) to any great extent'. Two days later the Japanese introduced, not just a change of code, but a major restructuring of their entire communication system. This meant that many aids to analysis developed over the years were nullified literally overnight. The identification of callsigns, for instance, was rendered much more difficult and once again traffic analysis became the major source of radio intelligence.

From the start of October the Japanese stepped up their reinforcements. Had they done so on the same scale six weeks earlier, they would have had little trouble in retaking Guadalcanal. Now, it was just too late – although that was not obvious to either side at the time.

It seemed almost as though the Japanese were timing their moves by the moon, for their assaults on Guadalcanal regularly began to take shape towards the middle of the month. On 6 October the CincPac Bulletin gave another warning: 'Desron 3 active Solomons associated with Seaplane Division 11, 17th Army and Landing forces Shortland and Guadalcanal areas. Predict another attempt recapture Guadalcanal Field impending'. Two days later: 'Expect continued enemy reinforcement Guadalcanal by destroyers and small craft almost nightly. Destroyers transporting landing force Guadalcanal believed to carry 150 men each'.

There was further evidence of the Japanese change of heart over Guadalcanal on 9 October, when General Hyakutake, commanding the 17th Army, arrived in Guadalcanal to take personal command of the campaign.

Another large 'Tokyo Express' of two seaplane carriers and six destroyers sailed from Rabaul, covered by *Aoba*, *Kinugasa* and *Furutaka*, under Rear Admiral Goto. As it happened, the Allies already had their version of the Express at sea. Task Force 64, of the heavy cruisers *San Francisco* and *Salt Lake City*, the light cruisers *Boise* and *Helena*, and five destroyers, had sailed from Espiritu Santo on 7 October to cover a troop convoy of two transports and eight destroyer-types.

Task Force 64's commander was Rear Admiral Norman Scott, who had commanded the Eastern Screen at Savo and had thus been a spectator of that débâcle. He had made up his mind that the same thing would never happen to him. He had drilled his squadron, paying special attention to night encounter techniques, and had them close under firm control – perhaps too firm, as events showed.

One of the seaplane carriers and its escort were sighted by aircraft and reported to Scott on 11 October. That night Scott steamed at 29 knots to close Guadalcanal and intercept. His force was in single line ahead, the destroyers disposed ahead and astern of the cruisers. Scott's line was an unwieldy two and a half miles long, and the latest radar was in *Helena* and *Boise*, not in the flagship *San Francisco*.

At 11 pm that night Scott's ships were about eight miles north of the extreme western tip of Guadalcanal, steering north-east at 20 knots. Unknowingly, Scott had achieved the perfect attacking position, having 'crossed his enemy's T'. *Helena* obtained a radar contact at 11.25, range fourteen miles, but did not report it.

Scott did not know of *Helena*'s radar contact until the enemy were within five miles of him, when he had already decided he had gone far enough to the north-east and had ordered his force to reverse course. He therefore encountered his enemy when his ships were changing formation, and all his carefully drilled cohesion broke down. His own destroyers were actually between him and the Japanese, and when *Helena* opened fire, having sighted ships at 2,500 yards, Scott at first ordered her to stop, thinking she was firing on friendly ships.

It was the turn of the Japanese to be surprised by night. Accustomed to having the Slot to themselves after dark, they were hopelessly caught, with their turrets still trained fore and aft. When the American cruisers opened fire, they hit *Aoba*, mortally wounding Goto, damaged *Furutaka* so badly that she later sank, and sank the destroyer *Fubuki*. *Kinugasa* and one destroyer, *Hatsuyuki*, turned away from Goto to port, and escaped attack. They met and shelled the destroyer *Duncan* who had gained a radar contact and steamed off to the west on her own. *Duncan* was later abandoned and sunk.

Pursuing Goto to the west, *Boise* ill-advisedly switched on a searchlight, giving *Aoba* and *Kinugasa* an aiming point. Both opened fire and *Boise* was badly damaged. After some more desultory firing, Scott broke off, at half past midnight, and reformed his ships.

It was believed that four Japanese cruisers and four destroyers had been sunk in this action, and the Battle of Cape Esperance, as it was called, was hailed as a great victory. It was less than that, as events would show, for Scott's line-ahead formation had been clumsy and the surprised Japanese had failed to get off their Long Lance torpedoes. But still, it was a victory, showing that the Japanese were not entirely invincible by night and with this good news of Cape Esperance, the US Navy took the opportunity to release the first details of Savo Island.

However, the Japanese had successfully landed the reinforcements Goto had been covering, including artillery, that night and now began a programme of bombardments of Henderson Field. The 14-inch guns of the battleships *Kongo* and *Haruna* shelled the airfield for ninety minutes on the night of 13/14 October and only desisted some five minutes earlier than planned because they were disconcerted by four attacking PT boats. The next night *Chokai* and *Kinugasa* fired 752 8-inch at Henderson and the night after that it was the turn of the cruisers *Myoko* and *Maya* with 926 8-inch shells while Tanaka's accompanying destroyers added 253 5-inch.

It was clear that another climactic point in the Guadalcanal struggle was approaching. ULTRA had once again given warnings of another impending Japanese attack. On 14 October: 'Enemy transports, cruisers, destroyers concentrated Buin Shortland, continued night infiltration into Guadalcanal anticipated', and two days later, 'At least two carriers believed Solomons area. C-in-C Combined Fleet is in direct tactical command present operation'.

By 16 October Japanese transports were able to unload boldly in daylight on the beaches near Tassafaronga. Although aircraft from Henderson bombed and set on fire three of the troop transports, a regular Tokyo Express had arrived at Cape Esperance that night and unloaded 1,100 troops. For the first time Japanese ground strength on Guadalcanal was approximately equal in numbers to the Marines, and they looked forward to 'Y' Day, 22 October, when, after a week's 'softening up', Japanese troops would at last take Henderson Field.

At Pearl Harbor Nimitz was under no illusions about the gravity of the situation. 'It now appears that we are unable to control the sea in the Guadalcanal area,' CincPac headquarters diary recorded on 15 October. 'Thus our supply of the position will only be done at great expense to us. The situation is not hopeless but it is certainly critical'. To his staff Nimitz said, 'I don't want to hear, or see, such gloom and such defeatism. Remember the enemy is hurt too, but our job here is to provide them with everything they need on Guadalcanal to fight this battle. We aren't going to do any good sitting here moaning or wailing or wringing our hands.'

In fact virtually the whole of the Combined Fleet – four battleships, five carriers, ten cruisers, and 29 destroyers – had been sent south and sailed from Truk on 11 October for an enormous blockade and bombardment operation. Early on 17 October Yamamoto detached Carrier Division Two of *Junyo* and *Hiyo* to launch a strike of eighteen Zekes and eighteen Kates against shipping off Lunga. But Yamamoto's message was partly decrypted. Fighters from Henderson were waiting and shot down seven bombers and one Zeke.

The CincPac Bulletin of 23 October was headed 'ULTRA', showing that the cryptanalysts had already made some progress in breaking back into the Japanese code system, and stated: 'Indications of another Japanese offensive soon. Exact date and place not known but believe will be within two or three days and directed against Guadalcanal. At least ten enemy submarines in Solomons-New Hebrides general area'. A corrected copy added: '8th Fleet Commander in Southern Bougainville Strait area in Japanese cruiser CHOKAI likely. Several signs of impending Japanese offensive very shortly probably with Guadalcanal as objective'.

The main Japanese fleet lay north of the Solomons, waiting, in Yamamoto's words, to 'apprehend and annihilate any powerful forces in the Solomons area' and to fly aircraft into Henderson once the field had been taken. The Combined Fleet, though at full strength, was once again deployed in three separate groups. A striking force, of the Main Body (3rd Fleet) was under Nagumo, with *Shokaku* (flagship), *Zuikaku* and the light carrier *Zuiho*, a heavy cruiser and eight destroyers. A Vanguard Force of the 3rd Fleet, under Rear Admiral Hiroaki Abe, lay some sixty miles south of Nagumo, with two battleships, three cruisers and seven destroyers. Over a hundred miles to the north-west was the Advanced Force (2nd Fleet) under Kondo, flying his flag in the heavy cruiser *Atago*, with two battleships, three more cruisers, the carriers *Junyo* and *Hiyo*, and an escort commanded by Tanaka, flying his flag in the light cruiser *Isuzu*, and ten destroyers. Yamamoto again had overall command from *Yamato* at Truk.

'Y' Day was twice postponed, from 22 October to the 23rd, and then to the 24th. By then *Hiyo* had suffered an engine-room fire on 21 October and was detached to Truk with two destroyers the following day.

At Henderson the Marines and the G.I.s of the 164th Americal Regiment (whose arrival on Guadalcanal Scott's forces had covered on the 12th) resisted much more strongly and held out far longer than the Japanese had expected and, though the Japanese naval liaison officer on Guadalcanal had prematurely signalled 'Banzai! The airfield is captured,' early on the 25th, Nagumo still had to wait, while his fuel and his patience dwindled.

The postponement of 'Y' Day and the stout defence of Henderson allowed the newly-repaired *Enterprise* to complete her long voyage from Pearl Harbor and rendezvous with Task Force 61, commanded by Rear Admiral Thomas C. Kinkaid, on 24 October, and permitted Kinkaid to bring TF 61, with two carrier task forces, TF 16 with *Enterprise* and TF 17 with *Hornet*, to a position north of the Santa Cruz Islands.

Catalinas from Espiritu Santo sighted two of Nagumo's carriers 350 miles west-north-west of TF 61 just before noon on 25 October. Kinkaid was in no doubt what was expected of him, having received the signal 'ATTACK REPEAT ATTACK' from Admiral Halsey (who had re-lieved Ghormley in command of the South Pacific Area on 18 October, Nimitz having decided that the theatre needed more aggressive, less defeatist leadership). Kinkaid steered for the reported enemy position at 27 knots and launched a strike but Nagumo, still uncertain of his enemy's position, had already withdrawn to the north.

The main battle of Santa Cruz, on 26 October, 1942, was once again a day of strike and counter-strike between carriers, in which the tactical balance went to the Japanese, who had 199 operational aircraft, to TF's 136, and still had, at that stage of the war, more experienced aircrews.

Enterprise launched an armed reconnaissance of 16 Dauntlesses, each with a 500-lb bomb, at first light. Two of them completely surprised and bombed *Zuiho*, putting her out of action in an unexpected and unmolested attack. Nagumo's aircraft reported the position of one American carrier at 6.58 am and his strike of 65 aircraft, half of them Zekes, was on its way twelve minutes later.

By 7.30 *Hornet* had launched a strike of 15 Dauntlesses, six Avengers and eight Wildcats. Thirty minutes later *Enterprise* contributed three Dauntlesses, eight Avengers and eight Wildcats. These were followed a quarter of an hour later by another force of nine Dauntlesses, nine Avengers and nine Wildcats from *Hornet*.

So, while the Japanese aircraft flew in one compact strike, the Americans set off in a procession. The two strikes actually passed each other on their way. Twelve Zekes peeled off and shot down four Avengers and four Wildcats from *Enterprise*, for the loss of three of their own.

When the Japanese strike arrived, *Enterprise* happened to be hidden in a rain squall and the attack fell upon *Hornet*, who was hit by two torpedoes, six bombs and two aircraft which made suicide crashes on her flight deck. In a few minutes *Hornet* had lost all power and steerage way and came to a dead stop, a blazing wreck.

Two hundred miles away to the north-west *Hornet*'s torpedo aircraft had become separated from their group leader Lieutenant Commander Widhelm, leading the dive-bombers, and attacked Abe's Vanguard Group with no success. The survivors of *Enterprise*'s strike joined in, also with no success. *Hornet*'s second strike badly damaged the cruiser *Chikuma*, but the results generally did not match the effort involved.

However, Widhelm's dive-bombers made up for it all. Although Widhelm himself was shot down, his dive-bombers hit *Shokaku* with between three and six 1,000 lb bombs, preventing her operating her aircraft. But her second strike, with *Zuikaku*'s, was already attacking *Enterprise*, having sensibly ignored the stricken *Hornet*.

Enterprise had fighters in the air but for the second time that day the fighter direction organization was found wanting. *Enterprise* was hit by two bombs. Her forward lift was put out of action, but her high speed was unimpaired and she managed to avoid a determined torpedo attack. Finally, a strike from *Junyo* scored a hit on the battleship *South Dakota*, who was part of *Enterprise*'s anti-aircraft screen, and dropped one bomb clean through the hull of the cruiser *San Juan*.

Attempts were made to take *Hornet* in tow but she was hit by another bomb from a *Zuikaku* strike and another torpedo from *Junyo*'s second strike. Both the tow and the ship were abandoned. Destroyers tried in vain to sink her with torpedoes and gunfire. When a signal to Kondo from Rear Admiral Ugaki, Yamamoto's chief of staff at Truk, ordering him to try to capture and tow *Hornet*, was decrypted, fresh attempts to sink her were made but she refused to go. Eventually the Japanese found her burning hulk that night and gave her the *coup de grace* with four Long Lance torpedoes.

Kinkaid had decided to withdraw, having no carriers left to oppose the Japanese battleships. So the Battle of Santa Cruz, the last of the great carrier confrontations of 1942, came to a close with another tactical victory for the Japanese. *Zuiho* and *Shokaku* were crippled, but they did not sink, although it was nine months before *Shokaku* was operational again. Against that, *Hornet* was gone and *Enterprise* was damaged. Until she was repaired the Allies had no carriers in the Pacific.

But it was a pyrrhic victory for the Japanese, who could not afford many more like it. Ninety-seven aircraft and, more important, 148 priceless aircrew, including a high proportion of experienced squadron and section commanders, had been lost. The Americans had lost 81 aircraft and 24 aircrew, four of them prisoners-of-war. The Americans could afford losses; new aircraft were beginning to roll off the assembly lines in their hundreds and a massive aircrew training programme was gathering way in the States. But Nagumo's dead airmen were gone for ever.

In November, 1942, the Japanese High Command decided, belatedly, that one more major effort, one more heave, would take Guadalcanal. In the first ten days of that month the Tokyo Express made 65 destroyer and two cruiser troop-carrying runs. By 12 November the Japanese actually outnumbered the Americans on Guadalcanal for the first time.

Despite another Japanese callsign change on 1 November, cryptanalysis and traffic analysis managed to trace at least the basic shape of that 'one more heave' by the Japanese. Yamamoto planned a major effort at sea to coincide with the attack on land, so as to reach a conclusion with Halsey's carriers once and for all.

Yamamoto issued his orders on 8 November and, by a truly staggering, almost incredible, feat of cryptanalysis, most of the key elements of his plans were available to Halsey by the 9th. A summary of Japanese radio intelligence that day stated: 'New operation involving Guadalcanal either already begun or is about to begin, with Z day fixed and at least one phase of the operation concerned with the airfield on Guadalcanal fixed for Z-3 Day. Likely date appears to be November 12.'

More details were given in the summary next day, the 10th: 'Opord from C-in-C Combined Fleet 1830 November 8, parts unintelligible as yet, (a) Army convoy will arrive Guadalcanal on Z Day, (b) air attacks on Blue installations on Guadalcanal from Z-3, (c) escorts, air patrol and patrols of certain sectors provided for protection of convoy from Z-3, (d) air forces will be under the command of the Striking Force from Z-3, (e) Striking Force will operate against Guadalcanal from Z-1. Z-Day now November 13.' The only part of Yamamoto's plan not known was his intention to carry out another battleship bombardment of Henderson.

The Combined Fleet was to sail from Truk with *Junyo* and *Zuiho* and possibly three escort carriers, four battleships, five heavy and six light cruisers, and twenty-one destroyers. The CincPac Bulletin of 10 November stated: 'Big Japanese offensive against Guadalcanal to begin soon. Believe enemy striking force intends to hit that place followed by attempted landings by army units from transports. At present striking force believed either at or en route to position east of Greenwich Island.'

On 11 November the summary of Japanese radio intelligence was: 'Indications strong C-in-C 8th Fleet [Mikawa] in *Chokai* directly concerned in the command and protection of two Army convoys scheduled to arrive Guadalcanal on November 13. Convoys are large and important.'

On 10 November a coastwatcher at Shortland had reported 61 ships in the harbour, including six cruisers and 33 destroyers. Among them were eleven transports with some 7,000 troops embarked, to be escorted by twelve destroyers under Tanaka. There were indeed two convoys, as the summary had revealed. Six transports were to go to Cape Esperance, five to Tassafaronga.

At sea was an even more powerful force than radio intelligence had forecast. Kondo, flying his flag in the heavy cruiser *Atago*, commanded an advance force of two battleships, *Kongo* and *Haruna*, six cruisers and 21 destroyers. Abe led a Bombardment Group of *Hiei* and *Kirishima*, a light cruiser and destroyers. The 8th Fleet under Mikawa provided two support forces of heavy cruisers and destroyers.

The only Japanese weakness lay in air cover. *Shokaku*, *Zuikaku* and *Zuiho* were all on their way back to the Empire to repair battle damage and/or replace aircrew losses. *Hiyo* still had defective engines. Therefore *Junyo* was the only carrier at sea with Kondo.

Halsey had only *Enterprise*, still at Noumea under repair with her forward lift unusable, the battleships *Washington* and *South Dakota*, four heavy and four light cruisers, and 22 destroyers. However, Halsey had no intention of avoiding battle. He ordered Kinkaid to sail *Enterprise* on 11 November and 'to be prepared to strike enemy targets in Cactus area'.

Large American reinforcements, due to unload on 11/12 November, sailed for Guadalcanal in two parts: three freighters escorted by Scott in *Atlanta* and four destroyers, and four transports escorted by Rear Admiral Daniel Callaghan in *San Francisco* with the cruisers *Portland*, *Helena* and *Juneau* and five destroyers. Kinkaid's task force of *Enterprise*, the two battleships, two cruisers and eight destroyers would provide distant cover and a counter to Yamamoto. If *Enterprise* could not reach the battle in time, the battlewagons and four destroyers would be detached to act independently, under Rear Admiral Willis 'Ching' Lee.

Thus the scene was set for the naval battle of Guadalcanal, which lasted from the afternoon of 12 November, 1942, until 1 am on the morning of the 15th. It was one of the biggest sea-fights of the whole war. Had it taken place in the North Sea, the Western Approaches or in the Mediterranean, it would now be as famous as Jutland.

Both American reinforcement groups arrived safely, and the action began on the afternoon of the 12th with a Japanese air attack, successfully beaten off, on the transports unloading at Guadalcanal. Aircraft and intelligence reported a very powerful Tokyo Express of two battleships, four cruisers and eight destroyers, heading down the Slot. Kinkaid's ships were too far away to assist. Callaghan would just have to do his best.

Drawing a mistaken lesson from Cape Esperance, Callaghan had his ships in line ahead, with four destroyers ahead, then *Atlanta* flying Scott's flag, then *San Francisco* and the three remaining cruisers, with four destroyers bringing up the rear. This was an admirable formation for navigation and for ship-to-ship communication, but for battle it was more suited to sailing-ship tactics.

Furthermore, the cruisers with the best radar were not in leading positions and the two destroyers with the most modern sets were actually in the back four. Many of the ships had not exercised together before, but no combat intelligence was passed to them, nor did Callaghan issue specific instructions. By placing four of his destroyers at the rear, and keeping all eight closely under his personal control, Callaghan deprived them of the chance to use their best weapon, independent torpedo attack. Callaghan himself had no previous battle experience and was given command over Scott, who had, because he was the senior by a few weeks.

The first radar indication of the Japanese was at 1.24 am on Friday the 13th. At that time Callaghan's ships were steaming westward past Lunga Point, having seen the transports safely to their destination.

The Japanese ships were, of course, Abe's bombardment group, of *Hiei* and *Kirishima* screened by destroyers and *Nagara*. Heading south-east into Ironbottom Sound, leaving Savo close to port, Abe's object was to pound Henderson into helplessness. He was not expecting battle. The Japanese still expected the American ships to leave the Slot and go home with the setting sun.

Callaghan did not turn boldly to starboard, to cross his enemy's T, nor did he send his destroyers on ahead. He appeared to aim for a head-on encounter, for he turned his force slightly to starboard, into an oblique crossing approach in front of the Japanese ships. The leading destroyer *Cushing* sighted two Japanese destroyers at close range at 1.41 am and had to make an emergency turn to avoid a collision. This threw Callaghan's following ships into some confusion, which soon became complete. Callaghan delayed a fatal eight minutes before giving the order to fire, and a wild mêlée in the darkness began.

Atlanta was lit up by searchlight, hit by one torpedo and by gunfire on her bridge. She came to a dead stop, and Scott was among those killed. *San Francisco* steamed between the Japanese battleships, *Hiei* to port and *Kirishima* to starboard; she was hit several times and Callaghan himself was killed. *Cushing* was sunk by *Hiei* and the destroyer *Laffey* was sunk by a Japanese destroyer. The cruisers' and destroyers' fire set *Hiei* ablaze from end to end and both battleships reversed course. The destroyer *Sterett* torpedoed and sank the Japanese destroyer *Yudichi* but was then torpedoed and put out of action herself. *Portland* took one torpedo hit astern and could only steam in circles. *Juneau* was also hit but survived until the morning, when she was sunk with very heavy loss of life by the Japanese submarine *I-26* as she was trying to retire. The destroyer *Barton* was hit by two torpedoes and broke in two. She was brand new and had been in action only seven minutes. Another destroyer, *Monssen*, was left a burning hulk. Altogether, Callaghan's ships had taken a grim mauling. But Abe cancelled the bombardment of Henderson and the radio intelligence summary of 13 November revealed that Z Day had been postponed to the 14th because of the action off Savo.

Later on the 13th torpedo and bomb attacks by aircraft from Henderson, from *Enterprise*, then steaming up from the south, and from Espiritu Santo, caught *Hiei* off Savo Island. She turned over and sank at 6 pm. That night the cruisers *Suzuya* and *Maya*, under Admiral Nishimura, bombarded Henderson for nearly forty minutes.

Halsey refused to allow *Enterprise* to operate north of Guadalcanal and as she was still under repair (with workmen still aboard her) he detached the battleships under Lee to go into Ironbottom Sound and 'clean up'.

Approaching Lee's force was Kondo, in *Atago*, with three more cruisers and *Kirishima*, intent on delivering the bombardment of Henderson which Callaghan's ships had forestalled the night before.

Lee's ships entered Ironbottom Sound from the north at 10.15 pm on 14 November. Unknown to Lee, he had already been sighted by the light cruiser *Sendai*, who was shadowing him. Lee opened fire on *Sendai* at 11.17 pm, whilst his four destroyers had a private battle with Japanese destroyers close under the shadow of Savo. The US destroyers had decidedly the worst of it. *Preston* and *Walke* were sunk, *Gwin* and *Benham* badly damaged.

South Dakota had a critical power failure at a crucial time, so that she was unable to fire and became nothing more than a target herself, but *Washington*, superbly handled and fought, opened fire by radar on *Kirishima* at a range of 8,400 yards just after midnight. In a brisk seven minutes of firing, she hit *Kirishima* with nine out of seventy-five 16-inch shells and another forty 5-inch. *Kirishima* was battered into a helpless blazing wreck, and was later scuttled. Kondo retired at twenty-five minutes past midnight and returned to Rabaul, where Yamamoto relieved him of his command (as he had already relieved Abe the day before).

Tanaka's convoy was attacked from the air several times on the 14th and eventually ten of eleven transports were sunk or beached, and only some 2,000 troops were landed.

In one of the very few battleship engagements of the war, *Washington* had held the ring for the Allies at a very important time, for the naval battles of November were the turning point of the campaign. The Japanese Navy now proposed that Guadalcanal be abandoned. But the Army insisted on carrying on.

Rear Admiral Raizo Tanaka – 'Tenacious Tanaka' – was one of the ablest admirals of the war on any side. Brave, wily and quick to recover from surprise, he continued almost to the end of the Guadalcanal campaign to teach the US Navy that any mistakes would be harshly punished. Ironically, Tanaka's last major action was against a special task force formed because CincPac's staff had decided that their ships and commanders lacked the true offensive spirit.

Kinkaid was appointed to command the new striking force, Task Force 67, based on Espiritu Santo, of the heavy cruisers *Minneapolis*, *Pensacola*, *New Orleans* and *Northampton*, the light cruiser *Honolulu* and a destroyer escort. But Kinkaid was relieved on 28 November, to take command in the North Pacific. His successor was the unfortunate Rear Admiral Carleton Wright, who was pitchforked into action, and against the redoubtable Tanaka himself, only two days after assuming command.

A message from Truk to the 17th Army on Guadalcanal, advising them of another Tokyo Express, was decrypted on 29 November and the CincPac Bulletin for that day forecast: 'Daily attempts to transport reinforcements to both Guadalcanal and Buna by destroyers predicted for next few days'. The next day's Bulletin was more specific: 'Believe attempt to transport supplies to Guadalcanal by destroyers possibly also Marus now under way. Enemy submarines also heading for Guadalcanal'.

On the 29th Halsey ordered Wright to take Task Force 67 to sea so as to arrive off Tassafaronga by 11 pm, 30 November, to intercept a Japanese reinforcement group of eight destroyers and six transports.

It was Tanaka's Tokyo Express again, but a Tokyo Express in somewhat reduced circumstances. There were no transports but there were eight destroyers, six of them with their decks crammed with troops and stores. But this was no massive reinforcement. The destroyers were to dash inshore off Tassafaronga, throw drums of stores overboard to be hauled ashore by lines, put troops over the side to be picked up by small craft, and retire again. But Tanaka's ships met Wright's force before arriving at Tassafaronga.

Once again the Americans had the precious advantages of fore-knowledge and prior radar contact. Once again the chance was fumbled. One of the leading destroyers, *Fletcher*, with the latest radar, picked up Tanaka's ships at 11.16 pm, broad on the port beam, heading in towards the Guadalcanal shore. *Fletcher* asked permission to fire torpedoes, but Wright delayed a priceless four minutes before replying. It was then too late. By the time the torpedoes were launched, the Japanese ships had passed on an opposing course and the range was too great. Not one of the American torpedoes hit. When the last had gone, Wright's cruisers opened fire.

Tanaka and his highly trained torpedomen reacted quickly and launched more than twenty Long Lances in a few moments. They were helped by the cruisers' concentrating their fire upon only one destroyer, *Takanami*. Only five minutes after the action had opened, the Long Lances began to score: two hits on Wright's flagship, *Minneapolis*, knocking her out of the firing line; one on *New Orleans*, blowing off her bows and fo'c'sle up to No. 2 turret; one on *Pensacola* amidships, and two on *Northampton*. *Honolulu* alone escaped by adroit seamanship.

Excellent damage control saved all but *Northampton*, who sank after a three-hour struggle to save her, but the damaged cruisers were out of the war for nearly a year. Of Tanaka's force, only *Takanami* was sunk. However, his ships had to turn back without delivering their troops or supplies.

The Battle of Tassafaronga, as both sides realized, reflected the greatest credit upon the Imperial Japanese Navy: eight destroyers, surprised and with their upper decks cluttered by men and gear, had inflicted great damage upon a superior force of heavy cruisers which had known exactly when and where they would be and had been lying in wait for them.

The failure of the Tokyo Express to deliver men and supplies on the night of 30 November/1 December resulted in even more desperate shortages for the 17th Army. In December, 1942, the Express continued to run every two or three nights and to be regularly revealed by radio intelligence and intercepted.

On 3 December destroyers managed to unload some 1,500 drums off Tassafaronga but aircraft attacked the destroyers and then sent all but 310 drums to the bottom with machine-gun fire. On the 7th an Express was bombed but pressed on until it was attacked by eight PT boats off Savo Island when it turned back. This was a remarkable success for the PT boats who had achieved, without any loss, as much as Wright's cruisers had achieved, at so much cost, on 30 November.

Latterly the Japanese used submarines to supply the 17th Army. In the first week of December submarines delivered some 20 tons.

But radio intelligence gave advance notice of nearly all submarine attempts to supply Guadalcanal. In the early hours of 9 December ULTRA pulled off the perfect ambush when, forewarned, *PT44* and *PT59* lay in wait off Kamimbo for the large submarine *I-3* which actually surfaced between them and was dispatched by one torpedo from *PT59* as it began unloading.

Throughout the rest of December, 1942, and in January, 1943, enemy activity seemed to increase, as though the Japanese were redoubling their efforts to reinforce Guadalcanal. On 23 January reconnaissance reported considerable Japanese shipping activity north of the island. This was believed to be another Tokyo Express but in fact was an evacuation force. The Japanese had at last decided to abandon what had become a costly and open-ended commitment, but they concealed their intentions superbly well behind a façade of furious activity.

Guadalcanal continued to teach basic lessons of modern sea warfare to the bitter end. If nothing else, it should have taught every commander that it was vital to have air cover at all times. On 29 January, 1943, Halsey sent up a decoy reinforcement group, covered by cruisers, destroyers and two *Sangamon* Class escort carriers, hoping to lure Yamamoto into action again.

This group, under Rear Admiral Robert Giffen, was off Rennell Island on the 29th when it was attacked at dusk by torpedo-carrying Bettys from the newly constructed airfield at Munda in New Georgia. Giffen's ships were poorly disposed to repel an air attack, his captains had no orders what to do, and, most culpable of all, Giffen had left behind his carriers for some minor reason, and had no air cover.

Trusting to his anti-aircraft fire, Giffen pressed on, but one torpedo hit *Chicago*, the sole survivor of Savo, and left her dead in the water. Attempts were made to take her in tow but Japanese aircraft found her again at 4 pm the next day and, despite air cover from *Enterprise*, sank her with four more torpedoes. This was the seventh and last naval battle of Guadalcanal.

A change of Japanese naval callsigns scheduled for 15 January was deferred for two weeks. A complete change took place on 1 February and the Japanese began to evacuate their troops from Guadalcanal the next day. Their security was magnificent and by the 7th the last Japanese soldier had been spirited away by the Tokyo Express, running in reverse, under the Allies' very noses. On 8 February it was noted that Japanese radio traffic on Guadalcanal had dropped off sharply and it was realized that Guadalcanal was being evacuated rather than reinforced. This was confirmed by a German broadcast of a Japanese dispatch that an evacuation of Guadalcanal had been made.

So, Guadalcanal was a victory in the end, to which ULTRA and traffic analysis had made an invaluable contribution. The US Navy had many bloody lessons off Guadalcanal, losing hundreds of men and many valuable ships. But in general they profited from experience and by the end the Allies had sunk as many Japanese ships – twenty-five – as they had lost themselves.

When Guadalcanal was secured for the Allies, Australian troops had already inflicted on the Japanese their first defeat of the war on land, in Papua, where the Australians had counter-attacked in September, 1942, forced the Japanese to retreat along the Kokoda Trail, and by 31 January, 1943, had fought their way across the Owen Stanley mountain range and reached Buna on the north coast of New Guinea.

The Australians, in this little known campaign, suffered almost twice the casualties sustained by the US Marines on Guadalcanal, but together the Australians in Papua and the Americans on Guadalcanal had shown that the Japanese were not invincible – not at sea, not in the air and, now, not in the jungle either.

VII

THE FALL OF THE PEACOCK –
THE YAMAMOTO AMBUSH

JUST after 9 pm on 29 January, 1943, two Royal New Zealand Navy corvettes, *Kiwi* and *Moa*, operating from Tulagi, were off Kamimbo Bay, on the western tip of Guadalcanal, when *Kiwi* (Lt Cdr G. Bridson RNZN) obtained a firm asdic contact at a range of 3,000 yards and made two accurate depth-charge attacks which blew the large Japanese submarine *I-1* to the surface.

Kiwi opened fire with her 4-inch and 20 mm Oerlikon guns, while Bridson altered course to ram and ordered full speed ahead. When his engineer officer protested Bridson shouted, 'Shut up! There's a weekend's leave in Auckland dead ahead of us!'

Kiwi rammed *I-1* on the port side, recoiled and rammed again, Bridson bellowing, 'That'll be a *week*'s leave!' Landing barges could be seen on the submarine's after casing and soldiers in full packs were jumping over the side. *I-1*'s gun's crew manned their gun and got off a few rounds (*Kiwi* reported that two narrowly missed her) before *Kiwi*'s fire cut them down and killed Lt Cdr Sakamoto, *I-1*'s captain. Her navigating officer rushed down the control room ladder shouting, 'Swords! Swords!'. He and the first lieutenant, both armed with samurai swords, appeared on the bridge. The navigating officer grasped *Kiwi's* upper deck rail and tried to board her when she came in again.

With Bridson's slogan 'Once more for a *fortnight!*' *Kiwi* rammed the submarine a third time, her forefoot riding up over the casing and holing an external fuel tank so that a gusher of diesel oil spouted over *Kiwi*'s fo'c'sle.

Until now *Moa* had been unable to fire because *Kiwi* had been so close to the submarine that there was a danger of hitting her. But as *Kiwi* slid clear after the third ramming *Moa* opened fire. *I-1* finally ran aground on a reef at 2320 and her stern sank leaving only her bows and foreplanes out of the water. Sixty-six men, including 19 of the 60 soldiers she had been carrying to Guadalcanal, got ashore from *I-1* to a part of Guadalcanal still held by the Japanese where, according to a later Japanese account, they tore up or buried some of the submarine's codebooks and secret papers.

Kiwi and *Moa* stood by the stranded submarine until morning, when *Moa* sent across a boarding party who took the wounded navigating officer prisoner. According to their report, they also took the submarine's code books which they handed over to the US Naval authorities at Lunga, Guadalcanal. However, this was not reported to Pearl Harbor for some days.

A jubilant COMNAVACTSOL (Commander Navy Solomons) signalled COMSOPAC (Halsey) at Noumea, and to Nimitz and King for information:

'DURING THE NIGHT 29TH–30TH LOCAL OFF CAPE ESPERANCE NEW ZEALAND CORVETTES KIWI AND MOA DESTROYED IN SURFACE ENGAGEMENT LARGE TYPE 4-INCH GUN SUBMARINE CARRYING TROOPS X SUBMARINE GUTTED AND BEACHED NEAR KAMIMBO BAY, GUADALCANAL X I OFFICER PRISONER X 3 INJURED ON KIWI X KIWI BOW AND ASDIC GEAR DAMAGED SO THAT SHIP CANNOT CONTINUE PRESENT OPERATIONS AND WILL REQUIRE REFIT X KIWI IS SEAWORTHY AND CAN MAKE 9 KNOTS X'

The loss of *I-1* was confirmed by a signal early on the morning of the 30th from the survivors at Kamimbo:

'FROM: 2ND DET. AT KAMIMBO (I–I2O)

TO: SUBFORCE FLAGSHIP

INFO: IITH AIR FORCE, 8TH FLEET

FROM: C.O. OF I–I X

ENGAGEMENT REPORT X

AT I900 WAS ATTACKED BY TWO TORPEDO BOATS AND TWO PLANES X

X ABANDONED LANDING OF PROVISIONS AND SUBMERGED X WHILE RUNNING SUBMERGED WAS DISABLED BY 2 DEPTH CHARGES OR BOMBS AND FORCED TO SURFACE X

AT I920, FURTHER ATTACKED AND SUNK AT 2I2O IN POSITION I KILOMETER NORTH OF KAMIMBO X

CAPTAIN KILLED X 47 SURVIVORS NOW AT KAMIMBO X'

Kiwi and *Moa* had not been waiting off Kamimbo Bay that night just on the off-chance of sinking a Japanese submarine. The Japanese had begun using submarines again to run supplies to Guadalcanal late in December, 1942. On 8 January, 1943, traffic analysis showed associations between submarine commands and the Guadalcanal garrison which appeared to be in some way connected with logistics.

Radio direction-finding, carried out in part (appropriately in view of what was to happen to *I-1*) by three stations in New Zealand, at Waipapakauri, Musick Point and Awarua, and by radio fingerprinting, also provided from New Zealand, by RNZN Station Raupara, Blenheim, assisted in the location and identification of Japanese submarines in the Solomons area in January, 1943, playing a direct part in the sinking of *I-1*.

But the main part was played by cryptanalysis. One important message of 23 January was intercepted and partly decrypted:

'FROM: RABAUL

TO: COMMANDER 'B' SUBMARINE FORCE, SEAPLANE TENDER DIVISION, 26TH AIR FLOTILLA, COLLECTIVE RABAUL AREA, SUBMARINE SQUADRON 3

INFO: COMMANDER SUBMARINE FORCE, CHIEF OF STAFF 8TH FLEET

FROM: CAPTAIN I-17 X

INFORMATION CHIEF OF STAFF 17TH ARMY, COMMANDER NO 1 SHIPPING GROUP X WILL TRANSPORT PROVISIONS TO KAMIMBO AS FOLLOWS:

WILL DEPART RABAUL 24 JANUARY (. . .words missed. . .)

EXPECT ARRIVE KAMIMBO VIA (. . .) ROUTE AT 1745 27 JANUARY X'

Other messages relating to kamimbo and the movements of 'I' Class submarines were intercepted and decrypted, including:

'FROM: (?)

TO: 2ND COMMUNICATIONS DETACHMENT, KAMIMBO

THE SENDING OF MEN BY THE I-2 SUBMARINE ON THE 26TH, THE I-17 ON THE 27TH, AND THE I-1 ON THE 29TH WILL BE STOPPED.

FROM: STAFF GUADALCANAL OPERATIONS FORCE

TO: CHIYODA BASE GUADALCANAL, 2ND COMM DET KAMIMBO

THE EVACUATION OF PERSONNEL BY THE SUBMARINE I-2 ON THE 26TH, I-17 ON THE 27TH, AND THE I-1 ON THE 29TH IS CANCELLED.'

(This was very probably the first reference to the evacuation of Japanese forces from Guadalcanal.)

When this traffic had been evaluated, on 25th January Halsey signalled COMGEN CACTUS, the Commanding General Guadalcanal, Major General Alexander M. Patch, and COMAIRSOPAC,

Commander Aircraft South Pacific, Rear Admiral Aubrey W. Fitch, and Nimitz and MacArthur for information:

'JAP SUBS X MAY ARRIVE KAMIMBO WITH SUPPLIES ON 26TH, 27TH AND 29TH X TIME OF ARRIVAL INDICATED AS 1945L (-11) X.'

This enabled COMNAVACTSOL (Commander Navy Solomons) to make dispositions to intercept, as promulgated in his signal of 26 January to all ships CACTUS amd RINGBOLT (codename for Tulagi):

THIS IS A REENCYPHERMENT OF MY 260446 SENT TO OTHER INTERESTED PARTIES BY ANOTHER SYSTEM X HAVE RECEIVED REPORT THAT JAP SUBS MAY ARRIVE KAMIMBO ABOUT 1945L (-11) TONIGHT WITH SUPPLIES X (KIWI) COMBINE SWEEP 25 DIRECTED AT 1500 PROCEED IN COMPANY WITH MOA AND UPON ARRIVAL KAMIMBO AREA ESTABLISH ANTI SUB PATROL NORTHWEST TIP OF GUADALCANAL FROM COUGHLAN TO TISALE X AT DAWN PROCEED LUNGA AND TAKE POSITIONS IN SCREEN X IF FLOATING SUPPLIES ARE FOUND IN WATER RECOVER IF PRACTICABLE OTHERWISE DESTROY X IF [TOKYO] EXPRESS RUNS RETIRE TO WEST AND SOUTH OF GUADALCANAL.'

The rest of this signal contained instructions to other ships and commanders.

A Tokyo Express (actually on an evacuation, not a supply, mission) of seven destroyers and a cruiser did run on the night of the 26th but it turned back after two bombing attacks by Catalinas. After two blank nights, *Kiwi* and *Moa* were ready for *I-1* on the night of the 29th. (For the sinking, Bridson was awarded the DSO and Lt Cdr Peter Phipps, *Moa*'s CO, a Bar to his DSC, and both were awarded the US Navy Cross.)

The Japanese continued to be uneasy about the possibility of code books and other cryptographic material being left on board *I-1*. There was soon evidence that another Japanese submarine, *I-2*, was about to try and destroy the hulk of *I-1*. A message was intercepted on 8 February, in which neither the sender nor any of the addressees was decyphered, but enough was read for the cryptanalyst to comment that 'this message is barely readable but the sender fears that the registered publications on board the *I-1* may have fallen into enemy hands'.

Another partially readable message was from 6th Fleet to an unidentified address at Rabaul:

'REFERENCE "B" SUBMARINE FORCE SERIAL 080815 AND 6TH FLEETS (. . .) X

IN ORDER TO (. . . something in connection with the destruction of the I-1) SUBMARINE I-2 WILL (. . .)
AS ALREADY ORDERED X.'

On 14 February, a badly garbled Japanese message, in which neither sender nor any addressees were identifiable, was intercepted and partly read:

'I–2 AT ABOUT 1530 THE 13TH
. . .ALTHOUGH APPROACHED TO WITHIN 1800 METERS COULD NOT.
. . .OFF KAMIMBO . . .
. . .IN VIEW OF PATROL . . .
. . .EXPECT TO CARRY IT OUT TOMORROW THE 15TH . . .'

As a result of this, Halsey sent a signal at 2319 on the 14th to COMNAVBASE CACTUS, for information to CINCPAC, SENAV CACTUS (Senior Naval Aviator, Guadalcanal) and COMGEN CACTUS:

'COMSOPAC 120345 X ULTRA X BELIEVE JAP SUB STILL TRYING TO CARRY OUT MISSION AT KAMIMBO X ANOTHER ATTEMPT INDICATED FOR 15TH REF X.'

Another signal followed on the next day:

MY 142319 (date-time-group of the signal above) X ULTRA X OBJECTIVE MAY BE INTERFERENCE WITH SALVAGE OPERATION OF JAP SUB X.'

The forecast was correct. *I-2* did make an attempt to salvage the code books and destroy the remains of *I-1* on the night of 15 February, but was driven off and quite badly damaged by a PT boat. This was revealed by a signal intercepted the next day from 'NETAYO 1' to an unidentified addressee, which was difficult to read but confirmed that *I-2* made an unsuccessful attempt to destroy *I-1* on the night of the 15th but was driven off by a patrol boat. *I-2* reported that she was now en route to the Shortland Islands, to arrive 0500 on the 18th. She would run on the surface after the 17th. In a second message, *I-2* reported that she had been damaged, which very probably accounts for the decision to run on the surface.

The salvage operation referred to in Halsey's signal of 15 February had been carried out by the submarine rescue vessel USS *Ortolan* two days earlier and the results reported by COMNAVBASE CACTUS to Halsey, information Nimitz, in a Priority signal the same day:

ORTLANS [sic] (ASR 5) PRELIM SURVEY 13TH LARGE JAP SUB X
NO DAMAGE TO PRESSURE HULL X SUPERSTRUCTURE DAMAGED X

I TYPE 319 FEET WITH 4.7 GUN X PLAN OF OPERATION CLOSE FOR-
WARD COMPT AND DEWATER FLOWING FORWARD AFT X FLOTATION
APPEARS FEASIBLE BUT UNABLE ESTIMATE COMPLETION TIME X
RECOVERED FROM CONNING TOWER 2 NAVY 4 KANA I PROBABLY
OTHER SUB CODE X ESTIMATE OTHER SUB 2 MAN TYPE CAN BE
FLOATED ABOUT 4 DAYS X ADVISE DISPOSITION OF CODES X.'

Nimitz's reaction to the news of the codes was swift, by Priority
signal to Halsey only hours later:

HANDLE AS ZEAL   [alternative US term for ULTRA] FROM
CINPAC X COMNAVBASE CACTUS 130817   [date-time-group of
'*Ortolan*' signal above] X REQUEST CAPTURED CODE BOOKS OR
ENEMY COMMUNICATIONS DATA BE FORWARDED CINCPAC BY AIR
AS SOON AS PRACTICABLE X INDICATIONS JAPS APPREHENSIVE
REGARDING SECRET PUBLICATIONS ABOARD THAT SUB MAY HAVE
A CIPHER MACHINE ALSO X HOPE ALL MAY BE FOUND PRIOR
FLOATING X.'

Exactly what codes, cyphers and other crypto material *I-1* had
on board when she was sunk will probably never now be known.
An *Operational History of Japanese Naval Communications, December 1941–1945*, written by former Japanese commanders and staff
officers of the General Staff and the War Ministry at the direction
of the Allies after the war, gives in Chapter III 'Communications
Security' a section on 'Security "Accidents" and Countermeasures'
which includes an account of the loss of *I-1*: 'While transporting
provisions to Guadalcanal island, the submarine was stranded on the
coast of Kamimbo during combat with an enemy motor torpedo boat.
It listed and exposed part of its hull above the water. The responsible
persons evacuated some of the military top secret documents from
the craft and buried them in the coastal sands of enemy territory
where there was every fear of their being dug out plus the fact that
water-soluble ink had been used for only a few of these documents.
The loss comprised many code books for future use in addition
to those in current use, totalling about 200,000 copies. This fact
was reported about a month after the "accident" when the crew
returned to Rabaul. Although the Submarine Squadron Command
issued orders to dig them out and destroy them immediately, one
or two of the numerous places where the documents were buried could not be located. Moreover, as there were a considerable
number of code books left in the submarine, aerial bombardment
and torpedoing by submarines was carried out, but complete destruction was not confirmed.'

Postwar Japanese accounts of wartime events displayed an understandable desire to put literally the 'best face' upon disasters, but even allowing for that, and discounting such errors as *I-1* being sunk by a motor torpedo boat (the writers may have been confusing her sinking with the attack on *I-2*), the figure of 200,000 code *books* is open to question. Certainly, it would mitigate some of the Japanese defeats to come after Guadalcanal, which was the turning point of the war in the Pacific, if they could be partly blamed on the loss of so many code books.

It could be argued that *I-1* was carrying secret documents to several places, of which Guadalcanal was just the first. But even accepting the colossal amount of space so many books would take up in even a large submarine, the figure of 200,000 is inherently incredible. The decision to evacuate Guadalcanal had been taken in Tokyo on 31 December, 1942, and it was actually completed on 8 February, 1943, only days after the loss of *I-1*. To send a submarine with so many secret documents on board into such dangerous waters and to a destination which was just about to be evacuated would have been madness, especially if only a proportion of those documents were to be delivered to Guadalcanal.

There are other inconsistencies. The *Operational History* stated that the loss was not reported until the survivors returned to Rabaul 'a month later'. But the Japanese knew of *I-1*'s loss on the morning after, when the officer who had assumed command signalled details from Kamimbo. If the submarine really had had 200,000 secret documents on board, then the Japanese were extraordinarily slow in taking any action to recover them. In fact, *I-2* had made attempts on 13 and 15 February, long before the survivors were reported to have returned to Rabaul.

The survivors had landed in Japanese-held territory. Yet they are supposed to have buried the books and had then been unable to discover one or two of the caches when, at some unexplained date, the Submarine Squadron Command gave orders to have them dug up. Yet, according to the *History*, this could not have been until a month later, by which time Kamimbo, and indeed the whole of Guadalcanal, was in Allied hands.

Burying the code books suggests that the survivors, whose one thought that night must surely have been to get themselves safely ashore, then spent the rest of the night wading and swimming out to the submarine and back again, ferrying 200,000 code books to shore, where they buried them. *Kiwi* and *Moa* kept guard over

I-1 all night and must have seen any such activity, whereupon they would have fired to stop it, and they would have reported it later. They neither saw nor reported anything.

Had the code books remained on board instead of being buried ashore, then *Ortolan*'s divers would have discovered them. But the signal reporting *Ortolan*'s survey mentioned only a few code books.

It is more likely that the *History*'s use of 'code book' was a routine, somewhat vague, translation to cover a range of crypto material, such as new and reserve code books, keys, tables, additive strips and regulations for various editions, and that '200,000' was the number of crypto documents necessary to supply Japanese naval ship and shore units throughout the Pacific. These had all now been compromised by the loss of *I-1*.

The simplest explanation is that *I-1*'s survivors were evacuated from Guadalcanal and arrived in Rabaul on 9 February or a day later, when they admitted that current crypto material had been buried ashore where it was possible the enemy might discover it, and that some out-of-date material had been left on board. When this was reported to Tokyo, first an unsuccessful attempt to destroy *I-1* by bombing was made on 10 February and then the 7th Submarine Division of the 6th (Submarine) Fleet at Rabaul, to which both *I-1* and *I-2* belonged, was ordered to destroy *I-1*'s hulk, hence *I-2*'s attempts on 13 and 15 February (the 'torpedoing by submarines' mentioned in the *History* was never achieved).

The *History* listed the countermeasures taken after the loss of *I-1*:
1. Emergency measures were taken and new code books were used.
2. The additive table of the wartime code book was immediately revised and the encoding procedure was altered.
3. The original of the strategic code book was not changed.

The most important outcome from the Allied point of view was a major change in Japanese codes on 15 February, 1943, which was very probably the result of *I-1*'s sinking. The summary of Japanese naval radio intelligence for the 16th said: 'Readability of the most important Japanese operational code has been greatly decreased by a shift on February 15 (LZT). Estimated that approximately 4 weeks will be required before the new system is brought to the same degree of readability as the one displaced. Two additional operational codes have also been replaced by entirely new systems. These changes, with the recent changeover to new callsigns, obviously decreases the reliability which can be placed on Radio Intelligence.'

By the time the crypto material recovered from *I-1* eventually reached Pearl Harbor it was out of date. But that did not mean that it was not welcome. According to Lt Cdr Jasper Holmes, a member of the staff of FRUPAC (Fleet Radio Unit Pacific, as HYPO was now called) it 'was as precious as a moon rock to an astronomer'. It included the red-covered five-digit code book and its additive tables. 'For many long hours,' Holmes wrote, 'they [FRUPAC's staff] had puzzled and schemed to work out the meanings of those five-digit code groups. Now they could turn the pages and verify their recoveries, reliving old triumphs and rationalizing old mistakes. With superseded call lists [they] could verify the Japanese fleet organization and check the names of new ships and stations. In a thin pamphlet, also red-covered, were all the two- and three-letter area designators. Sure enough, AFG was French Frigate Shoal and AF was Midway – or rather Otori Shima (Big Bird Island), the name the Japanese had given to Midway in expectation of its capture.'

Holmes said that *I-1* had been carrying 'not only the current codes but copies of reserve editions scheduled to go into effect before the submarine returned from its mission. More than 200,000 secret documents, widely distributed across the broad Pacific, had been compromised and had to be replaced. It was months before the mess was cleaned up and many of the compromised items had to remain in service for some time.'

The change in the Japanese codes continued to hamper decipherment for the rest of February, 1943. The summary of Japanese naval radio intelligence for 4 March, for instance, recorded that 'Inability to read large portions of intercepted Japanese radio traffic and difficulties in identifying callsigns makes it practically impossible to assess the damage claimed to have been inflicted on Japanese convoy by Allied air forces on March 2 and 3'.

This referred to a recent action of which even the partially read messages provided by ULTRA had given at least an inkling, mentioned in the CincPac Intelligence Bulletin of 26 February: 'Now believe that convoy of 6 ships will arrive Lae about 5 March. Date destroyers arrive Lae with troops unknown but thought prior arrival above 6 ships'.

Exasperated by their reverses in New Guinea, the Japanese dispatched a whole infantry division of some 7,000 troops from Rabaul on 28 February, bound for Lae in eight transports, escorted by eight destroyers. The convoy passed into the Bismarck Sea on 1 March and, though bad weather concealed it at first, it was sighted on the 2nd. Aircraft of the USAAF and RAAF from Papua began a series of bombing attacks which lasted intermittently for thirty-six hours.

By 4 March the whole convoy of eight ships, and four of the destroyers, had been sunk, for the loss of two Allied bombers and three fighters. Japanese survivors swimming in the water or crowded on to decks were machine-gunned by aircraft and PT boats. ULTRA provided some information about survivors, for instance that the destroyer *Yukikaze* picked up 1,000 men of the Lae convoy off Finschhafen on 5 March. The Japanese lost some 4,000 men.

This Battle of the Bismarck Sea was a smashing victory for air power at sea, one of the greatest of the war, equivalent to a major victory on land. The Japanese never again attempted to move anything larger than a small barge by daylight within range of Allied aircraft.

The battle in the South Pacific now shifted northwards from Guadalcanal into the central Solomons, where the Japanese, though constantly harassed by air attacks, ship bombardments and offensive minelaying, extended the airfield at Munda, and built others at Vila, on Kolombangara Island and in southern Bougainville, and seaplane bases in the Shortland and other islands.

But these were defensive measures, which did not satisfy Yamamoto. In April, 1943, he launched Operation 'I', which was intended to be a crushing air offensive against Allied shipping and bases in Guadalcanal, Papua and Australia. He disembarked some 170 aircraft from his carriers to double the existing air strength of the 11th Air Fleet ashore in Rabaul.

Huge formations of between 100 and 200 aircraft swept down the Slot on 1 April, attacked Tulagi on the 7th, Oro Bay near Buna on the 11th, Port Moresby on the 12th and Milne Bay on the 14th. The Japanese aircrews, understandably, claimed tremendous successes, which Yamamoto believed. In fact, they sank the US destroyer *Aaron Ward*, the US tanker *Kanawha*, the Australian minesweeper *Pirie*, *Moa*, and a handful of small merchant ships, and damaged several more, for the loss of some 40 aircraft and their priceless naval aircrews.

The offensive was not only a failure in material terms, but a gross strategic error. Instead of flinging his precious aircrews against greatly reinforced Allied land bases, Yamamoto would have done far better to have held them back against the day when they would surely be needed against Halsey's and Spruance's carriers.

Yamamoto himself did not live to know the full extent of his failure. He had flown down from Truk on 3 April to Rabaul where traffic analysis revealed his presence and, as the days passed, his special interest in the airfields around the southern end of Bougainville.

Yamamoto had decided to make a personal tour of inspection of air bases in the northern Solomons, to see for himself how matters stood and to boost the morale of personnel in the field. The itinerary for his tour was organized by Captain Yasuji Watanabe, Yamamoto's staff gunnery officer and a personal friend, who suspected the security of Japanese Army codes and ordered that the signal giving details of the Commander-in-Chief's tour should be transmitted only in Navy code. Contrary to his orders, the signal was sent by both systems, and both were picked up by two US listening posts, at Wahaiwa on Oahu and Dutch Harbor in the Aleutians.

In the early hours of the 14th the duty officer at FRUPAC, Major Alva B. Lasswell, US Marine Corps, had decoded part of the intercept, which was to be Yamamoto's death warrant. At 0108 Z (Greenwich Mean Time) on the 14th FRUPAC sent a dispatch to COMINCH, CINCPAC, COMSOPAC and COM7thFLT containing a fragmentary translation of a Japanese message in JN 25, dated 1755/I 13 April, 1943, from CINC SOUTHEASTERN AREA FLEET to several addressees, including COMDR BALLALE GARRISON.

A paraphrased version of the message was: 'On 18th April CINC COMBINED FLEET will —- as follows: Ballale Island —- —- —-. Comment by FRUPAC: This is probably a schedule of inspection by CINC COMBINED FLEET. The message lacks additives, but work will be continued on it'.

Later on the 14th, at 1910 and 2157Z, FRUPAC and OP–20-G sent out more complete translations of the same message, which now read:

FROM: CINC SOUTHEASTERN AIR FLEET

ACTION: SOLOMONS DEFENCE FORCE, AIR GROUP #204, AIR FLOTILLA #26

INFO: BALLALE GARRISON COMDR

ON 18 APRIL CINC COMBINED FLEET WILL VISIT RYZ, R—- AND RXP IN ACCORDANCE FOLLOWING SCHEDULE:

1. DEPART RR AT 0600 IN A MEDIUM ATTACK PLANE ESCORTED BY 6 FIGHTERS. ARRIVE RXZ AT 0800. PROCEED BY MINESWEEPER TO R—- ARRIVING 0840. (—- HAVE MINESWEEPER READY AT #1 BASE). DEPART R—- AT 0945 IN ABOVE MINESWEEPER AND ARRIVE RXZ AT 1030? (———-). DEPART RXZ AT 1100? IN MEDIUM ATTACK PLANE AND ARRIVE RXP AT 1110 —-. DEPART RXP AT 1400 IN MEDIUM ATTACK PLANE AND ARRIVE RR AT 1540.

2. AT EACH OF THE ABOVE PLACES THE COMMANDER-IN-CHIEF WILL MAKE SHORT TOUR OF INSPECTION AND AT —- HE WILL

VISIT THE SICK AND WOUNDED, BUT CURRENT OPERATIONS
SHOULD CONTINUE. EACH FORCE COMMANDER ——
3. IN CASE OF BAD WEATHER THE TRIP WILL BE POSTPONED ONE
DAY.'

FRUPAC had already identified 'RR' as Rabaul, 'RXZ' as Ballale, an island just south of Bougainville, and 'RXP' as Buin, on the southern tip of Bougainville itself. The Garrison Commander at Ballale Island was one of the message's addressees. Ballale was mentioned early in the message. Clearly Ballale was the first stop on Yamamoto's route. It was just within range of fighters from Guadalcanal.

When Layton showed the message to Nimitz on the morning of 14 April Nimitz checked his wall-chart to confirm that the itinerary really would bring Yamamoto within fighter range of Guadalcanal and then asked, 'Do we try to get him?'

Layton was in no doubt they should. Nimitz then asked if the Japanese had a better, younger fleet commander to put up in Yamamoto's place, and whether there was any effective retaliation Japan could take. Layton's answer was no on both counts. There was only one Yamamoto, he said. His loss would be a tremendous blow to both service and civilian morale in Japan. It would be as though the Japanese had shot Nimitz down.

Bougainville was, as Nimitz said, in 'Halsey's bailiwick', so he sent him an 'eyes only' message giving him the text of the message and asking if there was a good chance of intercepting Yamamoto during his tour and shooting him down. Halsey confirmed that the army air commander on Guadalcanal could arrange for the shoot-down by long-range P-38 Lockheed Lightning fighters. Halsey's only misgiving was that such a venture might betray to the Japanese the fact that their codes were being read.

Meanwhile Nimitz had informed Washington and obtained approval from everybody from President Roosevelt downwards. Only Frank Knox, the Secretary of the Navy, had any qualms about the assassination (which it was), but he was reassured by churchmen as to the Christian view of it, while General 'Hap' Arnold of the USAAF confirmed that the operation was militarily feasible.

After receiving the President's approval through Knox on the evening of 15 April, Nimitz signalled to Halsey to go ahead with Operation VENGEANCE, as it was codenamed, 'provided all personnel concerned, particularly the pilots, are briefed that the information comes from Australian coastwatchers near Rabaul', adding, 'Best of luck and good hunting'.

CincPac's daily ULTRA Bulletin of 15 April, issued to all Task Force commanders in the Pacific, stated: 'At 1000 on 18 April YAMAMOTO himself, via bomber escorted by six fighters, will arrive from Rabaul in the Ballale-Shortland area. He will leave Kahili at 1600 the same day to return to Rabaul. All dates and times are 'L'. In case of bad weather the trip will be postponed until 19 April.'

Later on the 15th FRUMEL (Fleet Radio Unit Melbourne, as Belconnen was now called) passed to COMINCH, CINCPAC, COMSOPAC and COM7thFLT the translation of another Japanese message of 14 April, from RABAUL BASE FORCE to an unidentified addressee, referring to 'the special visit of Yamamoto', and 'in view of the situation regarding air attacks on the post', certain precautionary arrangements were requested, including the moving of the 'post' to a new location.

That message was very probably initiated by Lieutenant General Imamura Hitoshi, commanding the Rabaul Army Group, who was worried about Yamamoto's safety. At lunch on 17 April Imamura warned Yamamoto of the danger of US air ambush and told him of a narrow escape he himself had had over Bougainville. Yamamoto said that there had been some enemy air activity over Bougainville but it had been largely reconnaissance flights. There had been few air raids. In any case, he promised he would have an adequate escort of six Zeros.

That afternoon Rear Admiral Joshima Takaji, one of Yamamoto's best friends, flew into Rabaul from Bougainville to plead with Yamamoto to cancel the trip, saying it was madness and an open invitation to the enemy. Yamamoto refused to change his plans.

Very early on 18 April FRUPAC noted a Japanese aircraft originating two encoded weather reports and commented that this was an 'unusual time for Nip plane weather mission'. Certainly, weather reports seemed to confirm that Yamamoto's tour was on.

Yamamoto took off in a two-engined Mitsubishi 'Betty' bomber from East Airfield, Rabaul, at 0600 on 18 April, with Rear Admiral Ugaki, his chief of staff, and other staff officers in a second Betty, escorted by six Zekes.

Rear Admiral Marc A. Mitscher, Commander Air Solomons (COMAIRSOLS), assigned VENGEANCE to the 339th Fighter Squadron, commanded by Major John W. Mitchell, USAAF. Sixteen P-38 Lightnings, four of them designated the attacking section, the rest giving them protective cover, took off from Henderson at 0725 on 18 April. They were all fitted with long-range belly tanks, specially flown up from New Guinea.

Yamamoto was known to be a stickler for punctuality. Mitchell and his pilots could rely on him keeping strictly to his timetable. Nevertheless, the ambush would have to be carried out with pin-point precision. There would be little time for waiting or searching. Southern Bougainville was more than 300 miles in a direct line from Henderson but the ambushers would have to fly very low, between ten and thirty feet over the water, the most radar-avoiding but fuel-consuming height, on a roundabout route of 410 miles out to sea. The flight had been calculated and timed so that the interception was planned to take place at 0935, as the P–38s were approaching the south-western coast of Bougainville.

The timing was perfect. The enemy was sighted dead on 0935, when the P-38s were at thirty feet, heading in from the west towards the coast and just about to climb for altitude. The enemy aircraft were in a 'V', about three miles distant, flying down the southern coastline towards the airfield at Kahili, where they were due to land at 0945. To the surprise of the four attacking P-38 pilots and causing them some momentary confusion, there were actually two Betty bombers, flying together at 4,500 feet, with the Zekes in two sections of three each, 1,500 feet above them and slightly to the rear.

As the enemy, apparently unaware of any danger, continued their course for Kahili, the covering group of P-38s climbed for altitude, eventually reaching 15,000 to 18,000 feet. Meanwhile, the attacking section of four P-38s flew nearly parallel to the enemy's course but closing slightly at a speed of 200 mph in a 35° 2,200 feet/minute climb.

When level with the enemy bombers and about two miles away from them, two P-38s dropped their long-range belly tanks and swung into the attack at 280 mph. A third P-38 had difficulty in releasing his tank and the fourth stayed with him to cover him until he could do so.

The two attacking P-38s were not observed until they were less than a mile away, when both Bettys dived towards the sea. One began a 360° turn dive, while the other headed for the shore line. The escorting Zekes dropped their belly tanks and three of them peeled down in a string to intercept one of the P-38s, flown by Captain Thomas G. Lanphier. When Lanphier saw the Zekes approaching and realized he could not reach the Betty, he turned up and into the Zekes, exploding the first and firing into the others as they passed.

By this time Lanphier had reached 6,000 feet, so he dived and flew down to tree top height to pursue the escaping Betty. He came into

110

it broadside on and fired. The Betty burst into flames, lost a wing and crashed into the jungle. Lanphier was then forced to out-run and out-manoeuvre the pursuing Zekes who had the advantage of altitude.

Meanwhile, the second attacking P-38, flown by Lt Rex T. Barber, followed the other Betty out to sea, overhauled it and shot it down. The other two attacking P-38s had by now jettisoned their drop tanks and flew in to help ward off the Zekes. A wild dog-fight took place in which it was difficult to observe results, but three Zekes were shot down and at some point one P-38, piloted by Lt Raymond K. Hine, was lost.

As the three P-38s were leaving the scene, they came upon a third Betty flying low over the water. One P-38 dived on it, setting the port engine on fire, and the other two P-38s finished it off. So close was the combat that a fragment of debris from the Betty cut through the port wing of a pursuing P-38 and knocked out the port inner cooler; other chunks left paint streaks on the port wing. The P-38s above had taken no part.

The remaining fifteen P-38s returned to Henderson, where later that day COMAIRSOLS issued the message which Halsey passed on to Nimitz: 'P-38s led by Major John W. Mitchell, USAAF, visited Kahili area. Two bombers, escorted by six Zeros flying in close formation, were shot down about 0930L. One other bomber shot down was believed to be on test flight. Four Zeros added to score sum total six. One P-38 failed to return. April 18 [the anniversary of the Doolittle Raid a year earlier] seems to be our day.' Halsey added: 'Sounds as though one of the ducks in the bag was a peacock'.

Although there was no doubt at Henderson or at Halsey's head-quarters in Noumea that Yamamoto had been killed (even the normally dour Kelly Turner 'whooped and applauded'), nothing could be said in public until the Japanese themselves announced it. But that could not prevent rumours and informed speculation which began when Mitchell and his excited pilots returned, arguing over who had shot down what, and gradually spread until it was general inter-Service 'scuttle butt' throughout the South Pacific area that the interception and shooting down of Yamamoto had been achieved through the breaking of Japanese codes.

It was a miracle that the story did not break in the American press at home. As it was, MacArthur was willing to risk jeopardizing all the Allied cryptanalytical achievements by publicizing the ambush of Yamamoto as a triumph of his command, and it took the direct intervention of the US Joint Chiefs of Staff to prevent him. In his postwar memoirs, MacArthur referred sourly to the incident: 'Washington lauded it as one of the most important bags of the war, but labelled it top secret and forbade publication'.

The Japanese, though always on their guard about communications security, were sublimely confident about JN-25. There was a cryptic reference in the *Operational History*: 'At any rate, the Americans reported that the disaster to Admiral Yamamoto at Buin, Bougainville, was due to cryptanalysis. However, this was impossible as his movement was never dispatched in the Navy code.'

Astonishingly, there were three survivors, all badly injured, from the Betty which was shot down into the sea: the pilot, Yamamoto's staff paymaster, and the chief of staff, Vice Admiral Ugaki Matome. But in the other, shot down in the jungle north of Buin, everybody was killed, including Yamamoto.

There was no doubt in Tokyo either that Yamamoto was dead, but no public announcement was made. A search party hacked their way through the jungle to the wrecked aircraft and identified Yamamoto's charred remains. He had been shot by a machine-gun bullet through the base of the skull and must have been killed instantly. His body was carried to Buin for ceremonial cremation and then taken in a small white box on board the giant battleship *Musashi* for transport to Japan.

On 21 May the Japanese Navy Department issued a statement in plain language, reading in part: 'The Commander-in-Chief of the Combined Fleet, Admiral Isoruku Yamamoto, died a heroic death in April of this year in air combat with the enemy while directing operations from a forward position'. The same day Chungking reported that, according to a Domei radio broadcast of that date from Tokyo, Admiral Yamamoto had been killed in April in an air combat somewhere in the South-West Pacific Area, and that he had been shot down by US fliers.

Particularly grief-stricken by Yamamoto's death was Watanabe, his friend and staff gunnery officer, who was furious when he discovered that his C-in-C's itinerary had also been broadcast in army code. He was never able to confirm his suspicions, but he always believed that his friend and chief had been betrayed by army rather than navy communications.

Yamamoto had stood second only to the Emperor in the eyes of his countrymen and his death was a great traumatic shock to the

Japanese navy and nation. He was given a state funeral in Tokyo on 5 June, the first commoner to have that honour since Admiral Togo. His passing and replacement by the staid and conservative Admiral Mineichi Koga, who had none of Yamamoto's flair and charisma, were in a way symbols of Japan's declining fortunes.

VIII

FORWARD IN THE SOLOMONS

AFTER Guadalcanal had been secured, Allied forces in the South-West Pacific advanced towards Rabaul on two fronts, with a sequence of 'leap-frogging' amphibious operations, along the north coast of New Guinea, and in the Solomons. MacArthur's troops were transported by the Seventh Amphibious Force under Rear Admiral Daniel Barby (known as 'Uncle Dan, the Amphibious Man') and supported at sea by the Seventh Fleet (so designated in March, 1943), commanded first by Admiral Carpender and then by Kinkaid. By December, 1943, they had landed at Nassau Bay, Lae and Finschhafen, and Cape Gloucester in New Britain; in the Solomons, New Georgia, Vella Lavella and Bougainville had all been invaded. But first there was some unfinished business in the Aleutians.

There had been indications of possible Japanese operations in the Aleutians as early as March, 1942. In April a decrypted message from the C-in-C Japanese 2nd Fleet asked for charts of the Gulf of Alaska, the Aleutians and the Bering Sea. In May continuing Japanese interest in air operations in Hawaiian, Samoan and Alaskan areas, their concern about Aleutian patrols and defences, and their constant gathering of weather reports from northern areas, all showed that an attack must be on the way.

On 14 May a decrypted operation schedule showed important departure dates for the Japanese Aleutian Forces. On the 15th one message mentioned the 'AOB Occupation Force', and because a message sent by the Japanese Naval General Staff on 5 December, 1941, had designated AOB as Kiska, it was deduced that this was the objective.

Increasing numbers of decrypted Japanese messages, with traffic analysis, made it clear that the Midway and Aleutian campaigns were developing simultaneously, and that the Japanese plan was for the

US Fleet to be diverted to the north while their main force struck at Midway. Traffic analysis enabled estimates to be made of the Japanese forces to be used in the Aleutians area and gave evidence of an increase in their air strength.

As the days ran out, all the familiar signs were apparent: co-ordination of Japanese submarine activities with fleet movements, preparations involving ammunition, oil, aircraft and personnel re-placements, consultation between Japanese Army and Navy leaders and, most ominously, a dramatic decrease in enemy radio traffic on 31 May, all showed that a Japanese offensive was imminent.

Thus, it was no surprise when aircraft from *Ryuho* and *Junyo* attacked Dutch Harbor in the Aleutians on 3 and 4 June, 1942. The islands were lightly defended and the Japanese were eventually able to land and occupy Attu and Kiska islands after some minor naval engagements and strenuous counter-attacks by the USAAF. To some Americans, the loss of these admittedly insignificant islands slightly tarnished the great victory to come at Midway.

With their foul climate and dreary scenery, the Aleutians were, as both sides found out, much better left to the native Aleuts. But as the Japanese had taken Kiska and Attu, they had to maintain them. This led to a curiously old-fashioned naval action, a gun battle between ships with almost a First World War period flavour about it, in which no aircraft took part, fought off the Komandorski Islands, between Kamchatka and the Aleutians.

Late in March, 1943, FRUPAC deciphered messages which re-vealed that the Japanese were about to send a reinforcement convoy, a sort of Polar Tokyo Express, from Paramushiro to Attu. A task group of the light cruiser *Richmond* (wearing the flag of Rear Admiral Charles H. ('Soc') McMorris), the heavy cruiser *Salt Lake City* and four destroyers, put to sea to intercept.

McMorris' force was equivalent to the intelligence estimates in March, 1943, of Japanese naval strength in the north which was one heavy cruiser, the *Nachi*, one light cruiser, the *Tama*, and four destroyers. But, unknown to intelligence, the Japanese had strength-ened their Northern Force with a heavy and a light cruiser.

Lookouts sighted the Japanese ships, some 180 miles west of Attu, on 26 March. Believing himself to be equal in strength, McMorris advanced confidently towards them, only to encounter a superior Japanese force of two heavy cruisers, *Maya* and *Nachi*, two light cruisers and four destroyers, under Vice Admiral Hosogaya, escorting the group of transports to the Aleutians.

The two sides met, the Americans to the south, the Japanese to the north, just after 8 am on a cold, clear morning, and began to exchange salvoes at ranges of between ten and twelve miles. McMorris tried to work northwards to reach the transports, but the Japanese cut him off, concentrating their fire on *Salt Lake City*, who scored hits on *Nachi* but was hit twice and at one point came to a stop in the water.

With *Salt Lake City* almost helpless, McMorris had to retire westwards under cover of a smoke screen which the Japanese, having no radar, found impenetrable. Had Hosogaya penetrated the smoke screen, he would have found *Salt Lake City* easy prey, but somewhat timidly he retired, hotly pursued by three of McMorris' destroyers. McMorris had succeeded in turning the Attu reinforcements back. Hosogaya was shortly afterwards relieved of his command.

Attu was retaken by the US 7th Infantry Division in May, 1943, despite a final suicidal 'banzai' charge by a thousand screaming Japanese on the 30th. At the end, there were only 28 survivors from a Japanese garrison of nearly 2,500, and the Americans themselves suffered a thousand casualties. Plans were made to capture Kiska, but when the assault took place on 15 August, after a two-day air-and-sea bombardment, there were no Japanese on the island. Keeping total radio silence and aided by fog, the Japanese had taken off 5,200 troops undetected some three weeks earlier, repeating their successful evacuation from Guadalcanal.

As Layton said, there were some red faces in Pearl Harbor intelligence. They had overlooked one reconnaissance photograph on which the photo interpreter had noted 'things strewn around beaches and other places as if the island had been abandoned'. The Aleutians then dropped out of the action picture for the rest of the war.

While the Japanese were leaving the Aleutians, pressure continued to make them leave the Solomons. The campaigns on land were accompanied by another series of sea fights, as at Guadalcanal, and still more attrition of Japanese aircrews. The Japanese lost an estimated 2,500 aircraft attempting to retain Guadalcanal and in the subsequent defence of the central Solomons.

At sea the actions showed once again the importance of radio intelligence and, once again, that, though there was ample scope for the flair and daring of individual American commanders, the Long Lance torpedo was still the arbiter of naval battle in the Solomons.

After an unopposed landing on the Russell Islands in February, 1943, the main landing on New Georgia took place on 30 June and another bitter campaign began, in tropical jungle conditions similar to

Guadalcanal, though not as protracted. Even so, the islands were not secured until October, the Japanese reinforcing themselves at every opportunity by another Tokyo Express which, once again, with the help of advance intelligence warning, the Navy had to interrupt as best they could.

On the night of 4 July – a date Tokyo Radio stressed in their account – the light cruiser *Yubari* and nine destroyers bombarded the US troops ashore on Rendova Island and sank the US destroyer *Strong* with a Long Lance. The main engagement took place in Kula Gulf, the stretch of water between the north coast of New Georgia and the island of Kolombangara, on the night of 5/6 July.

A decrypt of a message from Rabaul revealed that the Japanese had dispatched a large Tokyo Express of ten destroyers from Rabaul to land Japanese reinforcements behind the newly-established American beach heads on New Georgia. The Japanese force consisted of two transport groups of three and four destroyers respectively carrying troops and supplies, led by a support unit of three more destroyers, *Niizuki* (wearing the flag of Rear Admiral Teruo Akiyama), *Sukukaze* and *Tanikaze*.

To intercept them Halsey sent a support group (which had lost *Strong* the night before) of the 6-inch gun cruisers *Honolulu* (flag), *Helena* and *St Louis*, and four destroyers, under Rear Admiral Walden L. ('Pug') Ainsworth. The American ships were fitted with the excellent SG surface warning radar. The cruisers' 6-inch guns, in triple turrets, had a very rapid rate of fire. As off Guadalcanal, technological superiority lay with the American ships, and they also had intelligence warning, but the Japanese disadvantages were compensated by superior seamanship and tactics.

Akiyama's ships ran down the eastern side of Kolombangara, where Akiyama detached his first transport group of three destroyers and turned back to the north as Ainsworth's ships cleared the northeastern point of New Georgia. Ainsworth detected Akiyama by radar at 1.40 am, range over twelve miles. He turned to port to close the range and then to starboard again, in the standard line-ahead fighting formation, nine minutes later. It was the same unwieldy line, with destroyers disposed ahead and astern, which had so often been used off Guadalcanal.

Akiyama had detached his second transport group for Vila when his lookouts sighted Ainsworth's cruisers against a clear northern horizon. He recalled the transport group, ordered 30 knots, and attacked.

Ainsworth meanwhile waited until the range had come down

to 6,800 yards before opening fire. When his ships did fire they concentrated on *Niizuki*, leading. *Niizuki* was soon shattered and left sinking, and Akiyama was killed. But *Sukukaze* and *Tanikaze* fired their sixteen Long Lances and retired to reload. Ainsworth's destroyers were still tied ineffectively to their tactical formation.

Three torpedoes hit *Helena* and she sank in a few minutes, until only a portion of her severed bows, still floating, showed above water; 168 of her people were lost. She had been a much-loved ship and the feelings of the hundreds of men whose ships were sunk in those waters were well expressed by one of her survivors: 'It was a sad, an unbelievably sad moment. What does one say? Not what you might expect. Nothing smart or slick. Just the so-called corny phrases you have heard time and again in the movies or read in fiction: "She was a grand ship." "She sure was swell." She went down gracefully and quickly, like the queen that she was.'

Sporadic skirmishes and firing went on almost until dawn, as the Japanese continued their runs to Vila and the Americans paused to pick up survivors. *Niizuki* was sunk and a second destroyer, *Nagatsuki*, ran aground on the coast of Kolombangara and was destroyed by aircraft the next day.

But Ainsworth thought he had achieved a much greater victory and claimed to have sunk two cruisers, and other destroyers which had 'vanished' from his radar screens during the action. After many 'sinkings' which had proved to be nothing but wishful thinking, Nimitz had decided that CincPac would make no action reports until intelligence had assessed them.

Layton advised Nimitz that Ainsworth could not have sunk any cruisers because 'There were no Japanese cruisers within five hundred miles of the action' [in fact, there was *Yubari* at Rabaul and, as events in the next few days would show, there was still *Jintzu*]. But decrypts the next day indeed confirmed that one Japanese destroyer had been sunk by gunfire and another had run aground on a reef.

The upshot was a revealing encounter between an operational commander and a staff intelligence officer. When Ainsworth flew to Pearl Harbor to report personally to Nimitz and heard Layton's opinion of his claims, he was furious and scornful of staff officers. 'How can you sit here on your fat ass, thousands of miles from the action and make such a statement,' he demanded of Layton, who replied that he could only report what was obtained from radio intelligence. 'I have no stake in this matter personally,' he said, 'but I have a stake in the war.'

Twelve days later Layton was vindicated when a top-secret document was taken from a survivor of another sunk Japanese destroyer. It was the report of the Kula Gulf action, confirming that no cruisers had taken part and two destroyers had been lost.

Ainsworth's engagement in Kula Gulf was regarded as such a victory at the time that Rear Admiral Aaron S. ('Tip') Merrill, also commanding a task group, signalled: 'I am afraid you have spoiled the hunting by taking too much game on your last hunt'.

Merrill was mistaken, as was demonstrated when Ainsworth's ships were in action again, in the Battle of Kolombangara on the night of 12/13 July. A decrypted message from Rabaul again gave warning of another Express, a Support Group of four destroyer-transports carrying 1,200 troops, escorted by five destroyers led by Rear Admiral Shunji Izaki, flying his flag in Tanaka's old flagship, *Jintzu*. This force left Rabaul for Vila at 5 am on the 12th.

This was, in fact, Ainsworth's fourteenth mission up the 'Slot', either in support of reinforcement convoys for New Georgia or, as on this occasion, in search of the Tokyo Express. He flew his flag again in *Honolulu*, with *St Louis* and the New Zealand light cruiser HMNZS *Leander* – slower, more lightly armed and with a larger turning circle than the US cruisers. He also had nine destroyers, in two squadrons.

A Catalina sighted Izaki's Support group shortly after midnight, some 26 miles from Ainsworth, north of Vella Lavella and heading south-east at 30 knots for Kula Gulf. Ainsworth formed his ships in single line ahead, with one squadron of five destroyers ahead of the cruisers and the other squadron of four destroyers astern, steering west at 26 knots. The line was six miles long. However, Ainsworth was ready to let his destroyers go at an early stage in the action.

On receiving the Catalina's report, Ainsworth increased speed to 28 knots – the best *Leander* could do – and at 1 am gained a radar contact. *Jintzu* had no radar but was fitted with a new electronic device which detected radar transmissions at twice the range of radar detection. Using this, Izaki had a good idea of his enemy's position and track.

Dispatching his four destroyer-transports to unload on Kolombangara, Izaki advanced towards Ainsworth's ships. He was anxious to close the critical gap between the range at which Ainsworth's radar would detect him and the range at which he could fire his Long Lances.

Ainsworth was just as keen to close, having decided to open fire when the range was between eight and ten thousand yards, and

119

being still ignorant of the Long Lance. Both sides approached at a combined speed of 58 knots.

At 1.12 am, when the range had come down to 10,000 yards, Ainsworth turned his ships to port to bring all guns to bear, and opened fire. *Jintzu*, like *Niizuki* before her, took the brunt of the fire (the three cruisers fired 2,630 rounds at her) and was thumped to a dead stop.

After his rear destroyers had fired torpedoes, one of which hit the stationary *Jintzu*, which eventually sank, Ainsworth turned his ships through 180°. But the Long Lances were on their way. *Leander*, slower to turn, and suffering a TBS (Talk Between Ships) fade-away at a crucial moment, was hit in her bows and knocked out of the battle. She had to limp away to Tulagi and thence, because Nimitz wanted no more aged light cruisers in his fleet, as far away as Boston for repairs.

One Japanese destroyer was separated from the others and took no more part, but the remaining four retired to reload and half an hour later they were back. There was some doubt about whether they were Japanese or American and Ainsworth's ships steered steady courses, making perfect torpedo targets, while they made up their minds. *Honolulu*, *St Louis* and the destroyer *Gwin* were all hit. The two cruisers followed *Leander* back to Tulagi, but *Gwin* went down.

Although *Jintzu* was lost with nearly all hands, including Izaki, the 1,200 Japanese troops were landed on the west coast of Kolombangara on 13 July. Once again the Japanese had shown their truly superb night-fighting skill. Happily for the Allies, the true results of these encounters were not known for some time, and in fact Kolombangara was yet another Japanese pyrrhic victory. The Japanese Navy kept on winning these undoubted tactical victories, but every one left them with fewer ships, unable to replace their losses.

Success or failure in these night encounters in the Solomons ultimately depended on the quality of the men involved. New faces brought new ideas. One new arrival was Captain Arleigh ('Thirty-One Knot') Burke, a destroyer commander destined to rise to the highest ranks in the Navy. After studying reports of previous actions, he concluded that destroyers should be used more flexibly and given more freedom of movement.

Burke devised a night action plan to split his destroyer squadron into two mutually supporting divisions. On first radar contact, one division would approach the enemy on a parallel and opposite course, while the other stayed at maximum effective gun range from the enemy. The first division would fire torpedoes and turn away. As the torpedoes exploded, both divisions would open fire on the surprised enemy.

Burke was relieved in command of his squadron before he could put his plan into action, but its effectiveness was clearly demonstrated by his successor in one undoubted victory for the US Navy in the Vella Gulf, west of Kolombangara, on the night of 6/7 August, 1943.

ULTRA had again revealed another Tokyo Express on its way down from Rabaul. The Allies had no cruisers available (partly due to the depredations of previous actions) so six destroyers under Commander F. Moosbrugger USN, Burke's relief, were dispatched to do what they could. By 10.30 pm on 6 August Moosbrugger's ships were steaming up the west coast of Kolombangara at 25 knots in two divisions of line ahead, the second division of three destroyers in station some 60° abaft Moosbrugger's starboard beam.

The Japanese force consisted of four destroyers, *Hagikaze*, *Arashi* and *Kawakaze* carrying troops and supplies, with the flotilla commander Captain Sigiura in *Shigure*. For once the Japanese were unusually unwary by night and failed to see Moosbrugger's ships, masked by the blackness of Kolombangara Island. Their first inkling of danger was the sight of the white water boiling under the sterns of the American destroyers as they turned away, having fired torpedoes at 4,000 yards.

Hagikaze, *Arashi* and *Kawakaze* were all hit by torpedoes, or subsequent gunfire, or both, and sank, two of them blowing up with such a violent flash and detonation that men thirty miles away thought it was the volcano on Kolombangara erupting. Only *Shigure* escaped, Sigiura evidently deciding that discretion was the better part of valour. Moosbrugger took his own ships away triumphantly untouched, after one of the neatest and quickest tactical victories of the war.

The Japanese had been reinforcing Kolombangara, expecting it to be invaded. But Halsey decided to bypass it and take the next island, Vella Lavella, which was comparatively lightly defended and the island was invaded on 15 August, 1943.

By then there were indications from radio intelligence of an important change in Japanese strategy. Decrypts signalled that the Tokyo Express would run no more. On 13 August Imperial Headquarters decreed that no more reinforcements would be run down the Slot. Troops already in the Solomons were to fight holding actions for as long as possible and then withdraw by barge or destroyer-transport. It was decided to abandon Kolombangara.

At Guadalcanal the Japanese were able to conceal their evacuation until it had been completed and they then claimed that it had really been a 'voluntary' withdrawal carried out after 'annihilating' the enemy. At Kolombangara this was not possible. Japanese intentions were well known and a blockade of Kolombangara was established on 25 August. But, despite information from ULTRA, excellent radar, and the most strenuous efforts by US destroyers, PT boats and aircraft, and even though the Japanese escape route was known and patrolled every night, only about a third of the barge fleet was sunk and about 1,000 men killed. Some 15,000 Japanese troops were evacuated from Kolombangara and taken either to Rabaul or the nearby island of Choiseul. Four thousand men were taken off by destroyer and another 5,400 by barge in five nights between 30 September and 4 October. On the Allies' credit side, the submarine *I–20*, which was taking part in the evacuation, was caught on the surface and sunk by the destroyer *Eaton* on the night of 1/2 October.

By 1 October the last remaining Japanese troops on Vella Lavella, just under 600 of them, were pinned on the north-west shore of the island. It needed no radio intelligence to reveal their plight. It was clear by then that they must either be evacuated or abandoned. The Japanese operation to evacuate these troops led to the Battle of Vella Lavella on the night of 6/7 October.

The night of the evacuation was revealed by radio intelligence, and the location of the Japanese troops, and therefore the destination of the evacuation force, was known. Only the exact composition of the force was not clear. In the event the Vella Lavella Evacuation Force, commanded by Rear Admiral Matsuji Ijuin, consisted of a support group of six destroyers, three destroyer-transports, and a transport group of four sub-chasers, four motor torpedo boats and four landing craft.

With so much advance information, picking off Ijuin's ships should have been like shooting fish in a barrel. But the problem was that all but three of the destroyers, under Captain Frank R. Walker, were already committed to convoy escort. Walker was ordered to steam up the Slot to a rendezvous ten miles off Marquana Bay on the north-west of Vella Lavella, where three more destroyers, under Captain Harold O. Larson, having left their convoy south of New Georgia, would steam at full speed to join him.

Larson's three ships had not joined when the first radar contact was gained just after 10.30 pm and Walker very boldly decided to press on with his own three ships. It was another 'shoot-out' between destroyers and this time Walker was fastest on the draw, firing torpedoes first at 7,000 yards and sinking the destroyer *Yugumo*. But Long Lances sank *Chevalier* and Walker's own *Selfridge*, while *O'Bannion* was badly damaged in a collision with *Chevalier*.

Meanwhile, Ijuin's three destroyer-transports had retired when Walker's approach was first detected, but the small craft went on and successfully took off the troops. With their soldiers safely away, and two destroyers for one, the tactical balance again went to the Japanese. But this was not realized at the time and, in an atmosphere of general Allied euphoria, Vella Lavella was regarded as a victory. The Allies felt, justifiably, they were winning the war in the Solomons.

There was one more ominous statistic for the Japanese. *Yugumo* was the fortieth of their destroyers lost since the war began. Japanese shipyards simply were not making good that rate of attrition, while new ships of all kinds were daily coming off slipways in the United States.

The next step towards Rabaul was Bougainville. Halsey decided to avoid the Japanese airfields at the northern and southern ends of the island and land in the middle, and instead of capturing a Japanese airfield, as at Munda on New Georgia, the Allies would build their own and let the Japanese try and capture it if they could, as at Henderson.

After heavy air raids to damp down Japanese activity at Rabaul, US Marines and New Zealand troops landed at Cape Torokina, Empress Augusta Bay, halfway up the western side of the island, on 1 November, 1943. As expected, that night the Japanese Navy attempted a counter-coup such as they had achieved off Savo Island in August, 1942.

But this was not to be another Savo. The US Navy had come a long way and a hard way since that terrible night. The lives and ships lost, then and since, had not been lost in vain. Ships' routines had been changed to mitigate combat fatigue in the crews. Radar presentation and interpretation, ship-to-air radio liaison, TBS voice discipline and combat information centres had all been improved.

Radio intelligence had also improved (although 'Joe' Rochefort had left Pearl Harbor in October, 1942, the victim of Washington intrigues). The Allies had begun to realize the full potential of communications intelligence. 'In my opinion, the value of Radio Intelligence has been demonstrated to the extent that we can never again afford to neglect it as we did before the war,' said Commander (later Rear Admiral) Joseph N. Wenger, a member of OP-20-G, in a lecture on 'Future Co-operation between Army and Navy' on 1 June, 1943.

'Furthermore, the difficulties of obtaining Intelligence have increased so greatly that we shall have to maintain an organization constantly at work on high-speed electronic equipment if we are to be prepared for any future wars. The equipment necessary to obtain Radio Intelligence is growing so complicated that we cannot wait until war comes to provide it. Certainly we cannot afford to risk another Pearl Harbor.'

By 1943 the Allies were also coming to realize the scale of resources needed for communications intelligence. For instance, the number of personnel involved, both US Navy and Army – 300 in 1939 – had risen to 37,000 by the end of the war in 1945. There was an enormous expansion, in the United States and in the United Kingdom, in courses to train large numbers of people, many of them university students, to speak or read Japanese; classicists and students in dead languages usually learned to read Japanese, while modern language students learned to speak it.

Techniques had improved in every respect of intelligence, from the interrogation of prisoners-of-war to the evaluation of aerial reconnaissance photographs (colour-blind men and women were recruited because their disability enabled them to 'see through' camouflage).

By 1943 the Allies began to sense they were really winning the radio intelligence war against the Japanese. As more codes were decrypted, over longer periods, the cryptanalysts believed they were at last beginning to feel their way into the Japanese mind. As the Japanese suffered defeats on land and retreated, there were more opportunities to capture documents, such as diaries, operational orders and, as from *I-1*, actual code books.

This new Allied confidence was evident at sea off the Solomons where, at last, some idea of the true deadliness of the Long Lance torpedo had been realized. The naval force commander at Empress Augusta Bay was 'Tip' Merrill. Although he would still go into battle in single line ahead, he would give his destroyer captains much more independence much earlier in the action. He also intended to manoeuvre his enemy up to twenty miles from the transport anchorages, to stand off and engage at ranges of nineteen to twenty thousand yards, and, most important, to avoid steaming on steady courses. By the time the Long Lances reached where he should have been, he would be long gone.

Radio intelligence indications through the autumn of 1943 had been that Admiral Koga, a much more cautious man than Yamamoto, was keeping the Combined Fleet and most of the 8th Fleet at Truk, where they were beyond the range of Allied bombing. But at the end of

October, traffic analysis indicated the arrival at Rabaul of units of the 5th Cruiser Division. A decrypt of the 30th revealed that they were the 8-inch gun heavy cruisers *Myoko* and *Haguro*, who had escorted a convoy down from Truk.

The two cruisers sailed from Rabaul on 31 October, with Vice Admiral Sentaro Omori flying his flag in *Myoko*, to intercept Merrill's task force who were on their way to bombard airfields beside the Buka Passage. But Omori missed Merrill and returned to Rabaul. When the news of the landing at Empress Augusta Bay arrived the next morning, 1 November, Omori was ordered to carry out a counter-landing with a force of a thousand soldiers embarked in five destroyer-transports, and also to break up the Allied amphibious forces on the beaches.

Merrill had four new 6-inch gun light cruisers, *Montpelier* (flag), *Cleveland*, *Columbia* and *Denver*. Ahead, he had 'Thirty-One Knot' Burke's Division 45, of four destroyers, and astern, Commander B.L. Austin's Division 46, also of four destroyers. Merrill's task was to place his ships 'across the entrance to Empress Augusta Bay and to prevent the entry therein of a single enemy ship'. As darkness fell on 1 November he steered north so to do.

Omori sailed with his two cruisers, screened to port by the light cruiser *Sendai* (wearing Ijuin's flag) and three destroyers, to starboard by the light cruiser *Agano* and three destroyers. The destroyer-transports were not at the rendezvous where Omori expected them and when they did arrive he found they could only make 26 knots. He asked, and was given, permission to send the transports back to Rabaul and then pressed on himself at 32 knots, determined to do to the Allied landing forces at Torokina what Mikawa had failed to do to them on Guadalcanal.

While Omori came on south, unaware of Merrill's ships and expecting to encounter only troop transports, Merrill headed north, with the benefit of some excellent spotting and reporting of Omori's ships by two US Army reconnaissance aircraft.

When *Montpelier*'s first radar contact was gained at 2.30 am on 2 November, 1943, range just over eighteen miles, Burke's van destroyers altered towards at once to attack the nearest Japanese column, led by *Sendai*. Merrill then reversed his cruisers' course, so that Austin's destroyers now became the van, intending them to attack in turn. But his ships were illuminated by a Japanese aircraft flare and were seen from *Sendai*. Omori turned his ships to starboard to close, frustrating Burke's torpedo attack.

Merrill could wait no longer and opened fire. Radar-controlled fire tended to concentrate upon one target and the focus this time was *Sendai*, which was quickly hit several times and forced out of the action. While Burke's twenty-five torpedoes were missing, Merrill altered course outwards, to keep his stand-off range, while his cruisers made smoke to counteract the brilliant Japanese flares.

Maintaining a range of 19,000 yards, Merrill's cruisers shifted aim to the Japanese cruisers and hit *Haguro*. *Denver* was hit in return. Shortly after 3 am Merrill led his ships through an elaborate sequence of course changes, stepping and side-stepping, turning and weaving, to avoid giving a target for the Long Lances. His cruiser captains followed him with admirable skill, despite the smoke and din and confusion of battle.

Omori had always over-estimated the forces against him and when he thought he had sunk two enemy cruisers he broke off the battle at 3.37 am and ordered a general retirement.

The US destroyers regrouped, but had mixed fortunes. Austin, in particular, was fired on by his own side, lost *Foote* who was torpedoed and had to be towed in next day, collided in his own ship *Spence* with *Thatcher*, was hit once and holed by a friendly shell, came under fire from Burke, missed a perfect chance of a torpedo attack as Japanese ships passed close by on a reciprocal course, and exchanged shots with two retiring Japanese destroyers. Burke's Division 45 came upon and gave the *coupe de grace* to *Sendai* and later dispatched the crippled destroyer *Hatsukaze*. Merrill recalled his destroyers at first light.

In two and a half days of bombardment, surface and anti-aircraft action, Merrill's cruisers expended 27,000 rounds of ammunition of various calibres, while his destroyers fired 52 torpedoes, to sink *Sendai* and *Hatsukaze*, damage *Myoko* and *Haguro*, and slightly damage *Agano*. Yet it was certainly a victory, for which 'Tip' Merrill well deserved the kudos he received. Omori was relieved of his command.

Amidst the celebrations over Merrill's victory, ULTRA revealed that because of the landings at Empress Augusta Bay Admiral Koga had decided to reinforce the 8th Fleet at Rabaul. Decrypts and traffic analysis established that Koga had sent a formidable force of no less than seven heavy cruisers of the 2nd Fleet, commanded by Vice Admiral Takeo Kurita, a light cruiser, four destroyers and supporting oilers (although the exact composition did not become clearer until 4 November when aircraft sighted Kurita's force, of nineteen ships in all, off the Admiralty Islands).

Halsey had no heavy ships to put up against Kurita but he did have a carrier task group, on temporary loan to him, of *Saratoga* and the new light carrier *Princeton*. It was a very bold move to pit carrier aircraft against a base as heavily defended as Rabaul, but Halsey decided to risk it. On 5 November a strike of 97 aircraft – 22 dive-bombers and 23 torpedo-bombers escorted by Hellcat fighters – was flown off from a launching point some 230 miles south-east of Rabaul and about 57 miles south-west of Cape Torokina to attack shipping in Rabaul harbour.

No Japanese ship was sunk, but many of them were taken by surprise and could be seen, as a war correspondent in *Saratoga* described them, 'running every which way, like a flock of skittering cockroaches in a suddenly lighted dirty kitchen'. Four of the heavy cruisers, two light cruisers and two destroyers were damaged. Kurita abandoned plans for a heavy cruiser sortie against Bougainville.

This was a decisive tilt in the balance of power. Command of the sea round the Solomons now passed to the Allies. On 11 November a carrier task group of *Essex, Bunker Hill* and the light carrier *Independence*, escorted by ten destroyers, under Rear Admiral Alfred E. Montgomery, struck again at shipping in Rabaul, damaging a light cruiser and two destroyers with torpedoes.

The Japanese retaliated furiously with a massive strike of 67 Zekes, 27 Vals and fourteen Kates which seemed to fill the sky, so that one fighter pilot was heard to say, 'Jesus Christ! There are millions of them! Let's go to work'.

They went to work and shot down 32 Zekes, 24 Vals and twelve of the Kates, in exchange for a few bomb near misses on the carriers. Thus, only slight damage was inflicted on Japanese shipping but great slaughter wrought amongst Japanese aircraft. ULTRA eventually revealed that Koga withdrew naval aircrews from Rabaul the next day. A little more Japanese air strength had been bled away, just at the time when the 'Atoll War' was beginning in the central Pacific.

In the last week of November, 1943, ULTRA revealed that the Japanese were planning to revive the Tokyo Express, probably for the very last time, to take troops to Buka Island, north of Bougainville, which the Japanese thought the Allies would invade next, and to take away aviation personnel whose occupation was gone because the airfield had been put out of action by ship bombardment.

On 24 November Burke, whose destroyers were refuelling, received a typically crisply worded signal from Halsey: 'Thirty-One Knot Burke, get this. Put your squadron athwart the Buka-Rabaul evacuation line about thirty-five miles west of Buka. If no enemy contact by 0300 Love (local time) 25th, come south to refuel same place. If enemy contact you know what to do. Halsey.'

Burke certainly did know what to do. To assist him, he had his own Division 45 with *Charles Ausburne, Claxton* and *Dyson,* and Austin's Division 46, with *Spence* and *Converse.* His adversary was Captain Kiyoto Kagawa, with the destroyers *Onami* and *Makinami,* screening Captain Katsumori Yamashiro's three destroyer-transports *Amagiri, Yuguri* and *Uzuki* which were to land 900 troops on Buka and evacuate 700 redundant aviation personnel.

Burke placed his ships in two divisions, 5,000 yards apart, to the western end of his search area, guessing this would give a better chance of interception. He was rewarded at 1.41 am on 25 November by three radar contacts, eleven miles to the eastward. It was Kagawa's screen, returning from their mission.

Burke led his Division towards the enemy and attacked with fifteen torpedoes at 1.56 am, range 6,000 yards, torpedo running range 4,500 yards. The Japanese lookouts were slow and Kagawa had little time to evade. *Onami* disintegrated in a ball of flame 300 feet high. *Makinami*'s back was broken.

Charles Ausburne now had another radar contact: Yamashiro's three transports, 13,000 yards behind Kagawa. Telling Austin to finish off *Makinami* Burke went after his new quarry. But Yamashiro was equally anxious to get away and Burke had to settle for a long chase, first north and then east, at 33 knots. He opened fire on the rear transport when it came in range.

Eventually, some sixty miles east of Cape St George, the most southerly point of New Ireland, Burke had put so many shells into *Yuguri* that she slowed down and gunfire from all three ships sank her. Burke still chased westwards, but at 4 am, when he was only thirty-three miles off Cape St George, he had to break off, lest dawn catch him close to an enemy coast. Telling Austin, who had meanwhile dispatched *Makinami*, to join him, Burke retired to the east.

Three Japanese destroyers had been sunk, without a single Allied casualty. No Allied ship had even been hit. This Battle of Cape St George was, according to the President of the Naval War College: 'An almost perfect action that may be considered a classic'. It took place on Thanksgiving Day, and Burke and his crews duly gave heartfelt thanks for their victory on their return.

IX

THE SUBMARINE WAR – BREAKING THE MARU CODE

'PRESS home all attacks,' wrote Rear Admiral James Fife USN, Commander Submarines South-West Pacific, in his standing orders. 'Pursue relentlessly, remembering that the mission is to destroy every possible enemy ship. Do not let cripples escape or leave them to sink – make sure that they do sink.'

The American submariners in the Far East, very ably assisted by the British and the Dutch, put Admiral Fife's orders faithfully into effect and achieved devastating results. By VJ Day, 1945, Allied submarines in the Far East were actually running out of targets. By that time, although submarines still constituted only 2 per cent of the American war effort on the Pacific, American submarines had sunk two-thirds of the total Japanese merchant ship tonnage sunk during the war, and had also sunk one out of every three of the Japanese warships sunk.

The United States and the Imperial Japanese Navies were roughly equal in submarine strength in the Pacific at the outset of the war. Neither navy had had any operational experience of submarines in the First World War. Both had prepared for submarine warfare on a long-range scale, and primarily for use against enemy warships. The crucial difference in the Second World War lay in the US Navy's technological advances, its readiness to profit by tactical experience, and its proper strategic deployment of its submarines. In all three areas the Americans were superior.

At the time of Pearl Harbor the US Navy had some fifty-five submarines in the Pacific, about half of them at Pearl and the rest with the Asiatic Fleet in the Philippines. Some of the boats were of the older and smaller S-class, of 800 to 1,000 tons, but the standard *Gato* Class fleet-type submarine, which carried the heat and burden of the day in the Pacific submarine war, was an excellent long-range weapon, of some 1,500 tons, with a crew of seven officers and seventy men, a cruising range of 10,000 miles, stores for sixty-day patrols, a surface speed under diesel-electric propulsion of just over 20 knots, and a maximum submerged speed of just under 9 knots. The submerged endurance on batteries was 48 hours at 2½ knots. These submarines were armed with eight to ten 21-inch torpedoes, with eighteen reloads, a 3-inch and, later, 5-inch gun on deck and various outfits of .50 calibre anti-aircraft guns.

The Japanese had sixty submarines, forty-seven of the fleet-type I-Class and thirteen of the smaller RO-Class. The I-Class were of some 2,000 tons, with a surface speed of 24 knots and submerged speed of 8 knots, and a cruising range of 10,000 to 17,500 miles. They were armed with twenty-four 21-inch torpedoes in six to eight tubes, with eighteen reloads. They also had one or two deck guns of 4.7- to 5.5-inch, with several AA guns.

The one advantage the Japanese submarines had was the quality of their formidable 40-knot, oxygen-powered, longer ranged torpedoes, with twice the explosive charge of the American torpedoes.

American torpedoes were frequently defective and, incredibly, it was nearly two years before the US Navy established the causes of the defects and remedied them. Under operational patrol conditions American torpedoes nearly always ran eight to ten feet below their proper depth, so that their magnetic detonators, designed to be activated by the target ship's metal hull, failed to work properly. Similarly, the contact detonators only worked best after an oblique impact, thus, ironically, penalizing the very submarine captains who aimed best and hit their targets broadside on.

Design faults were compounded by bureaucratic obstruction: shore-bound officers and bureaucrats continued to insist that the whole fault lay with incompetent submarine captains who could not aim properly, and refused to believe submarine captains who said they had *heard* their torpedoes hitting the target and failing to explode.

For the first months of the war Japanese submarines had considerable success in sinking Allied warships, especially in 'Torpedo Junction' in the summer of 1942. But the fatal Japanese tendency to indulge in non-profitable peripheral activities soon began to drain away their submarine patrol strength.

The Japanese diverted their submarines to carry midget submarines, to no tactical purpose, or to act as communication links, or to wait at rendezvous to refuel flying-boats, or to carry out unimportant surface bombardments, which had no more than pinprick nuisance value, of Midway, or Canton Island or Johnston Island, or (in 1942) the coasts of Vancouver and Oregon.

The largest Japanese submarines carried aircraft – requiring an hour after surfacing to assemble and launch – which they transported thousands of miles for valueless reconnaissance flights. One submarine, *I-25*, launched her aircraft loaded with incendiaries with the serious intention of setting light to the forests of North America. As the war progressed more and more Japanese submarines were taken off patrols and used to carry men, ammunition and food to beleaguered Japanese island garrisons bypassed and left to 'wither on the vine' by the Allied advance.

Unquestionably the best strategic use the Japanese could have made of their submarines would have been to make a determined effort to cut the supply lines from Pearl Harbor to Micronesia and Australia. They made no such effort. There was never any submarine war in the Pacific remotely comparable with the struggle against the Atlantic U-boat. The US Navy began by escorting their ships in convoys in the Pacific, but by the end of 1943 there was so little enemy submarine activity that single ships were steaming across the Pacific unescorted.

To misuse of submarines in exotic sideshows the Japanese Navy added an almost complete failure to safeguard their own surface ships against submarines. The Japanese were obsessed by the idea of an 'offensive' war. Like the British in the First World War, they regarded convoys as 'defensive' and therefore somehow demeaning and unworthy of a warrior nation. Convoy did not appeal to the Samurai spirit.

The Japanese did not introduce even a limited form of convoy until April, 1942, and a First Convoy Escort Fleet, with eight old destroyers, not until July. A Second Convoy Escort Fleet was formed in March, 1943, and an escort-building programme began. But the Japanese never approached the standard of the highly-drilled escort groups of the Atlantic. At the same time they planned to build twenty more aircraft carriers, designed for the offensive, and began to convert the third *Yamato* Class battleship hull into a giant aircraft carrier, the 60,000-ton *Shinano*. With the personnel and materials involved in these projects, they could have built scores of invaluable escort vessels.

The Allies, too, used submarines for a great variety of purposes in the Far East: to land and take off secret agents, saboteurs, political VIPs, coast-watchers, refugees and commando parties; to carry out air-sea rescue, weather reporting and photo-reconnaissance of beaches and shore lines; to act as radar picket ships, radio beacons and navigational markers for ships and landing craft on their way in to an assault beach; to locate enemy minefields by sonar; to carry stores and aviation fuel (as at Guadalcanal); and to carry out shore bombardments with guns or rockets. Where a target was too small to warrant a torpedo, submarines in inshore waters sent boarding parties to lay demolition charges, or sank the targets by gunfire.

But these various duties were kept firmly subsidiary to the main purpose of carrying out offensive patrols against enemy warships and merchant ships. In 1942 American submarines were equipped with excellent SD air search and SJ surface warning radar sets, and began to make night attacks by radar. Japanese submarines and escort vessels were not fitted with radar until much later in the war and survivors of Japanese anti-submarine forces complained after the war that they were like blind men trying to fight the sighted.

The Japanese came nowhere near matching American technological invention. They ended the war with the same anti-submarine weapons with which they began it, a somewhat inaccurate depth-charge and a haphazardly aimed air bomb. They made no proper assessment of submarine actions and really had no way of knowing for certain whether they had sunk a submarine or not. They optimistically assumed that they had sunk a submarine every time they attacked one.

It was no wonder that after the war Tojo himself admitted that there were three main factors which had defeated Japan: the 'leap-frogging' tactics of advance across the Pacific, the strikes by the fast carrier task forces and the steady attrition of shipping caused by submarines.

To these he might have added superior radio intelligence. In the weeks after the attack on Pearl Harbor US tracking stations continued to pick up radio transmissions from I-Class Japanese submarines lingering in Hawaiian waters. Traffic analysis and D/F fixes revealed information about their patrol tactics.

For instance, it was discovered that their captains liked to expend their deck-gun ammunition against a shore target before leaving their patrol positions. *I-1*, which had two 5.5-inch guns at the beginning of the war, bombarded Hilo harbour in Hawaii at the end of December, 1941, and then left the area. Midway was bombarded on the night of 25 January, 1942, by *I-173*, one of three I-Class submarines en route back to Japan. *I-173*'s approach was detected by D/F in time for the Marines on Midway to be warned and return fire. As expected, the three submarines then left the area. Their courses, speeds and positions were tracked by D/F.

I-173's bombardment of Midway provided a 'fix' of its position that night and D/F of its progress to the westwards enabled a trap to be set.

The US submarine *Gudgeon* was then some 600 miles west of Midway, returning from the first American war patrol in Japanese home waters. Late on 26 January she received a signal from ComSubPac giving an enemy submarine's estimated course and speed, heading directly for *Gudgeon*'s position.

Next morning *Gudgeon* was dived and waiting when, at 0859, her sonar operator heard the sound of propellors. The submarine itself was soon visible through the periscope in bright sunlight, steering west on the surface at about 15 knots. At 0908 *Gudgeon* fired a salvo of three torpedoes, one of which hit.

Radio traffic from the Sixth Submarine Fleet at Kwajalein was monitored for Japanese reaction, but there was no evidence that the Japanese knew they had lost an I-boat. *I-173* had sunk with no chance to transmit a radio warning. D/F fixes, however, confirmed the kill. They continued to track two submarines back to Japan. From the third, there was only silence.

This first success for radio intelligence in the submarine war was an historic event: the first ever sinking of an enemy warship by a US submarine. (The first ever confirmed sinking of an enemy ship by a US Navy submarine was by *Swordfish* which sank the 8,663-ton freighter *Atsutusan* Maru in the South China Sea on 16 December, 1941.)

ComSubPac at Pearl Harbor had no direct access to ULTRA but in the early days ULTRA information was passed by an extraordinary, unofficial manner which broke every rule for the handling of ULTRA. Rochefort would pass it verbally to Jasper Holmes who would then walk over to ComSubPac's offices and tell his chief of staff, without giving away his source. If Holmes had to pass on the latitude and longitude of a possible target, he would write the figures in ink on the palm of his hand and later wash his hands.

Such passing of ULTRA information by one who could not know the complete intelligence picture ran the risk that one successful submarine interception might lose the whole ULTRA secret.

The low-grade code in which the harbour master at Truk reported arrivals and sailings was often being read, although his messages were normally decrypted too late to be of any operational value. But early in February, 1942, he reported a carrier leaving Truk whose course would take her through a route in the Caroline Islands where a US submarine was on patrol. Holmes asked Rochefort if he could pass this on to the Submarine Force.

'If I had known more about communications intelligence than I did then, I would never have asked him,' Holmes said. 'Rochefort knew all the risks. He knew that OP-20-G would have permitted him to use such information only if a major strategic objective were at stake. He also knew that the Japanese had eight or ten carriers in the Pacific to our four, and that the opportunity to ambush a Japanese aircraft carrier was worth considerable risk. Carefully, he instructed me to "sanitize" the information as much as possible: conceal its source, lie convincingly if questioned closely, and pass it orally to someone I had confidence would restrict it to as few people as possible.'

Holmes told the chief of staff, an old friend from his own submarine days, that 'I had some firm information that *Grayling*, patrolling off Truk, could use, but I could not tell him where it came from because a leak probably would destroy the source. Could he use it? He could and did.'

A signal was sent to *Grayling* telling her 'to guard the pass; an aircraft carrier was coming through'. (If Holmes' recollection of the signal text is correct, then even the mention of 'aircraft carrier' was strictly a breach of ULTRA security procedures. There was no need to be so specific: *Grayling*, already on patrol, should simply have been ordered 'if not already in contact with the enemy' to move to a new area between certain times – where and when she would have had a good chance of sighting the carrier). In the event, *Grayling* reached the pass in time to see the carrier go through, but did not get a shot.

The next chance came early in March, when a partially decrypted message revealed that *Kaga*, one of the Kido Butai carriers, had been damaged (by a torpedo, it was thought, but actually by running aground on a coral reef) and was returning from the East Indies to Japan via Palau.

There were five US submarines then on patrol off Japan and the Nansei Shoto. Four of them were positioned along the likeliest route. *Narwhal* fired one long-range torpedo at a carrier, possibly *Kaga*, but missed.

More chances arrived in May. After the Battle of the Coral Sea, *Shokaku*, badly damaged by three bomb hits, and *Zuikaku*, with her air group mauled, retired to Truk. Three US submarines were on patrol off Truk, but it was not known which of five openings in the atoll reef the Japanese were using. Three of the passes were mined

134

but there were swept channels across the lagoon to and through the North-East and South Passes. *Greenling*, waiting off the North Pass, saw a large carrier steam through the North-East Pass, out of torpedo range.

Carrier Division Five, of *Shokaku* and *Zuikaku*, and Cruiser Division Five, of *Myoko* and *Haguro*, were ordered to return to Japan. The damaged *Shokaku* could not keep up with the others so she sailed with a destroyer escort a day before the rest, to return to Japan by a roundabout route. Her sailing signal was intercepted and decrypted. It gave the points through which she would pass but the coordinates were in an unsolved secret grid used in many encrypted Japanese messages to conceal latitudes and longitudes.

Therefore ComSubPac knew only that *Shokaku* would depart from Truk and arrive at the Bungo Suido, the entrance to the Inland Sea. Four submarines were disposed along the probable route and *Triton* actually sighted her, making 16 knots, but she was outside torpedo range and reached Japan safely on 17 May.

A decrypted message revealed that *Kasuga* Maru (one of five large Japanese merchantmen converted to auxiliary escort carriers, later renamed *Taiyo*) was to arrive at Kwajalein on 4 May. *Gato* was already on patrol there and *Kasuga* Maru's expected time of arrival was signalled to her. She was thus in the right place at the right time to fire a salvo of five torpedoes, which all missed. Rochefort told Holmes that it did not seem to do much good for him to relay information to his submarine friends if their torpedoes missed.

There was a serious point behind the remark. The sinking of a Japanese carrier would have mollified Rochefort's critics in US intelligence, who thought he was taking too much of a risk in allowing Holmes to tip off the Submarine Force. That information originated from JN 25 and anything that caused the Japanese to change it or suspect it was compromised would be a cryptographic catastrophe.

Although given only occasional scraps from ULTRA, and only then when there was a chance of sinking a carrier, ComSubPac had the benefit of the fullest information on the movements of enemy warships from other sources of radio intelligence. Submarines sank one major Japanese warship in 1942, the heavy cruiser *Kako* (by *S*-44, on 10 August, off Kavieng in the Solomons, but not as a result of radio intelligence). They also sank four Japanese destroyers and five submarines.

However, a look at an atlas showed the main routes Japanese shipping would be likely to use to and from the Empire, and traffic analysis indicated the frequency and direction of shipping movements. So, despite unreliable torpedoes, submarines sank some 140 Marus, totalling nearly 600,000 tons, between December, 1941, and the end of 1942.

Nevertheless, there was a sense that submarines were still not operating at their utmost operational effectiveness. But at the beginning of 1943 there was a cryptographic breakthrough which transformed the situation.

For communicating with their merchant fleet the Japanese used a four-digit code with a cipher superimposed, known to FRUPAC as the Maru code. The cipher key was changed at intervals but, according to Holmes, it only made messages unreadable for two or three days at the most. After some five months' sustained effort, largely by FRUPAC, the Maru code was broken in January, 1943, and immediately opened up a new world of possibilities.

The Pacific Ocean was so big, and its chains of islands and choices of channels offered such a large – almost an infinite – number of alternative routes, that mounting an effective submarine offensive against Japanese convoys would have required an impossible number of submarines. But the Maru code provided the composition of each convoy, often the names of the individual ships and their cargoes, the strength of the escort, the convoy's route and final destination, and, most important of all, the convoy's planned position at noon each day. Furthermore, each ship dutifully reported her own position twice a day, at 0800 and 2000. With such information, ComSubPac could concentrate his forces.

Although messages derived from the Maru code were transmitted under the name of ULTRA, with the same precautions and security classifications, they were sent to submarines much more freely than messages derived from JN-25. It was always possible that the Japanese might realize that submarine attacks on their carriers at sea could not all be due to chance or coincidence. Even had US submarines actually sunk one or more Japanese carriers in 1942, the gain would not have been worth the loss of JN-25.

But the Maru code was concerned only with the movements of Marus. Even if the numbers and locations of submarine attacks on their merchant ships should lead the Japanese to suspect that the Maru code had been broken, it was very unlikely that that would lead them on to suspect that their main five-digit code had also been broken. As Holmes said, 'The limited risk taken in allowing submarines to use liberally information from the Maru code was justified by the large potential gain. Intelligence, like money, may be secure when it is unused and locked up in a safe. It yields no dividend until it is invested.'

In January, 1943, the first full month of the use of the Maru code, the number of potential targets indicated by ULTRA, as derived from the Maru code, was 57 (a convoy of an unknown number of ships being counted as one target). In February, it was 55, in March 72, in April 41.

The difficulties of finding and sinking targets, even with the benefit of ULTRA, are shown by a closer examination of the figures. Many potential targets were never sighted at all, because the ComSubPac message was not received, or the submarine addressed was not in the area, or was in the area but made no contact, or it was pursuing another target, or was frustrated by mechanical difficulties, rough weather or poor visibility, or the information was later cancelled as incorrect.

Of those 57 potential targets in January, 1943, for instance, 40 were never sighted. Of the fifteen potential targets which were sighted (the results were unknown for the remaining two), eleven were attacked, of which four were sunk and seven damaged.

January was a comparatively good month. The figures for February were nine targets sighted, of a potential 55, of which seven were attacked, two sunk and four damaged. For March the figures were 24 targets sighted of a potential 72, of which eleven were attacked, four sunk and six damaged. In April the number attacked sank to three, of which one was damaged.

The way in which the Maru code was used, the sequence of events, was clear by January, 1943, and was repeated almost unchanged for the rest of the war: the decrypt, the operational dispatch from ComSubPac to whichever submarine was judged best able to act upon it, and then success or failure at sea.

In January, 1943, ComSubPac sent 36 ULTRA signals addressed to seventeen submarines on patrol. *Whale* (Lt Cdr J. B. Azer) was on patrol off Kwajalein when, on the 13th, not due to ULTRA, she sighted the 3,550-ton cargo ship *Iwashiro* Maru, outward bound for Truk, and sank it with four torpedoes. On the 15th *Whale* received operational dispatches which showed the extraordinary amount of detail ULTRA signals contained: 'X 1 CARRIER 2 DESTROYERS X DEPARTED 07-42N, 151-47E [North of Truk] AT 1200 ON 15 JANUARY X.' *Whale* searched the given area but saw nothing.

The last half of the signal ran: 'HEIYO MARU TO ARRIVE AT 08-42N 152-59E ON 15 JANUARY X EN ROUTE TO 07-54N 153-06E

BETWEEN 15 AND 17 JANUARY X.' A signal next day, 16 January, gave additional information about *Heiyo* Maru's movements: '15 JANUARY – 17–30N 144–32E X 16 JANUARY – 13-43N 147-47E OR 57E X 17 JANUARY – 10-15N 151-25E X (ABOVE ALL NOON POSITIONS) X ARRIVAL AT NORTH DOOR OF TRUK SCHEDULED 0900 18 JANUARY X ALL TIMES MINUS 9.'

When he reached the area on 17 January Azer saw a Japanese patrol boat steaming in a square, north then west, south then east, as though waiting for something. He steered north along the track given in the ULTRA message and, only two miles south of the noon position forecast by ULTRA, he sighted the 9,815-ton cargo liner *Heiyo* Maru approaching. Through the periscope Azer could see troops on her upper deck. Clearly they were reinforcements bound for Rabaul and the campaign in the Solomons.

Azer fired three bow torpedoes, which all hit, and a stern torpedo which also hit but the troopship did not sink. In all Azer fired nine torpedoes, of which eight hit, before *Heiyo* Maru sank.

The highest scorer that month was *Silversides*, which was eventually to become one of the highest scoring US submarines of the war, under three captains. On 16 January, at that time commanded by Lt Cdr C. R. Burlingame, *Silversides* received an ULTRA: 'TOEI MARU AND POSSIBLE ESCORT X TO ARRIVE AT 4-54N 149-22E AT 1630 (I time – possibly an error for 1400 I time) ON 17 JANUARY AND AT 6-35N 150-5E AT 0400 ON 18 JANUARY X WILL ARRIVE SOUTH GATE TRUK AT 1000 ON 18 JANUARY X TRAVELLING 13 KNOTS.'

Burlingame placed *Silversides* on the target's track and sighted what he called a *Genyo* Class vessel just after 2 pm on 17 January, only a few miles off the ULTRA forecast position. He claimed three torpedo hits and it was confirmed later that he had sunk the 10,023-ton tanker *Toei* Maru.

On the 18th *Silversides* had another ULTRA: '"B" CONVOY COMPOSED OF FOUR SHIPS AND ESCORT X EN ROUTE FROM TRUK TO SHORTLAND X.' Burlingame searched along the route ULTRA had given where he saw three destroyers on the 19th, but no convoy, and had to abandon the search because of poor visibility.

The next day another ULTRA arrived: ' "C" CONVOY X FOUR SHIPS AND TWO ESCORTS X.' Positions were given for the convoy on 20 and 21 January. Again *Silversides* lay in wait and this time Burlingame was rewarded. The convoy, of four ships and two escorts, as forecast, appeared dead on time and track on 20 January. Burlingame made a night attack and claimed five hits. In fact he had sunk the 5,154-ton passenger-cargo ship *Somedono* Maru, the 4,391-ton cargo ship *Surabaya* Maru and the 8,320-ton cargo ship *Meiu* Maru in the same attack. *Silversides* was damaged in a depth-charge counter-attack by the escorts, and headed for Pearl Harbor on the 23rd, but her total score for the month was 27,798 tons, entirely due to ULTRA.

In the spring of 1943 American torpedoes were still behaving erratically and failing to detonate correctly, while the bureaucrats ashore still fought their long, bitter and entrenched battle to prove that the faults lay entirely with the submarine captains' failure to aim their salvoes properly. ULTRA was able to provide some ammunition for the submariners' case that it was the torpedoes that were to blame.

In April, 1943, traffic analysis, decrypts of JN-25 messages to the carriers and the Truk port director's arrival and departure messages revealed that Japanese carriers were ferrying reinforcement aircraft down to Truk, whence they would fly on to Rabaul to take part in Yamamoto's Operation I.

On 8 April FRUPAC decrypted a message giving details of the arrival of a task force, including three carriers, at Truk early on 10 April. For some reason (probably to enable extra escorts from Truk to meet them) the message also gave the force's position on the evening before it was due to arrive at Truk. This was sent in an ULTRA signal to *Tunny* (Lt Cdr John A. Scott), patrolling south-west of Truk.

On 9 April Scott made a night attack using radar, actually penetrating the task force's formation. According to Holmes, 'With consummate skill, he manoeuvred *Tunny* into perfect position between two columns of Japanese ships. In quick succession he fired both bow and stern tubes, ten torpedoes, at two aircraft carriers at ranges between six hundred and eight hundred yards. Diving deep, to avoid escorts, Scott heard seven torpedo explosions at the proper intervals.'

There was naturally jubilation when this news reached Pearl Harbor, but it was short-lived. Next day Truk's port director reported the safe arrival of all three carriers. Evidently *Tunny*'s torpedoes had exploded prematurely.

By now misfires and 'prematures' in American torpedoes were well known to the Japanese. Several Japanese ships had arrived in harbour with unexploded torpedoes actually embedded in their sides. There was even a Japanese saying: 'A tanker cannot sink if it is torpedoed.'

Finally, in May, June and July, 1943, there were other missed chances due to defective torpedoes which brought the crisis to a head. Once again ULTRA played an important part.

Wahoo was one of the most successful US submarines and her captain, Lt Cdr Dudley ('Mush') Morton, one of the best submarine COs. In May, 1943, *Wahoo* returned from a patrol off northern Japan in which, with ULTRA help, three Marus totalling 10,376 tons had been sunk (making *Wahoo's* total since 10 December, 1942, 46,609 tons).

Morton had to go temporarily to hospital after his return and Holmes went to see him. He found Morton angry and bitter about the poor performance of his torpedoes and convinced that, but for misfires, he would have sunk another three ships.

Later that month *Sculpin* (Lt Cdr Lucius H. Chappell) was passing Marcus Island on her way to her patrol area off Honshu when she was diverted by ULTRA signal some 400 miles off her track to intercept a Japanese task force including two carriers. The targets were sighted by night making 22 knots. Chappell made a surfaced attack but could not gain a favourable attacking angle and eventually had to fire at long range. None of a salvo of four torpedoes hit and one blew up only a few hundred yards ahead of *Sculpin*.

More and more instances of torpedo failures occurred, while ULTRA continued to provide evidence of unsuccessful attacks.

When the US 7th Army invaded Attu in May, 1943, Admiral Koga, C-in-C Combined Fleet, reacted by sailing from Truk with battleships, cruisers and the aircraft carrier *Hiyo* and arrived on 22 May at Yokosuka, intending to join more battleships and carriers in the Empire and sail for the Aleutians. But Japanese resistance on Attu ended before he could sail.

On 10 June the carriers began to disperse to carry out exercises and pilot training in the Inland Sea, their movements closely watched by ComSubPac through ULTRA. But fast-moving carriers were difficult targets and two attempts, by *Sawfish* and *Trigger*, and by *Trigger* again with *Salmon*, were unsuccessful.

However, there was to be another chance. On 9 June ComSubPac sent an ULTRA signal to all submarines guarding NPM Fox (the submarine broadcast), with the most urgent priority of 'OP OP OP'. The text, a typical example of ComSubPac vernacular, showed that, although COs of submarines based in Western Australia had recently been warned by Admiral King in a circular of 18 May not to mention the word ULTRA in their war diaries and to delete such mentions from all past and future war diaries, ComSubPac continued to use the word in signals: 'ANOTHER HOT ULTRA COMSUBPAC SERIAL 27 X LARGEST AND NEWEST NIP CARRIER WITH TWO DESTROYERS DEPARTS YOKOSUKA AT 5 HOURS GCT 10 JUNE AND CRUISES AT 22 KNOTS ON

COURSE 155 DEGREES UNTIL REACHING 35-55 NORTH 140 EAST WHERE THEY REDUCE SPEED TO 18 KNOTS AND CHANGE COURSE TO 230 DEGREES X SALMON AND TRIGGER INTERCEPT IF POSSIBLE AND WATCH OUT FOR EACH OTHER X WE HAVE ADDITIONAL DOPE ON THIS CARRIER FOR THE BOYS NEAR TRUK WHICH WE HOPE WE WON'T NEED SO LET US KNOW IF YOU GET HIM X UNKNOWN IF SPEEDS GIVEN ARE SPEEDS THROUGH THE WATER OR SPEEDS MADE GOOD X DISTANCE THEY WILL TRAVEL ON COURSE 230 IS UNKNOWN BUT BELIEVED TO BE ABOUT 100 MILES X.'

Thus, when *Hiyo* and two destroyer escorts steamed across Tokyo Bay at 21 knots on the night of 11 June *Trigger* (Lt Cdr Roy S. Benson) was waiting. Benson got to within 1,200 yards of *Hiyo*, fired six torpedoes and heard four explosions at the right time interval. He arrived at Pearl on 22 June, delighted that *Trigger* was the first submarine to sink a Japanese aircraft carrier.

He was to be disillusioned. FRUPAC had already established through decrypts that four of *Trigger*'s torpedoes had indeed hit *Hiyo* but only one exploded properly, in a boiler-room. *Hiyo* was badly damaged and only struggled back to Yokosuka with her upper decks almost awash. But she was not sunk.

On 24 July, 1943, *Tinosa* (Lt Cdr L. R. 'Dan' Daspit) hit and stopped a large 19,262-ton Japanese tanker, *Tonan* Maru No. 3, west of Truk. While his target lay stationary, Daspit lined up his submarine and fired another nine torpedoes, each individually aimed. All hit. None exploded. Daspit then had the presence of mind to bring his remaining torpedo back for examination.

Tinosa's experience would have been the last straw, but, after *Tunny*, *Wahoo*, *Sculpin* and *Trigger*, Nimitz and Rear Admiral Charles A. Lockwood (who had become ComSubPac in February, 1943) decided enough was enough. Despite acrimonious exchanges with the Bureau of Ordnance, on 24 June, 1943, Nimitz ordered the deactivation of magnetic exploders on torpedoes in all ships and aircraft under his command, although submarines in the South-West Pacific Command continued to use magnetic exploders.

The figures of sinkings by submarines were expected to improve in July and August, but they did not, although on 1 August, fore-warned by ULTRA, *Pogy* (Lt Cdr G. H. Wales) torpedoed and sank the 7,497-ton aircraft ferry *Mogamigawa* Maru on its way from the Empire to Truk. ULTRA also gave Wales notice of a Japanese task force of two carriers, an auxiliary carrier, several cruisers and escorting destroyers. He did sight them but they were making 25 knots and he was unable to overhaul them and gain an attacking position.

The figures had not improved because the torpedoes were *still* defective. The Mark VI contact exploder, which detonated the torpedo on impact with the target, was badly designed. Modifications were carried out at Pearl Harbor which greatly improved performance although, as Holmes said, 'It still produced some duds.' It was not until the end of September, 1943, that Pacific submarines' torpedoes had reliable exploders.

An analysis of results made in January, 1946, derived from ULTRA between 1 January and 31 October, 1943, showed that the total number of potential targets revealed by ULTRA was 810. Of those, 445 potential targets were not sighted, for a variety of reasons such as ComSubPac message not received (4); submarine not in area (100); submarine pursuing other targets (86); submarine in area – no contact (223); mechanical difficulties in submarine (5); rough weather or poor visibility (20); and information cancelled as incorrect (7).

The number of potential targets sighted was 354. Of these, 120 were attacked, 33 of them being sunk, 56 damaged, 16 had no perceptible damage and 15 missed. Almost twice as many, 234, were sighted but not attacked because of unfavourable position of submarine (65); rough weather or poor visibility (16); submarine attacked by escorts (9); target showed hospital ship markings (3); submarine engaged with other targets (137); or targets not worth a torpedo (4). For eleven potential targets the results were unknown.

With torpedoes which, at last, ran at the correct depth and detonated upon impact, the submarines' success figures began to rise. In September, 1943, submarines sank 38 Marus, of 157,002 tons, the highest monthly figure of the war so far. In October 27 Marus were sunk, of 119,623 tons. The number of potential targets provided by ULTRA in October rose to 126, but, for the usual reasons, the number of targets actually sighted and attacked was nineteen, and five were sunk.

Of those five three were sunk from one convoy by *Silversides*, on her seventh war patrol, with another successful CO, Lt Cdr John S. Coye. On the 17th *Silversides* joined with *Balao* to attack a convoy off New Ireland and sank the 1,915-ton *Tairin* Maru on the 18th.

Acting on an ULTRA message, both submarines went north to intercept a convoy of seven Marus, with two escorting patrol craft, on its way from Truk to Rabaul. After an aborted surface attack on 22nd, when a 'premature' from *Balao* alerted the escorts who drove *Silversides* off, Coye made one attack on the evening of 23 October and a second the following morning and sank the 5,407-ton *Tennan*

Maru, the 1,893-ton *Kazan* Maru and the 6,182-ton passenger-cargo *Johore* Maru. *Silversides* had to finish off the last with gunfire and her crew were allowed up on deck to witness the sinking. Coye's patrol total of 15,397 tons was one of the highest of the war.

On 4 November *Halibut* (Lt Cdr I. J. Galantin) was on patrol in the Van Diemen Strait, off the southern tip of Kyushu, when she received an ULTRA message 'to be in a certain position at a given time' to intercept a Japanese task force emerging from the Bungo Suido the next day.

Halibut steered north and detected the enemy by radar just after 5 am on 5 November. As dawn broke Galantin identified through the periscope four large ships – a *Tone* Class heavy cruiser, two battleships, one of them of the *Nagato* Class and, best of all, an aircraft carrier, with a silhouette similar to *Shokaku*.

Galantin fired a bow salvo of six torpedoes at the carrier and saw one hit through the periscope. He then fired two stern-tube torpedoes and heard two more hits. With his target stationary, he intended to fire again but the torpedo 'ran hot' in the tube. At the same time destroyers counter-attacked with depth-charges. Galantin managed to evade, while his torpedomen got the rogue torpedo back in the tube.

From decrypts FRUPAC identified the carrier as *Junyo*, sometimes known as *Hayataka*. She had suffered one hit starboard side aft and had to be towed back to the Inland Sea.

It was a very good start to what was to be an excellent month for ULTRA and for the submarines. In November, 1943, submarines sank 43 ships, of 285,820 tons, and damaged another 22 of 143,323 tons, for a total of 429,143 tons, the best of the war so far.

During the month 120 ULTRA messages were sent out to submarines: 76 of them gave information about enemy ship movements – fifteen were of task forces of one or more warships, six of submarines, four of naval auxiliaries, and 51 of convoys of one or more merchant vessels. Another 40 messages added to or corrected the originals. Four other ULTRA messages gave general warnings of task forces, submarines, mine fields etc, for which no direct result was seen.

On 29 November a message from the port director at Truk to various local ship and shore addressees and for information to 1st, 3rd and 6th Fleets, was decrypted: 'Entries and departures, 30 November. Departing via North Channel: 0530, ZUIHO, CHUYO, UNYO, MAYA [heavy cruiser], destroyers AKEBONO, USHIO, SAZANAMI, URAKAZE, course 241. After 0840 course 000.' These ships were all bound for Yokosuka. Their noon positions en route were also decrypted.

The first ULTRA, and two later amplifying ULTRAs, were primarily addressed to *Skate*, on patrol near Truk, who attacked on the 30th and claimed one hit, which was not confirmed by ULTRA.

The fourth ULTRA on 29th was an 'OP OP OP' from ComSubPac, to *Sawfish*, *Gunnel* and other subs in vicinity: 'CHANCE OF A LIFETIME X ULTRA SERIAL 66V FOR ACTION SAWFISH GUNNEL AND ANY OTHER SUBS IN VICINITY X 28 AND 36 PEANUTS X 2 AUXILIARY CARRIERS AND 4 DESTROYERS X 0330 X 2ND X 23-30 NORTH 148-56 EAST X POSITION AT SAME TIME FOLLOWING DAY 30-08 NORTH 146-15 EAST X SUCCESSIVE POSITIONS OF THIS UNIT TIME AND DATE INDICATED ARE AS FOLLOWS 2100 3RD 33-52 NORTH 142-20 EAST AND 6 HOURS LATER 34-40 NORTH 140-20 EAST X AVOID DETECTION OR RADIO TRANSMISSIONS IN VICINITY OF TRACK UNTIL AFTER CONTACT.'

Gunnel, on patrol off Chichi Jima, attacked without a hit two days later, on 2 December. The following day *Sunfish* sighted two carriers and two or more destroyers at a range of ten miles but was unable to get closer than 12,000 yards and broke off the approach.

It fell to *Sailfish* (Lt Cdr R.E.M. Ward), waiting some 250 miles south-east of Tokyo Bay, to take the 'chance of a lifetime'. *Sailfish* surfaced in the midst of a tropical storm, with mountainous waves, 50-60 knot winds and driving rain, on the evening of 3 December. 'Can't see a thing,' said Ward, 'but blackness and water with the water mostly in my face.'

Just before midnight *Sailfish* had a radar contact, range 9,500 yards, followed shortly afterwards by three more contacts. *Sailfish* dived just after midnight on 4 December, fired four torpedoes at 0012 and heard two hits. The target, actually *Chuyo*, signalled to Tokyo: 'Hit by one torpedo at 0010. Fire in crew's quarters forward. Able to proceed.'

Sailfish surfaced to follow the damaged carrier and at 0552, just after dawn, fired three more torpedoes from the surface and 'observed and heard two torpedo hits'. *Chuyo* signalled again that she was hit. *Sailfish* dived and just before 8 am Ward saw an aircraft carrier through the periscope, range 10,000 yards, lying dead in the water. *Sailfish* passed down the carrier's port side at a range of about 1,500 yards. Ward could see 'many planes on deck forward and enough people on deck aft to populate a fair size village'.

Finally, at 0942, *Sailfish* fired three stern tube torpedoes and heard two hits followed by 'loud breaking-up noises heard not only on sound but also very clearly throughout the boat'. When Ward next put up the periscope there was nothing to be seen. After nearly being run down by *Maya* and one counterattack 'not too close', *Sailfish* 'set course to proceed to area' at 1400.

Decrypts later confirmed that *Chuyo* had indeed sunk. After so many disappointments, near-misses and misfires, a US submarine had at last sunk a Japanese carrier. It was a great success – not least for ULTRA.

In December, 1943, submarines sank 32 ships of 121,351 tons, but during the year the US Navy lost 15 submarines and 1,129 officers and men.

X

THE ATOLL WAR

'LAST week,' wrote *Time* magazine in November, 1943, 'some two to three thousand U.S. Marines, most of them now dead or wounded, gave the nation a name to stand beside those of Concord Bridge, the *Bonhomme Richard*, the Alamo, Little Big Horn, and Belleau Wood. The name was Tarawa.'

The great Allied drive across the Central Pacific, from fortified island to fortified island in what became known as the 'Atoll War', had begun with an assault on a hitherto totally unknown atoll in the Gilbert Islands. At Tarawa, as on Guadalcanal, there were some hard and bloody lessons to be learned.

For much of 1943 there had been a comparative lull in the Central Pacific, as though the theatre had been awaiting the arrival of its queen, the *Essex* Class aircraft carrier. These magnificent new, 27,000-ton, 32-knot vessels were heavily armed with anti-aircraft guns but were designed primarily for attack; they were lightly armoured, but carried an impressive complement of 90, later 100, aircraft. The first of them arrived at Pearl in May, 1943, and by the autumn the Fifth Fleet (formed on 13 March, 1943, out of the Central Pacific component of the Pacific Fleet and commanded by Raymond Spruance, promoted Vice Admiral) had six heavy carriers, including a new *Yorktown* and a new *Lexington*, five new *Independence* class light carriers, twelve battleships and a host of cruisers, destroyers and landing craft of various types and sizes.

The Fifth Fleet combined extraordinary mobility with fearsome hitting power, being able to surprise one target with a punishing strike and then vanish into the distance of the Pacific, using the very vastness of the ocean as a defence, before reappearing to strike at another target, hundreds of miles away, a short time later.

The Fifth Fleet's spearhead was the Fast Carrier Task Force, designated Task Force 58, commanded by Rear Admiral Charles Pownall and later by Rear Admiral Marc A. ('Pete') Mitscher. The task force was organized in separate task groups, each under its own admiral, and each normally containing two heavy and two light carriers, with its own escort of fast battleships, cruisers and destroyers. Task groups could operate independently or in company as a task force. By detaching individual task groups to refuel and rearm, the task force as a whole could exert constant pressure on the enemy.

TF 58's tasks were to carry out pre-invasion strikes on the target atoll's defences; give tactical air support to the troops on or approaching the beaches during the assault phase; maintain air cover while the atoll was secured and air strips set up ashore; strike at distant Japanese island bases to prevent them flying in reinforcements; and to intercept any Japanese attempt by sea or air to counter-attack the troops on the target atoll.

While the carriers and battleships held the distant ring, the Marine and Army assault troops – the Fifth Amphibious Corps, under Major General Holland M. ('Howlin' Mad') Smith, US Marine Corps – were carried to the target beaches by Rear Admiral Richmond Kelly Turner's Fifth Amphibious Force, which was a further large fleet of transports, cargo ships and landing ships and craft, with its own escort of carriers, battleships, cruisers and destroyers. The Fifth Fleet also had its own shore-based air force, under Rear Admiral John Hoover.

The first target in the 'Atoll War' was to have been the Marshall Islands, mandated to Japan in 1920 and closed to foreigners for years before the war. But Nimitz decided that the Gilberts must be attacked first, because of their threatening position on the flank of any advance towards the Marshalls.

Intelligence, especially from photo-reconnaissance, showed that the Gilberts were formidably defended. This was very largely the Allies' own fault. The Japanese had taken the Gilberts in December, 1941, but had only token forces there until August, 1942, when Colonel Carlson's Marine Raiders arrived by submarine for a 'hit and run' raid on Butaritari Island, in Makin Atoll. The raid was only an irritant, but it had the effect of causing the Japanese to reinforce the atolls, build an airfield on Betio Island in Tarawa Atoll, and begin to construct gun emplacements and defences.

By November, 1943, Tarawa had a garrison of 4,500 troops and was defended by fourteen coast defence guns, ranging from 5.5-inch to 8-inch, and batteries of field guns ensconced in pillboxes strengthened with logs and armour plate, anti-aircraft guns, and immobile tanks mounting fourteen 37-mm. guns. The troops also had bombproof shelters, and the beaches were obstructed by wire and log barricades.

There were no ship-to-ship engagements in the Atoll War, no equivalent of the Tokyo Express, and no chance of laying ULTRA ambushes which had led to so many actions off Guadalcanal and Bougainville. Intelligence efforts were therefore largely directed at estimating the strength and armament of enemy garrisons and the nature of their defences.

FRUPAC's task was made easier because there were very few army troops in the Gilberts and the Marshalls, which were defended by special naval units who used naval radio circuits and naval codes. Traffic analysis and decrypts revealed the order of battle of the Tarawa garrisons. On Betio, for instance, FRUPAC identified the Sasebo 7th Special Naval Landing Force, the 3rd Special Base Force, the 111th Pioneers and a 4th Fleet construction unit. In the event, FRUPAC's estimate of the Tarawa garrison's total strength was accurate to within a couple of hundred men.

Very little was known about the islands themselves and a great deal of effort was devoted to such matters as the likely weather and the topography of the atolls, gradients of beaches, contours of hills, heights of prominent features, depths of water offshore, positions of coral reefs and tidal variations.

ULTRA did provide chances of attacking the enemy. There had been no major reinforcement of Betio since May, 1943. That month FRUPAC decrypted a message revealing that two Marus were on their way to Betio, one of them carrying four 8-inch guns captured from the British in Singapore.

The submarine *Pollack*, on patrol off the Marshalls, was ordered to lie in wait for the Marus off Jaluit and on 20 May sank the 5,350-ton ex-light cruiser *Bangkok* Maru. She was not carrying the guns, but she did have 1,200 troops for Betio. Most of them survived and were taken to Jaluit, where they spent the rest of the war.

D-Day for Operation GALVANIC, the assault on the Gilbert Islands, was 20 November, 1943, five days later than originally planned but the fact that it took place at all on that date was a miracle of determination and planning by 'Howlin' Mad' Smith and his staff.

Some 200 ships took part, together with 108,000 men, including 27,000 assault and 6,000 garrison troops, with 6,000 vehicles and 117,000 tons of cargo. The first elements of the Northern Attack Force, under Turner, taking one regiment of 27th US Army Division to Makin, began to sail from Pearl on 21 October. The

Southern Attack Force, under Rear Admiral Harry W. Hill, taking the 2nd Marine Division to Betio, sailed from New Zealand and Efate, beginning on 12 November.

Preliminary bombing of the targets began next day, 13 November. The carriers had begun 'warm up' strikes on Marcus and Wake Islands as well as the target atolls on 1 September. After a pause for replenishment, the carriers returned, deployed in four groups, for a programme of heavy strikes on Tarawa, Makin, Rabaul, Nauru and Jaluit between 11 November and D-Day. The bombing did little damage to the islands' defences but did cause their garrisons to fire off much ammunition, which they had not replaced by D-Day.

D-Day air strikes at Betio began just after dawn (later than planned and required) and were followed by two and a half hours of naval bombardment by three battleships, four cruisers and several destroyers who pounded the island with more than 3,000 tons of high explosive shells.

All this greatly encouraged the Marines, waiting to disembark. Physically hard, superbly trained, many of them Guadalcanal veterans, the 2nd Marine Division was probably the best military formation in the US armed forces at that time. However, although they had unshakeable confidence in themselves, the Marines devoutly hoped that all the Japs on that island were now dead or dazed.

Intelligence could estimate the strength of a garrison and its defences, but could not forecast how many of the enemy would survive bombardment. It could draw up tide tables and maps but could not allow for every idiosyncrasy of tide and reef. On Betio more Japanese survived the bombardments than was believed humanly possible. There were crucial lapses in radio communications, and lulls in the bombardments allowed the Japanese precious minutes to move their troops into position.

There was unexpectedly heavy and alarmingly accurate gunfire from the beaches. The landing craft and the amphibious tractors could not all get ashore quickly enough because an unforeseen low tide stranded them on a coral shelf. Marines had to wade the last hundred yards, thigh deep, under withering fire. Many died in the water and many more were killed as they stepped on the sand. Whole platoons were pinned down, wherever they could find any cover, for hours.

It took the Marines three days to secure an island which was 2,000 yards long and 500 wide at its broadest point. The last island, Lone Tree, to the north was not taken until the 28th. Casualties among the Navy and Marines engaged were 1,009 dead and 2,101 wounded.

Of the defenders, who had been ordered to fight to the last man, one officer, sixteen men and 129 Korean labourers survived. At Makin, a hundred miles to the north, the 17th Division took Butaritari in three days, with only 64 killed and 150 wounded.

The assault on the Gilberts caught the Japanese off balance. Reinforcements for Tarawa had only reached Kwajalein when Tarawa fell. Vice Admiral Takeo Takagi, who had taken command of the Sixth Fleet submarines that month, sent nine submarines to operate against American ships in the Gilberts and issued orders which he hoped would convince the Americans that he had more submarines than he actually had. He constantly changed the deployment of his submarines. Three separate sentry lines were formed, one north of Makin on 26 November and a second and a third the next day. He ordered some to dive and others to stay on the surface and send radio messages to confuse US intelligence.

Takagi succeeded only in confusing his own submarine commanders. His subterfuges soon produced a state of near chaos. For example, when on 1 December *I-174* was some three miles off Makin, waiting for a US convoy (which never came), her captain said: 'Other submarines were dashing back and forth between various stations assigned to them by Sixth Fleet. First an order would say "move". Then it would be changed to "move, navigating on the surface". Still later it would become "wait, remaining on the surface".'

The Japanese lost six of those nine submarines but scored one success, at dawn on 24 November, when *I-175* torpedoed the escort carrier *Liscome Bay*. The explosion detonated the bombs in a bomb store and the ship was torn apart, sinking in 23 minutes, with the loss of 53 officers and 591 of her ship's company.

For GALVANIC, mobile radio intelligence units embarked in Spruance's flagship, the heavy cruiser *Indianapolis*, in Pownall's flagship *Yorktown*, and in *Enterprise*, wearing the flag of Rear Admiral A. W. Radford, commanding the Northern Carrier Group, TG 50.2. Japanese air reaction to the first carrier strikes on 19 November was immediate. The task groups were constantly being spotted and one LST Group at Makin was attacked. But the aircraft used well known frequencies and the radio units found it easy to predict attacks by listening for requests for weather reports between one island and another.

However, there were so many American ships in a small area that it was sometimes difficult to tell from a Japanese report which group had been sighted. Task Group 50.3 was spotted on 20 November but no attack message had been originated by the Japanese when the light carrier *Independence* was hit by one torpedo that evening. Significantly, TG 50.3 had no RI Unit embarked.

The Japanese made skilful use of torpedo attacks by night which, in Admiral Radford's opinion, were tactically better than anything the US Navy could do at the time. Fortunately the Japanese almost always used plain language tactical signals to get their aircraft into attacking positions and the RI Units' warnings enabled the task groups to manoeuvre to avoid the torpedoes.

On one pitch black night some Japanese aircraft flew directly over *Enterprise*'s task group at a height of not more than 500 feet. The RI Unit had been in contact with them and as the aircraft approached was able to assure Radford that the aircraft were not attacking and did not even know the ships were below them. The ships forbore to fire and the aircraft flew on in ignorance.

As soon as the airstrip on Tarawa was serviceable the carriers began to retire from the area. The *Enterprise* RI Unit transferred at sea to *Essex*, in TG 50.3, for a dawn strike on Kwajalein on 4 December. The force, of six carriers, ten cruisers and eleven destroyers under Pownall, began its run in from about 500 miles north-east of Kwajalein and achieved complete surprise, the first reaction from Kwajalein being the alarm '50 small planes overhead'.

Four ships in the lagoon were sunk and 55 aircraft destroyed. The Japanese retaliated that evening with the same skilful night torpedo attacks and just before midnight hit *Lexington* with one torpedo aft, damaging her rudder. *Lexington* was able to make her own way to Pearl, steering by main engines.

The RI Unit in *Essex* thought it 'almost miraculous' that the force had escaped detection during the approach. It was not 'almost miraculous', but the result of patient FRUPAC decryptions of Japanese naval air force messages, which revealed the Japanese naval air order of battle and their air search schedules.

From decrypts and analysis of Kwajalein traffic, it was established that despite reinforcements of 40 bombers from Hokkaido and 35 fighters from Rabaul flown in to Kwajalein on 25 November, the Japanese did not have enough aircraft to carry out air searches through the full perimeter and were concentrating their searches to the south and south-east, the likeliest directions from which they expected attack. Pownall was thus able to approach from the un-guarded area to the north-east.

After 'Bloody Tarawa', as it became known, everybody assumed that the next target would be somewhere in the outer rim of the Marshalls. That was certainly what the Japanese assumed, because by the end of the first week in December, 1943, decrypts and traffic analysis had made it unmistakably clear that the Japanese were heavily reinforcing the outlying atolls of Jaluit, Wotje, Maloelap and Mili with troops and artillery from Kwajalein.

When Nimitz had digested this intelligence, he startled all his force commanders by announcing that the next assault would be on Kwajalein itself, the very heart of the Marshalls.

Despite the losses, which caused great alarm among press and public at home in America, 'Bloody Tarawa' was an invaluable testing ground. Bombardment patterns, landing craft designs, disembarkation procedures, ground-to-air radio liaison, rescue of aircrew by submarines, protection of bomb stowages in carriers, clothing for combat personnel, methods of assaulting armed strong-points, and scores of other techniques, routines, designs and plans were all improved as a result of experience in the Gilberts.

Intelligence techniques were also improved. For example, General 'Howlin' Mad' Smith complained bitterly that the first knowledge he had that the Japanese on Betio had 8-inch guns was when 8-inch shells exploded along loaded transports in a supposedly safe anchorage.

Holmes was sure the guns had been mentioned in the intelligence summaries, albeit 'sanitized' to protect their ULTRA source by being described as '20-centimeter coast-defense guns'. He discovered that indeed they had, but the only reference to them was buried in obscure small print in a long descriptive paragraph. Henceforth intelligence bulletins and summaries made much less use of text and much more of maps, photographs, sketches, diagrams and tables.

Kwajalein was Tarawa writ large – except in American casualties. The largest coral atoll in the world, Kwajalein was even more strongly and formidably defended than Tarawa, indeed it is very probable that without the invaluable experience and indispensable bases the Gilberts provided, the Marshalls invasion would have failed.

The majority of the Japanese garrison of some 8,700 men were about equally divided between the main air bases on the adjacent islands of Roi and Namur, in the north-eastern corner, and the main naval base on the largest island of Kwajalein in the south. They were entrenched in massive steel pill-boxes and bunkers and were as determined to resist to the last man as those at Tarawa.

For the Allies, some 300 ships took part, not counting the carrier task groups or the submarines, to escort or carry 54,000 assault troops.

The Northern Attack Force, under Rear Admiral Dick Conolly, conveyed the 4th US Marine Division to assault Roi-Namur. The Southern Attack Force, under Turner, took the 7th US Army Division to Kwajalein. A third force in reserve eventually went on to take Eniwetok.

D-Day for Operation FLINTLOCK, the assaults on Kwajalein and Majuro (an atoll on the outer rim), was 31 January, by which day the fast carrier raids had eliminated the last Japanese air opposition. The whole operation took place with no Japanese air intervention of any kind. The undefended Majuro, which the Japanese had abandoned in November, 1942, (FRUPAC had forecast there were six Japanese on Majuro – in fact, there was only one) was soon occupied on D-Day and its magnificent lagoon quickly became a base for the ships of the mobile service squadron.

At Roi-Namur the Marines went ashore in their improved amphtracs and landing craft after a naval bombardment lasting three days which was so heavy and prolonged and delivered from such close range that the grateful Marines dubbed their Admiral 'Close-In' Conolly. Once ashore, the Marines cleaned up Roi and Namur and neighbouring islands in a brisk operation lasting just over twenty-six hours.

At Kwajalein, after an equally heavy bombardment (of some 6,000 tons of shells) the 7th Infantry met fierce opposition but worked methodically through the island from the east and round up to the north, captured it on 4 February and mopped up the final remains on the 5th. Total US casualties for the landings were 372 killed and about 1,500 wounded. Of the Japanese, only 100, and 165 Korean labourers, survived.

Four RI Units were embarked for FLINTLOCK in *Indianapolis*, *Lexington*, *Essex* and *Saratoga*, but with no air opposition they had little to do except hear Kwajalein going off the air and Truk taking over control.

At Kwajalein co-operation between Navy, Army and Marines had been unusually good. Admiral King, never lavish with praise, signalled: 'To all hands concerned with the Marshalls operation: Well and smartly done. Carry on.'

As the Japanese evacuated or were driven out of islands, there were many more opportunities for finding documents, although the Joint Intelligence Centre Pacific Ocean Area (JICPOA) was hampered by over-enthusiastic US personnel who 'liberated' vital intelligence material as souvenirs. Holmes recalled one instance of a code-book picked up by a sailor on Makin Atoll containing a code still in use in the Marshalls. To the chagrin of JICPOA staff, by the time the code book was found during a routine inspection of messdecks back in Pearl, the code had been superceded. Special teams were formed to recover such material before the souvenir-hunters could get their hands on it.

As a major Japanese regional headquarters, Kwajalein yielded an unusually rich haul of intelligence documents. For example, a Japanese patrol vessel was driven ashore in Gehh Island in Kwajalein atoll early in the operation. Later, one Army raiding unit mistook its intended landing objective and went ashore on Gehh instead, where they captured a Japanese officer and recovered from him a roll of seventy-five red-edged charts.

Any Japanese documents with red edges were known to be important intelligence material. These charts revealed the locations of minefields and other obstructions in the lagoons and harbours of Micronesia, including the minefields at Kwajalein and at Eniwetok – the next objective.

Eniwetok was just over 300 miles west-north-west of Roi-Namur and only 670 miles from Truk, the great Japanese stronghold in the Carolines. Known as the 'Gibraltar of the Pacific', Truk was in fact not nearly as strongly defended as legend had it, but it was the best fleet anchorage anywhere in the Japanese mandated islands and had been the regular base for the Combined Fleet since July, 1942.

Truk's geographical layout, of scattered volcanic islands inside a triangular-shaped coral reef, made it virtually impregnable to surface attack from outside its perimeter. But it was open to the air. After the same FRUPAC analysis of air search patterns from Truk as from Kwajalein, a powerful task force including six fleet and four light carriers in three groups under Mitscher (who had relieved Pownall in January) made a fast and undetected run towards Truk in the night of 16/17 February, 1944, to carry out Operation HAILSTONE.

Spruance himself was present, flying his flag in the battleship *New Jersey* (the fleet commander had also been present during the Marshalls landings, ready to take over command if the Combined Fleet sallied out). But there was no chance of that. Truk was just within bombing range of Kwajalein and Bougainville, and its supply route from the Empire was constantly beset by US submarines. Thus, Truk was no longer the safe base it had once been.

Photo-reconnaissance of Truk on 4 February showed plenty of targets, but the same reconnaissance flight had given the game away to Admiral Koga, who sent most of his warships to Palau and went back to Japan himself in the giant battleship *Musashi*.

The last cruiser, *Agano*, left Truk on 16 February and was torpedoed and sunk by the submarine *Skate* the next day. But the fleet auxiliaries, the oilers, seaplane carriers, submarine tenders and many Marus of the support force were due to leave later and were still in Truk when the first fighter sweep, launched from a point 90 miles north of Truk before dawn on 17 February, caught the defenders by surprise.

Seventy-two fighters followed by eighteen Avengers with incendiaries found some fifty merchant ships in the harbour and 365 aircraft ranged on the airfields. The strike put all but a hundred of the aircraft out of action. The carriers then mounted more or less continuous strikes of fighters, bombers and torpedo-bombers to work over the airstrips and attack shipping. That evening the Japanese made their only reply, a torpedo attack by Kates who scored a hit on the carrier *Intrepid* (a somewhat unlucky ship, nicknamed 'The Evil I'), putting her out of action for some months.

In the meantime Spruance in *New Jersey* with another battleship, *Iowa*, two heavy cruisers, four destroyers and the light carrier *Cowpens* to give air cover, made one anti-clockwise sweep round Truk to catch any would-be escapers. They sank the light cruiser and Sixth Fleet submarine flagship *Katori* and the destroyer *Maikaze*.

That night a strike of Avengers, specially equipped and trained for night bombing, attacked shipping in the lagoon. It was the first time in the war such a raid had been made and it was a signal success: one-third of the total tonnage destroyed at Truk was sunk by these Avengers.

Strikes resumed the next day, 18 February. Everything that moved or floated had now been sunk or strafed and the aircraft turned their attention to fixed fittings – hangars, fuel tanks, storage dumps, buildings and vehicles. When the carriers retired at noon their aircraft had flown 1,250 sorties, dropped 400 tons of bombs and torpedoes on shipping and 94 tons on airfields and shore installations. They had sunk the cruiser *Naka*, auxiliary cruisers *Aikoku* Maru and *Kiyosumi* Maru, destroyers *Oite*, *Fumizuki* and *Tachikaze*, the armed merchant cruiser *Akagi* Maru, two submarine tenders, an aircraft ferry, six tankers and seventeen other ships – a total of about 200,000 tons. This was a crushing blow to the Japanese Navy. The loss of so many fleet supply and support vessels was as grave an operational defeat as the loss of capital ships. Truk was never the same again. The Eniwetok landings were carried out with no air interference at all, and even Allied pilots as far away as Rabaul suddenly noticed the lessening of Japanese air opposition against them.

Operation CATCHPOLE, the invasion of Eniwetok, began with landings by the 22nd Marine Regiment on the northerly island of Engebi on 17 February 1944, after the 1,000 defenders had been pounded by a massive air and sea bombardment. The island was taken the next day, in a simple invasion, inexpensive in lives.

On the two neighbouring southerly islands of Parry and Eniwetok, however, matters went awry. The Japanese there had concealed themselves so well that air reconnaissance failed to detect them and it was believed that both islands were unoccupied. At the last moment intelligence material found on Engebi revealed the truth. It was too late to mount a proper bombardment on Eniwetok and the assault troops of the 106th Infantry Regiment, slower and more cautious than the Marines, made heavy weather of their advance and the island was not taken until the 21st. Parry was bombarded for three days; then the Marines landed on the 22nd and took the island in a day. Of the 3,500 men in the Japanese garrison on Eniwetok, there were 64 survivors.

After attacking Truk, most of the carriers went on to strike at the Marianas, leaving *Saratoga*'s TG 58.4, with an RI Unit still embarked, to cover the Eniwetok landings. The first enemy reaction to the landing was a plain language message from the airstrip on Engebi, to Truk, via Jaluit: 'Enemy is in the lagoon in large force; evidently intends to land; request aid.' Two and a half hours later another plain language message read: 'Because of enemy [blanks] am suspending communications. I pray for the long life of the Emperor.' That was the last heard from Eniwetok.

The loss of such important atolls in the Gilberts and the Marshalls, and MacArthur's steady progress in New Guinea, forced the Japanese High Command to abandon the strategy of defending an outer line extending to the Bismarcks, and to set up instead a new inner defensive line, more than a thousand miles to the west, running from the Marianas, to the Palaus, to western New Guinea.

Many other islands and atolls to the east of this line, such as Nauru and Ponape, and Jaluit, Mili, Wotje and Maloelap in the Marshalls, and bases such as Rabaul and Truk, were never invaded at all, but were simply 'leap-frogged' and neutralized by air strikes from time to time. They remained in Japanese hands until the very end of the war, but their garrisons, bypassed by the Allied advance and many of them cut off from all assistance except from submarines, were left to wither on the vine, being decimated by starvation and disease and by repeated attacks by Fifth Fleet carrier aircraft, which used these isolated Japanese outposts as 'live' practise targets for aircrews new to the Pacific.

In New Guinea South-West Pacific Command began the new year of 1944 with landings at Saidor on 2 January. A plan for capturing Kavieng in New Ireland was dropped and the invasion of the Admiralty Islands north of New Guinea brought forward when a reconnaissance in force on 29 February, with MacArthur himself present, was turned into a proper invasion. The islands were secured on 24 March.

MacArthur wanted to attack Rabaul but was overruled by the Chiefs of Staff, and so sidestepped the main Japanese 18th Army at Wewak, where ULTRA indicated the Japanese were concentrating their strength for their main resistance, by landing further along the coast at Hollandia, where ULTRA had revealed that the Japanese were reducing their resources, with a secondary landing at Aitape, between Wewak and Hollandia, to seize the airstrips there.

For these operations MacArthur had the assistance of the Fifth Fleet. Ever more confident of their power to stay at sea within range of Japanese air bases, the carriers of TF 58 steamed south and secured MacArthur's seaward flank in March and April, 1944, with further strikes at Truk, on the Palau Islands and the western Carolines.

After the strikes on Truk in February, 1944, many units of the Combined Fleet went to Peleliu, in the Palau Islands, some 1,300 miles west of Truk. The C-in-C, Admiral Koga, was much more conservative and much less charismatic than his predecessor, but he shared Yamamoto's desire to have – one day – a decisive engagement with the US Fleet. On 8 March he issued a plan, later called 'Zebra Operation Order', to bring the American fleet to action in the area of the western Carolines, overcoming the handicap of a shortage of carrier aircraft by using the favourite Japanese device of a decoy. When the Allies attacked the Philippines, Palau or the Marianas, the aircraft-less Japanese carriers would be used to draw off the enemy carriers while shore-based aircraft and the Japanese surface fleet fell upon and destroyed the Allied expeditionary force.

Koga had had no chance to put his plan into action before Operation DESECRATE, the fast carrier task force strikes at the Palaus on 30 March. The carriers were sighted by an aircraft from Truk on 25 March, probably by one from Peleliu on the 28th and certainly the next day, so giving Koga warning.

Although the task force's aircraft sank 36 ships of some 130,000 tons in Kessel Passage, the fleet anchorage, the forewarned Koga had withdrawn his main warships – the third time in a year that the Combined Fleet had had to leave its base. US submarines had been placed in a ring round the Palaus to act as plane guards for US airmen shot down and to intercept any Japanese ships attempting to get out from under the carrier strikes. On the 29th *Tunny* scored one torpedo hit far forward on *Musashi*, doing slight damage.

Koga was not flying his flag on board *Musashi* at the time. He had decided to abandon the Palaus and move his fleet headquarters to the Philippines. He, his chief of staff, Admiral Shigeru Fukudome, and other staff officers took off from Peleliu in two flying boats on 30 March, bound for Davao in the Philippines. A FRUPAC decrypt the following day reported an air crash near the island of Cebu in the southern Philippines.

One version is that Koga's aircraft vanished in a tropical storm, while Fukudome's came down in the sea off Cebu. Still clutching his briefcase, Fukudome was captured by Filipino guerrillas. He was released after threats of reprisals but his briefcase was retained. Another version is that Koga's aircraft crashed on Cebu on the 30th and he was captured by guerrillas. The Japanese commander on Cebu got to hear of it and threatened Colonel Cushing, the guerrilla leader on Cebu, that he would conduct a campaign of reprisals against native villages unless Koga was released, and proceeded to carry out his threat. Cushing decided to trade Koga, but Koga died a few days after he had been given up to the Japanese and his body was returned to Palau where he was buried.

Whatever the truth of the matter, the most important outcome for the Allies was the recovery of a copy of Koga's 'Zebra Order'. It arrived in Pearl Harbor marked 'Secret. Not to be copied or reproduced without permission of General MacArthur.' Realizing its importance, Layton asked Nimitz to send an urgent message asking for clearance. The text was translated, edited, duplicated and sent to fleet commanders at sea. Its content was to affect Spruance's judgement and decisions in the confrontations to come.

The landings at Hollandia were successfully carried out on 22 April, 1944, and on the offshore island of Wakde on 17 May. MacArthur's next main target was the large island of Biak. But the landings there, on 27 May, met much stiffer resistance than expected.

Biak was important to Japanese strategy. Its airfields were needed to give land-based air support for the Japanese First Mobile Fleet in Operation A-GO, a refinement of Koga's plan devised by the new

C-in-C Admiral Soemu Toyoda to bring the US Fleet to battle.

In March, 1944, the Japanese had reorganized their Navy so that virtually 90 per cent of all their seagoing ships except for submarines formed the First Mobile Fleet, under a most able commander, Vice Admiral Jisaburo Ozawa. On 3 May Toyoda issued his orders for Operation A-GO. The plan was for a 'special force' to lure the American fleet to certain 'designated areas' either off the Palaus or the western Carolines, where it would come within the range of the maximum number of Japanese air bases. (There was another deciding factor: the Japanese Navy did not have enough fuel to venture much further afield than the 'designated areas'.) The American fleet would then be crushed between the 'hammer' of Ozawa's ships and the 'anvil' of land-based air power.

As always, Japanese plans were somewhat complicated and relied upon the enemy doing the right thing. In fact, by that stage of the war the Japanese were no longer capable of 'luring' the Allies anywhere, or of imposing any sort of plan upon them. Toyoda's only hope of success lay in a mistake by Spruance.

For A-GO the Japanese built up their shore-based air power to some 540 aircraft disposed in a great ring from Chichi Jima in the north to New Guinea in the south, with the majority in the south, where an attack would suit the Japanese better, and which they therefore expected would be the most likely place for the Allies to strike.

The same wishful thinking governed their positioning of submarines used, as usual in the Japanese Navy, for scouting rather than direct offence. The Japanese worked out which way the American carriers had gone to attack Hollandia, hoped they would do the same again, therefore expected them to, and placed their submarines accordingly in the 'NA' line, running north-east to south-west some 130 miles north of the Admiralty Islands.

Patient decrypting at FRUPAC and OP-20-G revealed the 'NA' line's position, line of bearing and length, with submarines disposed along it at regular intervals some thirty miles apart. In all, seventeen of the twenty-five Japanese submarines deployed for A-GO were sunk (though not all from the 'NA' line) without themselves sinking a single Allied ship or even making one useful sighting report.

The most astonishing performance along the 'NA' line, and indeed in the whole war against Axis submarines, was put up by the destroyer escort USS *England* (Lt Cdr W. B. Pendleton USN) who sank six Ro-Class submarines in twelve days in May, 1944. Named after an ensign killed in the battleship *Oklahoma* at Pearl Harbor, *England* was a new ship with only some ten weeks' sea experience, but she worked methodically along the line, picking off submarines one by one with her 'Hedgehog' ahead-throwing weapons so successfully that eventually the officer in tactical command of her escort group held her back to give the other ships a chance.

But, when their attacks failed, *England* was called up, moved smoothly in, and nailed the submarine with her Hedgehogs every time. 'Goddammit,' the group commander signalled, 'how do you do it?' *England* replied: 'Personnel and equipment worked with the smoothness of well-oiled clockwork. As a result of our efforts, Recording Angel working overtime checking in Nip submariners joining Honourable Ancestors.' From Washington Admiral King signalled, uncharacteristically, 'There'll always be an *England* in the United States Navy.'

The First Mobile Fleet assembled at Tawitawi, at the western end of the Sulu Archipelago, in May, 1944. There they were well placed for a naval battle in the area chosen by them, and were only 280 miles from the oilfields of Tarakan, whose oil was of such quality that it could be burnt in ships' boilers without refining.

CincPac's daily bulletins continued to report summaries of intelligence on enemy movements and intentions, and particularly any evidence that the Japanese were about to implement the 'Zebra Order'. On 22 May the Bulletin mentioned the indication that a new Cardiv Four was being formed, of the battleships *Hyuga* (flag) and *Ise* which had possibly been converted to carriers. The same bulletin referred to an officer's notebook captured in the Marshalls which had entries 'pertaining to proposed fleet carrier actions and mentions use of a decoy group consisting of one *Taiho* Class carrier plus *Hyuga* and *Ise*.'

The Bulletin for 30 May, 1944, stated: 'Japanese communications Intelligence units throughout central Pacific, in Japan and Kuriles warned on 28 May to have, quote, All in Readiness to join action in present operations, unquote, providing further indication enemy expecting Able Major Blue operation shortly and slightly suggesting Japs preparing for fleet action to counter such a Blue operation.'

In fact, a strong Japanese naval force under Vice Admiral Matome Ugaki had begun to assemble at Batjan in the Moluccas, to carry out Operation A-GO, when, quite suddenly, the whole strategic position for the Japanese was utterly changed by events a thousand miles to the north.

XI

'THE GREAT MARIANAS TURKEY SHOOT'

On 11 June, 1944, 200 Hellcats from TF 58 made a series of fighter sweeps over airfields in the Marianas. The next day two carrier groups attacked Saipan and Tinian while the third struck at Guam. On the 13th seven new battleships under Rear Admiral Lee conducted a heavy but none too accurate bombardment of coastal towns. A much more effective bombardment was carried out the following day by older battleships, some of them restored survivors of Pearl Harbor. The meaning of all this activity suddenly dawned on the Japanese; the Allies were about to assault the Marianas.

For the Japanese this overrode any other consideration. Important atolls in the Gilberts and the Marshalls could be lost. Great fortresses like Rabaul and Truk could, if necessary, be abandoned. But if the Marianas fell, including Saipan, the naval and administrative centre of the Japanese inner defence ring, then the Empire itself was threatened.

The decision to attack the Marianas, with a target date of 15 June, was taken by the Joint Chiefs of Staff as late as 12 March, when the main Allied strategic preoccupation was the imminent invasion of Normandy. But there were three US Marine and two US Army Divisions in the Pacific, and the Fifth Fleet was growing stronger every week – ample resources for another landing.

The four main islands, Guam, Saipan, Tinian and Rota, were centrally placed for further advances west to the Philippines, north-west to Formosa, or north up the Bonin and Volcano Islands to Japan itself. They would provide advanced naval bases and airfields for long-range Superfortress bombing of the Japanese mainland. Last, but not at all least, Guam belonged to the United States.

The Expeditionary Force had some familiar names: Spruance commanded the Fifth Fleet, and Mitscher the fast carriers. Richmond

Kelly Turner, now making his fifth major amphibious operation, commanded the Joint Expeditionary Force, with 'Howlin' Mad' Smith commanding the troops; these two also commanded the Northern Attack Force, of the 2nd and 4th Marine Divisions, mounted in Hawaii and the American West Coast and intended for Saipan and Tinian.

The Southern Attack Force had 'Close In' Conolly and Major General Roy Geiger USMC, with the 3rd Marine Division, mounted in Tulagi and Guadalcanal and aimed at Guam. Admiral Blandy and General Ralph Smith commanded the Floating Reserve, of the 27th US Army Division.

In time and distance and numbers, the scale of the Marianas invasion dwarfed anything that had preceded it in the Pacific. Saipan was more than 3,500 miles from Pearl Harbor, and more than a thousand even from the nearest advanced base at Eniwetok, itself only a coral atoll harbour, to which everything for the assault had to be brought.

The huge distances involved meant that the entire expeditionary force was afloat and on its way at the same time, and the ships concerned were needed for more than three months. But such was the command of sea and air that the Allies had won over such vast areas of the Pacific that the 535 ships for the invasion, carrying or escorting 71,000 troops from Hawaii and another 58,000 from the Solomons, were able to assemble, sail and reach their destinations unharmed. In spite of the gigantic scale of the operation and the short time allowed, Turner set the date of 15 June for Saipan, and the 15th it was. The date for Guam was left open, depending upon events.

Before Operation FORAGER, the invasion of Saipan, Guam and Tinian (Rota was not invaded), JICPOA supplied the Fifth Fleet and the Joint Expeditionary Force with what Holmes called 'literally tons of maps and charts, air target folders, information bulletins, photographs, estimates and translations'.

For an attacker, the Marianas posed all the problems of the coral atolls, and some new ones. Their coasts had the same tidal quirks, coral reefs and shelves. Ashore, the enemy had room for manoeuvre, with mountains at hand and limestone complexes ideal for defence. For the first time the target islands were populated by Japanese and people friendly to the Japanese.

The Saipan garrison, under Lieutenant General Yoshitsugu Saito, consisted of 22,000 soldiers, identified by intelligence as belonging to the 43rd Division and 47th Independent Mixed Brigade. Sinkings by American submarines had greatly reduced the flow of reinforcements to Saipan but the enemy strength was still twice that estimated by intelligence. There were also some 7,000 officers and men of the Japanese Navy, under Nagumo – the same Nagumo of Pearl Harbor, but now demoted to a subordinate position.

Shore defences, gun emplacements and bunkers were nothing like as strong as they had been for the coral atolls, because until 1944 the Japanese had not believed that they would ever have to fortify the Marianas. But the materials were there and, given another three months' construction time, Saipan would have been a much more formidable proposition than it was in June, 1944.

Intelligence about the Marianas was assisted by most informative photo-reconnaissance flights by specially fitted Navy Liberators flying from Eniwetok and by the new Underwater Demolition Teams: expert swimmers, trained to reconnoitre and survey beaches (they actually had black rings, twelve inches apart, painted on their bodies so that they could measure depths of water) and later, covered by naval gun-fire, place underwater demolition charges to blast paths through the coral for the incoming landing craft.

With such assistance, and with the usual massive air cover and bombardment support, the assault troops were in very good heart, being especially cheered by the news of the D-Day landings in Normandy while they were on their way.

When the sun rose on 15 June the people of Saipan looked out in astonishment at the huge fleet which had materialized offshore overnight. Accompanied by naval guns and ground strafing by cannon-firing Hellcats and rocket-bearing Avengers, some 8,000 Marines were ashore in the first twenty minutes and 20,000 troops were on land by nightfall. That night the Japanese counter-attacked with screaming banzai charges and the assault troops had a sleepless time. But the next morning they were still there. At sea, the Navy hoped that the Japanese fleet would come out.

These hopes were on the point of being realized. On 13 June, the day the battlewagons began their pounding of Saipan, Ozawa's First Mobile Fleet sailed from Tawi Tawi, observed and reported as they went by the submarine *Redfin*. Rear Admiral Ugaki, who had taken a force including the two monster battleships *Yamato* and *Musashi* south to assist the hard-pressed army on Biak, was recalled and sailed from Batjan the same day.

Although for the most part Ozawa observed strict radio silence in the conflict to come, the contribution of radio intelligence up to the eve of the battle is well illustrated by the almost eerily accurate forecast in CincPac's intelligence bulletin of 14 June, 1944:

163

'My estimate that Cinc Combined in Empire determined that present Blue activity Marianas was occupation and not a diversional strike. Cinc Combined issued Opords to "Able" Force, Information Naval General Staff but due to separation of Batdiv One Task Group [*Yamato* and *Musashi*] from rest of 1st Mobile Fleet he also issued certain relevant instructions.

'I believe that the former "Zebra Operation Order" of 8 March is in general effect with slight modifications and it is observed that the pattern of Japanese reaction thus far rather closely follows that plan. Estimate Cinc 1st Mobile Fleet sortied with his striking force from Tawi Tawi to fuel near entrance to Surigao Strait to be joined there by Cardiv Two and that the Task Unit under Combatdiv One will fuel either at Davao or at sea and then join the striking force to the east of the Philippines.

'It is possible this first Striking fleet will proceed to a point about 350 miles west or northwest of Saipan where it can utilize shore-based searches and patrols based at Iwo Jima, Yap, Palau, Woleai and Truk also utilizing floatplanes based Ulithi and planes of cruisers and battleships for A/S patrols.

'The decision of the Cinc Combined would probably be required for day surface engagement depend on the situation and efficiency of Jap scouting and reconnaissance. Believe Com 1st Mobile Fleet would have freedom to make night torpedo hit run attack should reconnaissance show such opportunity. Jap carrier strikes would be dependent on situation stressing surprise from flank.

'The movement of 1st Striking Fleet towards Marianas Area is suggested by inclusion of Cinc Central Pacific Area Fleet in two dispatches involving Cinc 1st Mobile Fleet Combatdiv One and Cinc Combined Fleet. However Cinc 1st Air Fleet has not been a direct addressee but suspect his subordinate position to Cinc Central Pacific Area Fleet might account for this.

'Estimating carrier task force departing Tawi Tawi 131000 taking speed 18 knots to arrive Surigao 141300 and allowing 6 hours fuelling period could sortie Surigao at about 141900. Batdiv One Task Unit speed to 140630 position was 20 knots if continued could arrive Davao for fuel at 150200. After 6 hours fuelling can sortie at 8 hours. R/V position unknown but for purpose of estimate placed at 16N 140E (approximate locus of all enemy search coverage).

'At 20 knots Batdiv One Task Unit can R/V at 170930 in above position, carrier force having made 14.5 knots any higher speed by carrier force will increase required speed by Batdiv One. In short consider Jap

164

force of six BBs and 9 carriers with attendant CCs and DDs might be at optimum position approximately 16N 140E by dawn D+2 at earliest. All foregoing are deductions largely based on submarine sightings and traffic analysis with only meager amount of cryptanalysis. In estimating enemy capabilities it may be well to consider possibility his launching a/c at extreme range to land in Marianas after attack.

'US submarine reports Task Force of 6 carriers (with planes aboard) 4 BBs 8 CCs and about 6 DDs in northern Sibutu Passage at 131000 on course 320 speed 18. Cinc Pac ULTRA to Usuals. Estimate carriers this force as Cardivs One and Three, BBs as Batdiv 3 (*Haruna, Kongo*) *Yamashiro* and *Nagato* and CCs as either Crudiv 7 or 4 + *Mogami Yahagi* + 2 CCs of either Crudiv 7 or 4.

'Urgent associations afternoon and evening 13th between enemy naval high commands and probable directives from Cdr 1st Striking Fleet to 1st and 2nd Replenishment forces suggest enemy had reached a decision and Oports were being issued in regard to surface action against Blue force in Marianas.

'Above sub sighting tends to confirm this and further suggests probable passage of Surigao or San Bernardino Straits by above Task forces. Believe Cardiv Two now in Philippine area and will join other Cardivs soon.

'It is known that force consisting of BBs *Musashi* and *Yamato* of Batdiv One along with Crudiv 5 (*Haguro* and *Myoko*) and *Noshiro* (CL) + 5 DDs left Batjan Island (00-38S 127-28E) at 132200 passing through position 01-50N 126-50E at 140600 and thereafter proceeding so as to join 1st Striking Fleet. This R/V position not known but estimated some place between Mindanao and Marianas. Estimate this sudden demand on services of Batdiv One Task Force to the northward will seriously hamper previous Jap plans for reinforcing Biak and other points in West New Guinea area.'

On receiving and assessing this, Spruance concurred that it would be the 17th before the enemy could be in position, so he detached two carrier groups under Rear Admiral 'Jocko' Clark to race 650 miles north-westwards and destroy aircraft at Chichi Jima and Iwo Jima on 15 and 16 June. These aircraft would otherwise have been staged through to reinforce Guam and Saipan.

Ozawa's ships were sighted and reported emerging from the San Bernardino Strait by the submarine *Flying Fish* at 6.35 pm on 15 June. An hour later *Seahorse* sighted Ugaki's battleships steaming north-wards, about 200 miles east-south-east of the Surigao Strait. Also on the 15th a coastwatcher reported three carriers and 17 warships in the Visayan Sea, approaching the San Bernardino Strait, at 10.10 am, and a second coastwatcher reported no less than nine carriers, three battleships, ten cruisers and eleven destroyers emerging from the Strait at 5.30 pm. These sightings were all passed to Spruance by CincPac 'ULTRA to Usuals' Bulletins on 16 and 17 June. So Spruance knew that two enemy forces were heading towards him. But, incredibly, these were the last enemy reports he was to get for a very long time, although a third submarine, *Cavalla*, reported oilers and destroyers early on the 17th.

The Bulletin of 16 June stated: 'Evidence dated 14th that CinC Combined Fleet placed "Able Operations" in effect at 131727 with remark these operations to be decisive. Cincpac estimates Able operations generally similar to Zebra operations translations of which forwarded fleet and type commanders as ATIS [Allied Translator and Interpreter Section, at MacArthur's headquarters] limited translation No. 4.'

It all came to pass as ULTRA had forecast. Ugaki's ships met the First Mobile Fleet at 4 pm on 16 June, about 300 miles east of the Philippines. In battle order, Ozawa had his ships in three groups. A van force commanded by Vice Admiral Takeo Kurita had Cardiv 3, of three light carriers, *Chiyoda*, *Chitose* and *Zuiho*, with 88 aircraft under Rear Admiral Sueo Obayashi, escorted by *Yamato*, *Musashi*, *Haruna* and *Kongo*, four heavy cruisers of Crudiv 4, and destroyers.

This force was some 100 miles ahead of the main fleet, which was in two groups: 'A' Group, under Ozawa himself, with Cardiv 1, of the new carrier *Taiho* (flag), *Shokaku* and *Zuikaku*, carrying 207 aircraft, escorted by cruisers and destroyers; and 'B' Group, under Rear Admiral Takaji Joshima, with Cardiv 2, of *Junyo*, *Hiyo* and the light carrier *Ryuho*, with 135 aircraft, escorted by the battleship *Nagato*, one cruiser and destroyers.

It was hoped that Kurita's van would act as 'bait' and draw the enemy on to the main fleet. If that happened, it would be a climactic moment in the Pacific war, as Ozawa well knew. He made the signal Admiral Togo had made to his fleet before Tsushima nearly forty years earlier: 'The fate of the Empire rests on this one battle. Every man is expected to do his utmost.'

Between Ozawa and Saipan lay Task Force 58, a vast armada thirty-five miles by twenty-five, covering an area of 700 square miles of sea, with seven fleet and six light carriers in four task groups, 965 aircraft, seven battleships, twenty-one cruisers and sixty-nine destroyers. Spruance flew his flag in *Indianapolis*, Mitscher in *Lexington*.

Even at this stage of the war, even such a brilliant employer of air power as Spruance evidently still had a vestigial, almost atavistic, belief in the battleship as the ultimate arbiter of naval battles; a special battle group of seven battleships was formed under Lee. No battleship came within 300 miles of an enemy at any time during the battle, and one carrier task group had to stand by to cover them.

Ozawa had planned his approach carefully so as to elude air search but, in any case, Spruance's fleet was superior to the Japanese in every way except air search, where it was markedly inferior. TF 58's searches and those of land-based aircraft were in general too few, too short and mostly wrongly aimed. But *Cavalla*'s report on 17 June showed that the Japanese were still standing on. Mitscher suggested a night battleship action, with a possible air strike at first light on the 18th. But Lee, possibly with memories of the chaotic night engagements off Guadalcanal, refused.

Much better served by air reconnaissance, Ozawa received two good sighting reports on the afternoon of the 18th, one of the northern end of TF 58 and the other of the southern. Ozawa's plan had always been to make use of his aircrafts' greater striking range by keeping a minimum of 300 miles from his enemy. Now, he made the important decision to steer away to the west and attack the next morning, having his van at 300 and his main body at 400 miles' range from the enemy.

Obayashi in the van force began to launch a strike of 67 aircraft on his own initiative, but on receiving Ozawa's signal of his intention to attack in the morning he cancelled the strike and recalled the aircraft that had taken off. This was a chance lost. A strike then, arriving at dusk, might well have caught TF 58 off guard and done some damage.

That evening, 18 June, Ozawa broke radio silence for the first time to alert the airfields on Guam. The signal was picked up by direction-finders and FRUPAC sent Spruance an accurate position, putting the Japanese fleet some 350 miles west-south-west of him.

Spruance, then steering east, might have turned back. Mitscher thought he should have turned back. Mitscher suggested TF 58 steam to the westward so as to be ready for a strike early on the 19th. Spruance thought about the suggestion for over an hour and then rejected it. His orders were to capture, occupy and defend Saipan and he allowed nothing, neither the prospect of defeating the Japanese fleet nor the fear of being 'shuttle-bombed' by Japanese carrier aircraft which could attack his ships and then land ashore to rearm and refuel, to deflect him from that main purpose. He had always in his mind the possibility of an outflanking 'end run' by Ozawa.

Ironically, a search aircraft from Saipan obtained a radar contact early the next morning which confirmed the direction-finder's estimate of the Japanese fleet's position. The report was not received in *Indianapolis* for some eight hours but, even had Spruance received it earlier, he very probably would have acted no differently.

For one reason or another, none of the US air searches found the Japanese fleet and when 19 June dawned Spruance still had only the stale submarine and D/F reports of where his enemy lay. But, as it happened, he had TF 58 perfectly positioned to take the Japanese onslaught which sporadic air activity on the night of 18/19 June showed could not be far off.

The day's action began with fighter sweeps over Guam, Rota, Tinian and Saipan, in which Japanese aircraft on the ground were shot up and aircraft in the air, some of them reinforcements from Truk, were shot down. With the losses already suffered, the Japanese 'anvil', on which they had placed such hopes, was shattered before the main battle had opened. (Jocko Clark's strikes, and the belief that Mitscher would attack Yap or the Palaus, had in any case caused the Japanese to bring fewer aircraft to the Marianas.)

Ozawa began flying off searches at 4.45 am, well before dawn. Some were shot down, but Ozawa soon had reports of part of TF 58's great array of ships. By 8.30 Obayashi was flying off the first Japanese strike of the day: 45 Zekes with bombs, eight Jills with torpedoes, escorted by sixteen Zekes, which were detected by radar at about 150 miles range. The attacking aircraft were accompanied – shepherded – by a co-ordinator who, at a range of about 70 miles, assigned targets to the strike and generally lectured the pilots, who were apparently inexperienced, on how to attack.

For FORAGER, RI Units were embarked in *Indianapolis*, *Lexington*, *Hornet* and *Yorktown*. *Lexington*'s usual RI officer, Lt(jg) Charles A. Sims, picked up the co-ordinator's frequency and relayed his instructions to the fighter direction officers. With such long-range radar detection, the co-ordinator's detailed instructions, and the delay he caused while he imparted them to his charges, TF 58's fighter direction officers had ample time and scope to deploy the Hellcats, who were thus given space and height enough to intercept.

The Hellcat pilots were experienced men who had been flying for two years and had more than 300 hours. According to them, their opponents were mostly greenhorns, with a few old hands as stiffening. These were not the hardened veterans of Nagumo's day. The raw crews broke their formations prematurely, forfeiting precious collective security, made elementary errors in formation flying, fell for the simplest attacking ruses, and, worst of all, failed to press home or co-ordinate their attacks properly. It was not a contest but a massacre. Only twenty-four of the raid survived, having scored one bomb hit on *South Dakota*.

It was suggested in *Lexington* that 'Co-ordinator Joe', as he had been nicknamed, also be shot down, but wiser counsels prevailed. *Lexington*'s fighter directors then had the tricky task of warning pilots in the air to leave Joe alone, without revealing to the enemy that they knew Joe was there.

The second strike was a big one, of 53 Judy bombers, 27 Jill torpedo-bombers and 48 Zekes, launched from Ozawa's own division of large carriers at 9 am. As the flagship *Taiho* was steaming up into the wind to launch aircraft, she was hit by one of six torpedoes fired by the submarine *Albacore*. No serious damage appeared to have been done and *Taiho*'s speed was only reduced by one knot.

Eight of the strike returned prematurely, and two were shot down by 'friendly' fire as they flew over Kurita's ships. The remainder had an even hotter reception over TF 58. Although one or two of the carriers were near-missed and a torpedo-bomber crashed onto the battleship *Indiana*, fortunately without exploding its torpedo, 97 of the aircraft in this raid never returned to their carriers.

As *Shokaku* was landing on the pitifully few survivors of her air group, she herself was hit by three torpedoes from *Cavalla*. *Shokaku* fell out of line and began to lose power. Explosions started fires which, as in her predecessors at Midway, were spread by petrol. Just after 3 pm a bomb magazine exploded, tearing *Shokaku* apart.

Shokaku was quickly followed by *Taiho*. That single torpedo had damaged her petrol tanks and the vapour was spread throughout the ship by an inexperienced damage control officer opening up ship's ventilation. Fumes from the crude Tarakan fuel were added to the petrol. Very soon *Taiho* was a giant petrol bomb awaiting a spark. It came just after 3.30 pm with an explosion which lifted the armoured flight deck and blew out the hangar sides and the very hull-plates in the bottom of the ship. Ozawa and the Emperor's portrait were transferred to a destroyer and then to the cruiser *Haguro*. Only about 500 of *Taiho*'s crew of 2,150 were saved.

The third raid of 25 Zekes with bombs, seven Jills and fifteen escort Zekes was flown off from *Junyo* and *Hiyo* at 10 am. They were directed by Co-ordinator Joe to a false sighting position and, fortunately for them, missed TF 58. Only about a dozen of them were engaged and seven were shot down.

The fourth and last strike, another big one of 30 Zekes, nine Judys, 27 Vals, six Jills and ten Zeke fighter-bombers, began taking off from *Junyo*, *Hiyo*, *Ryuho* and *Zuikaku* at 11 am. With Co-ordinator Joe once more in charge, they first flew to a phantom contact southwest of Guam and then turned north.

Once again the interpretative skills of TF 58's fighter direction teams matched the aggressive flying of the Hellcat pilots. Six Judys who attacked one carrier group did no damage and all except one were shot down. Eighteen more aircraft were intercepted by Hellcats and only half survived. Forty-nine remnants, trying to land on Guam, were caught by twenty-seven Hellcats from *Essex*, *Hornet* and the light carrier *Cowpens* and thirty of them were shot down. Another nineteen were lost operationally and in deck-landing crashes. So only nine of the 82 on that strike ever returned and none of them had done any damage to TF 58.

There had been at least two 'Co-ordinator Joes' during the day, relieving each other when their fuel ran low, but TF 58's fighter direction teams had a mental image of just one. Whoever he was, he continued to provide priceless information on when and where strikes were coming in. When Joe finally signed off after the fourth strike and started for home, eager voices asked, 'Can we go get him now?' But Mitscher said 'No indeed! He did us too much good!' So, as the American naval historian Samuel Eliot Morison wrote, 'Little Joe flew home, proud of having done his duty to his Emperor, and followed by the blessings of American fighter-directors.'

However the official US Navy account, *The Employment of Mobile Radio Intelligence Units by Commands Afloat During WWII*, declassified in 1981, says of the RI Units in FORAGER, including Sims in *Lexington*, 'Most of the Japanese planes were shot down 50-75 miles from the U.S. force. This may account for the RIU not being able to hear any radio telephone or VHF. Most communications were encoded, and RI units were disappointed in the amount of information on specific tactical activity they could provide without the code.'

Throughout the day a fighter sweep from *Yorktown* patrolled Guam, and TF 58's bombers, which had flown off to keep clear, raided airfields on all the islands, bombing cripples and generally keeping the enemy quiescent.

After one sortie that day, a fighter pilot at debriefing told the air intelligence officer, 'Why hell, it was just like an old-time turkey shoot down home!' The apt description stuck and that day's hectic eight and a half hours' battle over the Philippine Sea became known as 'the Great Marianas Turkey Shoot'. Ozawa had lost two carriers and 346 aircraft. TF 58 had lost thirty aircraft and suffered hits on *Indiana* and *South Dakota*. If the Coral Sea had been a battle in which no ship sighted an enemy ship, then the 'Turkey Shoot' was the day the US Navy scored a great victory without one ship or aircraft sighting an enemy ship.

The victory might have been greater, for at this point an opportunity was lost. Incredibly, TF 58 flew no searches that night of 19/20 June. Possibly Mitscher thought his aircrews had done enough for one day, or conceivably there was some lingering 'mental block' in the carrier groups about night-flying. As it was, the first search flight at 5.30 next morning fell some 75 miles short of Ozawa's ships, which were milling about and preparing to fuel for another day's operations.

For Ozawa had by no means given up. Huddled with his staff in a cramped cabin under *Haguro*'s bridge, and with only her limited communications systems at his disposal, he still had no clear idea of what had happened. He knew he had lost two carriers and many of the aircraft had not returned, but they had probably landed on Guam for the night. Vice Admiral Kakuta, commanding the base air force in the Marianas from Tinian, constantly under-reported his losses. Even when Ozawa shifted his flag to *Zuikaku* he was still unaware, as Yamamoto had been at Midway, of the catastrophe which had befallen the Japanese Navy.

There was worse to come. Ozawa's ships were sighted at last at 4 pm on 20 June. This was the first sighting of the enemy by a TF 58 aircraft in the whole battle. The range was 275 miles. Dusk was at 7 pm. It was very late, but not too late. Mitscher decided on an all-out strike. A full deckload – 85 Hellcats, 77 Helldivers and 54 torpedo-Avengers from *Hornet*, *Yorktown*, *Bunker Hill*, *Wasp*, *Enterprise*, *Belleau Wood*, *Bataan*, *Monterey*, *Cabot* and *San Jacinto* – was launched in the astonishing time of ten minutes.

There was no time for the niceties of co-ordinating attacks. The strike had to get in and out again before darkness fell. In such hurried circumstances they did very well, sinking the light carrier *Hiyo*, damaging *Chiyoda* with one bomb hit and sinking two tankers.

The resistance put up by Ozawa's combat air patrol (CAP) confirmed the Hellcat pilots' suspicions that only the greenhorns had been chopped down over TF 58 and the veterans had survived. But, with further losses, Ozawa had only thirty operational aircraft left at the end of the day, out of the 450 with which he had begun the battle. After ordering Kurita to carry out a surface engagement, and then cancelling the order, Ozawa recognized defeat and, like Yamamoto, turned for home. On the way he composed a letter of resignation (which Toyoda did not accept).

Complete darkness had fallen before TF 58's aircraft returned to their carriers. Every carrier and every ship in the screen turned on masthead lights, deck lighting and red and green navigation lights and flashed signalling lamps until, as one pilot said, the fleet looked like 'a Mardi Gras setting fantastically out of place here, midway between the Marianas and the Philippines'.

Recovery took two hours. Aircraft ran out of fuel yards away from their carriers and landed in the sea. Others landed on where they could, on the wrong carriers or even on carriers which tried desperately to wave them off because their deck was cluttered. Many ditched aircrews were picked up the next day and on subsequent days. TF 58 lost 130 aircraft on 19 and 20 June and 76 aircrew, compared with Japanese losses of 476 aircraft and about 445 aircrew.

Spruance began a stern chase that evening but it was soon obvious that the enemy was outdistancing him and he called off the chase at 8.20 pm on 21 June. The invasion of Saipan could now go on without interruption and the island was secured on 9 July after a bitter campaign. General Saito committed suicide, as did Admiral Nagumo. The victor of Pearl Harbor, and the man who had taken Japanese arms across the world from Hawaii to the shores of India, shot himself in a cave and was buried in an unmarked grave.

Tinian was invaded, after days of heavy bombardment, on 24 July and secured by 2 August, although mopping up of small parties went on for months. The date for the Guam invasion had been postponed when Spruance heard of the approach of the Japanese fleet on 16 June. It finally took place, after thirteen days' bombardment, on 21 July and the island was recovered by 12 August (although isolated Japanese soldiers, who had not heard of the surrender, were still emerging on Guam into the 1970s).

The successes of *Cavalla* and *Albacore* were not known for some time and there was disappointment at Pearl Harbor over the outcome of the battle. Spruance was criticized for not taking the offensive on 18 June or chasing more vigorously on the 20th. Eventually even Spruance himself seems to have been persuaded that somehow the battle had not been conclusive.

In fact, by staying on the defensive on the 19th and letting the enemy come to him, Spruance had won a smashing victory. In Spruance's hand the Hellcat fighter had been a trump card. Once again ULTRA had played its part in a victory where it could be said that the Japanese had not only been outfought but outthought. It was true that some Japanese carriers had escaped, but they were neutered animals without their aircrews. The Japanese carriers were never a force again and the next time they were used in battle it was only as almost impotent bait.

XII

THE EASTERN FLEET –
IN THE SHADOW OF LEYTE GULF

WHEN Nagumo's carriers threatened Ceylon in 1942, the FECB moved again, from Colombo to Kilindini, the naval base at Mombasa in East Africa. The cryptanalytical unit attached to the Chief of Intelligence Staff (COIS), Eastern Fleet, was housed in HMS *Alidina*, a requisitioned Indian school in Alidina on the rocky northern shore of Kilindini where, as Hugh Denham, one of the linguists who served there wrote, 'The "front line" of the unit were the wireless operators who intercepted the enemy messages; then the analysts and their staff stripped off the additive keys; the linguists established the meanings of the code-groups and translated the texts for prompt reporting to COIS at NHQ. At the end of each day we went round to the back of the building and supervised the incineration of the secret waste.

'It was a coherent operation, in a way self-contained, although of course, as the Japanese code-books and key-tables began to change more rapidly, it was dependent on the results exported from the large, vigorous party at Washington – normally referred to by us by its cover-name, Susan. However, although our cryptanalytic contribution was eclipsed in quantity by that of Susan, we felt that our recoveries of additives, code-group meanings etc were not insignificant and we prided ourselves on their quality.'

Alidina pulled off a notable coup in November, 1942, when one of their cryptanalysts, Brian Townend, broke into JN-40, the merchant shipping code of four-syllable kana groups, used to report attacks on Allied submarines or aircraft and often revealing the detailed routes of convoys and the identity of some of the vessels in them. The messages usually followed a common pattern: latitude, longitude, ship's number, name (—— Maru) and cargo in November, 1942. It was solved from a situation which normally occurred only in text books. The Japanese sent a message that left out an easting and northing from the plain text. They then re-enciphered the correct complete text using the same keys. Comparison of the two cipher messages enabled the deciphering method to be diagnosed and solved.

One section of *Alidina* worked on JN-40 and another on JN-14, a four-digit reciphered naval code, which sometimes revealed coastal vessel movements and also major fleet movements. But the main effort was directed against the main code, JN-25. 'We worked in one of the big schoolrooms,' said Denham, 'and we spread the additive sheets, the texts and the indexes out on huge laboratory tables which we pushed together into the centre of the room. With regard to the translated decrypts which went to COIS, we scrupulously distinguished between what we could categorically guarantee and words or passages where there was an element of doubt – perhaps because of garbled intercept (the bulk of a decrypt) or uncertain code-group meanings. Nor were garbled texts the only bane of life at *Alidina*. There were so many power cuts at Mombasa that they had a saying "Power corrupts. Auxiliary power corrupts absolutely".'

In August, 1943, FECB moved back to Colombo, to HMS *Anderson*, for the rest of the war. *Anderson* – a collection of single storey buildings surmounted by numerous large radio antennae, on the southern outskirts of the city, near the race course and a couple of miles from the sea – was the control centre of an extensive communications intelligence intercept and tracking organization. Its main task was the interception of Japanese radio traffic. It was the hub of a wide network of direction-finding stations spread around the Far East. There were sections – from March, 1944, manned 24-hours a day, seven days a week, 365 days a year – for cryptanalysis, including Japanese naval air codes; radio monitoring; direction-finding; traffic analysis; 'fingerprinting' of individual radio operators; and REB, said to stand for 'Radio Elimination of Bloodstains', when the received carrier waveform, showing the unique radio 'signature' of a transmitter, was displayed on a cathode ray tube or oscilloscope and then photographed.

Throughout 1943 the Eastern Fleet had been the 'Orphan Annie' of the Navy, neglected and starved of ships. Consequently it was a quiet year operationally, indeed so quiet that the Americans, and especially Admiral King, accused the British, with some justification, of not pulling their weight in the Far East.

But with the turn of the new year of 1944 reinforcements began to arrive from other stations. In January the Admiralty planned to send a total of 146 ships to join the Eastern Fleet in the next four months. On 27 January Vice Admiral Sir Arthur John Power, commanding the 1st Battle Squadron and Flag Officer Second in Command, Eastern Fleet, arrived in Ceylon with the battle-cruiser *Renown*, the battleships *Valiant* and *Queen Elizabeth*, the fleet aircraft carrier *Illustrious* and the repair carrier *Unicorn*, which was temporarily used as an operational carrier because of the shortage of aircraft carriers on the station.

There was also a shortage of destroyers. The Eastern Fleet did not have enough to escort both the Indian Ocean convoys and the fleet itself. The convoys had priority. It was not until April, when the fleet had been reinforced by more destroyers, the escort carriers *Shah* and *Begum*, the French battleship *Richelieu* and most important of all, by the US carrier *Saratoga* and three American destroyers, that Admiral Sir James Somerville was able to attempt an offensive sortie against the Japanese.

The Eastern Fleet's operations in 1944 were a kind of muted accompaniment in a minor key to the great themes of the Pacific. Operations were timed to have a distracting effect, in the hope that the Japanese would divert forces to the Indian Ocean.

Thus Operation COCKPIT, on 19 April, 1944, was intended to pin down Japanese air and surface forces in the Singapore area while MacArthur's landing at Hollandia took place. Aircraft from *Illustrious* and *Saratoga* attacked the harbour and oil storage tanks at Sabang, an island off the north coast of Sumatra.

On 17 May, shortly before *Saratoga* and her escorts returned to the United States, a second strike (Operation TRANSOM) was carried out, on the Wonokrono oil refinery and the harbour of Surabaya in Java. The enemy appeared either indifferent or taken by surprise and neither strike met much opposition.

Part of the credit for this can be taken by *Anderson* who devised W/T deception plans for the operations, and provided from ULTRA-based intelligence 'Eastern Fleet Special Summaries' on U-boats in the Indian Ocean, and Japanese naval forces, major fleet units, and air strengths in South-East Asia and the Netherlands East Indies.

For TRANSOM, for instance, the W/T deception plan, dated 28 April, 1944, as promulgated to the fleet was: 'The C-in-C intends to simulate by W/T Deception that the Fleet is returning and later has returned to harbour.

'2. The Fleet sails from Trinco on 7 May and the above deception plan will be carried out on 11 May.

'3. After inference of 3 days in harbour, it will be indicated that the

Fleet has sailed again and the attached Deception Plan implementation in (c) and (d) will be laid on.

'*Scenario*. On "D" Day of TRANSOM an air strike against Port Blair from carrier-borne aircraft will be indicated. Note: This fits in with the enemy's recent reactions (ULTRA 1 0101 24th April para. 8).

'*Story*. We shall tell the enemy that, owing to Bombay disaster [the freighter *Fort Stikine*, loaded with cotton and ammunition, had caught fire and blown up in Bombay harbour on 14 April, causing immense damage and loss of life] and loss of landing craft and equipment, the landing troops who had been training in Ceylon for a raid on the Andamans cannot now be used. CinC EF, however, was so well satisfied with Sabang that he intends a similar strike against Port Blair, mid May.

'*Implementation*.

(a) We can pass this over quickly through certain channels which have already been building up something in this direction.

(b) Fleet W/T cannot assist as no ships will be available.

(c) RAF should be asked to assist by an aircraft making fictitious sighting report on D-1 in a position 10°N 87°E.

(d) RAF should also be asked to carry out an actual strike on Port Blair on "D" Day, if possible using a proportion of US planes.'

Also for TRANSOM, Cdr W. Bruce Keith RN, a Japanese linguist, who was in charge of the cryptanalysis section of *Anderson*, distributed a surprisingly detailed information sheet about Japanese cyphers to ULTRA-indoctrinated officers in the fleet before the operation. Headed 'Anderson W/T Station' and dated 4 May, 1944, it was classified 'Top Secret':

'*Main Cypher (JN25)*

'Disregarding the very high grade tables in which there is little traffic, there are two recyphering tables which carry about ¼ and ¾ of this traffic. The less used table is the more secret one and contains operational orders to major Warship and Air Units, messages to and from Submarines etc. and can be regarded as "Flag Officers' Table".

'The other table is used mainly for administrative and convoy messages and can be roughly called a "General Table".

'The traffic in the "Flag Officers Table" is too meagre to produce results except on lucky occasions. These normally will not be current messages.

'The last three changes in tables have occurred after their being in use for only 3 weeks. Messages were readable currently for about the last week.

'The present table came into force on 1st May. There is still some doubt as to whether this is a normal change and Washington appears to think that there is some added complication. If this is correct we will not be able to read current messages at the end of 2 weeks. It is not possible to say more at this stage.

'The underlying book, as far as we can say at the moment, has not changed, having come into force on 10th January. It is probable that it will remain in force for about another 6 weeks.

'*Minor Cyphers*

'JN11 (Merchant Ship Liaison Cypher). Code book and cypher table changed on 1st April 1944 – not yet readable.

'JN40 (Merchant Ship Code, Enemy Submarine Warnings). Readable currently until 15 May when it is due to change.

'JN163 and 183 – Reporting Codes, both readable.

'JN14 – Operational Reporting Code – changed 1st May – not readable.

'JN147 – Operational Reporting Code – just beginning to be read.

'*Air/Ground Operation Code* (JN166)

'Current version has been in force for a few days. Reasonable prospect of being able to read some messages within the next ten days.

'*Met. Code* (JN36)

'In production and translations increasing. No change expected.

'*W/T "I"*

'All call signs are identifiable.

'*Summary*

'It is impossible to say what messages will be sent or whether they will be read, but a generalisation can be made.

'If our forces are sighted, sighting reports will be made and broadcast over many lines. Some of them we will be able to read and to report to Commander-in-Chief.

'We may be able to supply other information but owing to state of cyphers this should not be relied on.

'Weather reports should be available.

'Information from W/T "I" should be available.

W. Bruce Keith.'

Similar intelligence summaries and forecasts were provided by *Anderson* for Operations PEDAL in June and CRIMSON in July, 1944.

Admiral King had asked again for more effort in the Andamans-Malay area, to help the US Pacific fleet by keeping pressure on the Japanese. While the climactic battle of the Philippine Sea was fought, the Eastern Fleet did their best to divert Japanese effort in PEDAL, a carrier air strike at Port Blair in the Andamans.

Two more fleet aircraft carriers, *Victorious* and *Formidable*, joined the fleet in July and on the 22nd Admiral Somerville led a considerable force (for the Eastern Fleet) of two battleships, one battlecruiser, the two carriers, seven cruisers and ten destroyers for CRIMSON, a second and more ambitious attack on Sabang, which in the event was 'James' Farewell Party'. Sir James had his 62nd birthday on 17 July and CRIMSON provided satisfactory festivities: the capital ships bombarded the harbour, while aircraft from *Illustrious* and *Formidable* attacked airfields and the destroyers steamed off the harbour entrance, firing guns and torpedoes at close range in a most spectacular manner. Somerville was relieved as C-in-C Eastern Fleet by Admiral Sir Bruce Fraser on 22 August.

After the battle of the Philippine Sea in June, 1944, there was a major change in the command of the Pacific Fleet. Halsey relinquished command of the South Pacific Force and Area and in September relieved Spruance. Thereafter he, as Commander Third Fleet, and Spruance, as Commander Fifth Fleet, alternately commanded the Pacific Fleet. While Halsey and his staff were at sea, Spruance and his staff were ashore, planning the next operation, and vice versa. The ships of the Third and Fifth Fleets were the same; only the fleet commanders and their staffs changed. So too did the numerals of the various task forces and groups. Thus, the Fast Carrier Task Force was Task Force 58 under Spruance, Task Force 38 under Halsey.

Early in September, 1944, to support forthcoming landings in the Moluccas and the Palaus, aircraft of the Third Fleet under Halsey carried out strikes on Yap, the Palaus, Mindanao and, on 12-14 September, the central Philippine islands.

The latter strikes met startlingly feeble opposition. Some two hundred enemy aircraft were destroyed and several ships sunk, for the loss of eight aircraft from TF38. Halsey, excited and convinced that the central Philippines were just 'a hollow shell with weak defenses and skimpy facilities', urgently suggested to Nimitz that the planned assaults on Yap and the Palaus be cancelled and all Allied forces be concentrated for an assault on Leyte as early as possible.

In fact, the weakness of the Japanese defence was due to a planned withdrawal of their resources, until the Allies were plainly committed to a major offensive in the Philippines. Nimitz agreed to bypass Yap, but insisted on the landings in the Palaus.

One of the intelligence bonuses from the capture of the Marianas was the delivery at JICPOA in Pearl Harbor of fifty tons of captured Japanese documents, amongst them the Japanese order of battle in the Palaus, as of 8 June, 1944. This information was amplified and confirmed by a message of 28 July from the staff of the Japanese 14th Division to Tokyo, partially decrypted by 5 August and fully available on the 17th, giving the complete detailed disposition of the garrisons, unit by unit, on the larger Palau island of Babelthuap, and the three islands of Peleliu and Angaur (which were chosen for the assault) and Koror, as well as the garrison on Yap.

After the familiar and practised overture of air strike and bombardment by the Fast Carrier Task Force, the 1st US Marine Division landed on Peleliu, 470 miles east of Mindanao, on 15 September, for a campaign which, it was thought, should last four days.

ULTRA could accurately forecast the garrison strength of 10,000 men, including the 14th Division, but could not reveal the nature of the island's terrain. Submarine and aerial reconnaissance provided reasonable information about the beaches but almost nothing about the interior (JICPOA had been unable even to find anybody who had ever been to the Palaus, and nothing of any relevance had been written about them for over a century).

The Japanese were ensconced in natural caves and strong interlocking fortifications and, abandoning their usual tactic of 'annihilation of the enemy at the beach' in favour of stubborn defence in depth, they put up as bitter a resistance as anywhere in the Pacific. By the time organized resistance on Peleliu ended on 25 November, the Palaus had cost nearly 2,000 American casualties killed and over 8,000 wounded, most of them on Peleliu. The island was not finally cleared of Japanese until early in 1945. Angaur fell in three days and the neighbouring atoll of Ulithi, which had been abandoned by the enemy, was taken on 23 September without opposition.

Ulithi lagoon was a superb natural harbour, which quickly became the Third Fleet's main advanced base, but Peleliu proved to be of very limited strategic value. The costly assault on it was unnecessary and one of Nimitz's rare mistakes.

Meanwhile, MacArthur's forces in the South-West Pacific by-passed the strong Japanese garrison in Halmahera, in the Moluccas, and landed virtually unopposed on the more northerly island of Morotai. Thus by the beginning of October, 1944, the Allies held an inner ring of islands running from the Marianas, south and west to the Moluccas, and were in an excellent position to launch an attack on the Philippines.

While these events were taking place, the Eastern Fleet carried out diversionary operations in the Indian Ocean, attempting to distract Japanese attention and forces away from the Pacific. In September, to coincide with the Peleliu and Morotai landings, the carriers *Victorious* and *Indomitable* sailed from Trincomalee to attack the port of Sigli in northern Sumatra (Operation LIGHT). On 17 and 19 October, the eve of the Leyte landings, Admiral Power himself sailed with the main Eastern Fleet to carry out a series of air strikes and bombardments on the Nicobar (Operation MILLET) and Andaman (Operation MILLER) Islands. *Anderson* picked up Japanese radio reaction to these operations, which was also noted in CincPac Bulletins, but the Japanese diverted neither attention nor resources away from the Pacific as a result.

Events in the Pacific now hurried towards the largest battle in naval history, the second of that year in the Philippine Sea, known as the Battle of Leyte Gulf, although it was in fact four separate major engagements.

The Joint Chiefs of Staff, at the Quebec Conference, considered the implications of Halsey's news of weak Japanese reactions. The landings at Yap, the Talauds and Mindanao were cancelled. Nimitz and MacArthur were ordered to join forces for a landing at Leyte on 20 October, two months before the date originally set for the invasion of the Philippines. Such was the flexibility of the Allies' planning, and so wide the options open to them, that the 24th Army Corps, then actually embarked for the Yap assault, was diverted to Manus in the Admiralty Islands to join MacArthur's force for Leyte.

After Leyte, an invasion of Luzon was inevitable, and indeed the Chiefs of Staff ordered MacArthur, in a directive of 3 October, to invade Luzon on a target date of 20 December, 1944, and then to support Nimitz's subsequent invasion of the Ryukyus. Nimitz, similarly, was ordered to support MacArthur's operations in Luzon, occupy an island in the Bonins, with a target date of 20 January, 1945, and an island in the Ryukyus, with a target date of 1 March, 1945. Thus the long argument between the 'Army' and the 'Navy' plans was finally resolved by the pace and pressure of events. But, even now, Roosevelt did not appoint one man, either MacArthur or Nimitz, as supreme commander in the Pacific. This divided command was to have serious results off Leyte.

On 10 October, 1944, TF 38's fifteen carriers began preliminary strikes in support of the Leyte landings. The attacks were so widespread, from the Ryukyus down to the northern Philippines, and so heavy, with up to a thousand aircraft taking part, that the Japanese were convinced that the main assault was underway.

This belief was strengthened on Friday 13 October, south of Formosa, when Japanese aircraft penetrated TF 38's screen and hit the heavy cruiser USS *Canberra* with one torpedo. The next day they scored another hit, on the light cruiser *Houston*.

Returning Japanese aircrew vastly overestimated their successes, claiming to have sunk two American battleships and eleven carriers, damaged another eight carriers and two more battleships and sunk or damaged many other ships. Tokyo Radio triumphantly announced the sinking of nineteen carriers (more than TF 38 actually had) and the Emperor ordered a mass celebration for the 'Victory of Taiwan'.

ULTRA provided proof that the Japanese High Command really did believe most of the claims. An intercept of a message of 17 October from the Chief of the Japanese General Staff claimed the destruction of ten carriers and damage to three more. Vice Admiral Shima, with the heavy cruisers *Nachi* and *Ashigara*, and destroyer escort, was sent to mop up the 'cripples'.

In fact, Halsey was using the two damaged cruisers as 'bait'. Shima realized this and withdrew in time. By notable seamanship and damage control, the two badly damaged ships were towed clear to Ulithi. On 19 October Nimitz countered Japanese propaganda with the joyful message that 'Admiral Halsey is now retiring towards the enemy following the salvage of all the Third Fleet ships recently reported sunk by Tokyo Radio'.

The loss of the Philippines would effectively cut Japan off from the resources of the Dutch East Indies and Malaya. The Japanese had a plan – codenamed SHO-GO – for the defence of the Philippines which Admiral Toyoda, in Tokyo, prematurely activated. He committed hundreds of land-based and naval aircraft to the Philippines, where they were severely mauled by TF 38's aircraft. The Japanese lost some 500 aircraft in trying to stop an invasion which had not yet begun.

However, that invasion was imminent. In the early hours of 20 October, 1944, after a two-day bombardment, the first assault troops went ashore on Leyte beaches, meeting very slight opposition. The Japanese Navy first heard of the invasion force on the 17th and put into operation their own part of SHO, which as usual had a complicated command structure involving several detached forces – and a decoy.

Considering the scale of the battle, Leyte Gulf was comparatively little influenced by ULTRA. Unlike Midway, there was no uncertainty about the enemy's ultimate intention. Once it had been established that the Japanese fleet had sailed, their objective was obvious. They must surely try to attack the landing forces at Leyte, and must emerge through either the San Bernardino or the Surigao Strait, or both, to do so.

Radio intelligence, largely traffic analysis, had already revealed that the surviving heavy ships of the Japanese Navy were mostly based at Singapore, because it was nearer their fuel supplies and because Truk had been made unusable as a base, while the surviving carriers were based in Japan, attempting in home waters to train up fresh air groups to replace those massacred in the Philippine Sea in June. This training was nowhere near complete when SHO-GO began.

Radio intelligence again disclosed that Vice Admiral Takeo Kurita sailed from Lingga Roads, off Singapore, with the First Striking Force, on 18 October, and called at Brunei on 22nd to refuel. After leaving Brunei this force split into two. Kurita's Force 'A' (known to the Allies as Centre Force) was itself in two sections; the first, under Kurita himself, with the battleships *Yamato*, *Musashi* and *Nagato*, six heavy cruisers with Kurita flying his flag in *Atago*, the light cruiser *Noshiro* and nine destroyers; the second, under Vice Admiral Yoshio Suzuki, with the battleships *Kongo* and *Haruna*, four heavy cruisers, the light cruiser *Yahagi* and six destroyers.

Both these sections headed for the Sibuyan Sea and, ultimately, the San Bernardino Strait. Force 'C' (Southern Force) under Vice Admiral Shoji Nishimura, with the battleships *Yamashiro* and *Fuso*, the heavy cruiser *Mogami* and three destroyers, headed for the Surigao Strait. Nishimura was to have been reinforced by Shima's two heavy cruisers, but Shima was to act independently, and the two forces in fact never met.

At the same time Ozawa's main body (Northern Force) sailed from Japan with four carriers, *Zuikaku*, *Zuiho*, *Chitose* and *Chiyoda*, two hybrid battleship/carriers *Ise* and *Hyuga*, three light cruisers, nine destroyers, some escort vessels and oilers. But Ozawa's was only a shadow force. The four carriers had just 116 aircraft between them, less than half their normal strength, and the two hybrids had none at all. Ozawa was sailing on a voyage of self-sacrifice, offering his ships as live bait, in the hope of drawing Halsey's carriers away from Leyte

Gulf whilst the Japanese capital ships penetrated the Philippine archipelago, Kurita through the San Bernardino, Nishimura and Shima through the Surigao, to emerge on the eastern side like the two claws of a giant pincer and crush the Leyte troop anchorages. This time their opponent was not Spruance but Halsey. This time the bait was taken.

Halsey, flying his flag in *New Jersey*, had spent much of 24 October wondering where Ozawa's carriers were. He was sure they were at sea somewhere to the north. Honour, past frustrations, his own reputation as 'scourge of the Japs', his criticism of what he called Spruance's failure to get the Jap carriers in the Philippine Sea, all made Halsey give the Japanese carriers priority as targets. To a certain extent he was obsessed by them, so their destruction tended to blot out all other considerations from his mind.

Ise and *Hyuga*, whom Ozawa had pushed forward, were sighted at 2.20 pm and the main body an hour later. Now, at last, Halsey had the information he wanted. He was no man to sit idly by, watching what he called the 'rathole' of the San Bernardino, hoping his enemy would come out, when his main opponent had been sighted.

Misled by over-optimistic aircrew reports, Halsey believed that Kurita could no longer be a danger after the hammering he had received. That evening of the 24th Halsey led three carrier groups, with all their battleships, cruisers and destroyers, 67 ships in all, away to the north at 16 knots.

Lee and Admiral Bogan, commanding one of the carrier task groups, both signalled their misgivings but were ignored. Two intelligence officers on board *New Jersey* later told Holmes that they had produced documents to support their opinion that the Third Fleet was being enticed away from its position covering the San Bernardino, but nobody would listen to them. Halsey and the Third Fleet staff seemed determined that night to reject any facts that might discourage pursuit of the Japanese carriers. So Halsey set off to engage Ozawa. Not one ship, not even a destroyer, was left to guard the San Bernardino.

At Leyte the misunderstandings inherent in a divided command – with Halsey responsible to Nimitz and Kinkaid to MacArthur – were compounded by faults in communication. On the afternoon of the 24th Halsey had signalled to his ships that he was going to form a Task Force 34 of four battleships, with cruisers and destroyers, under Lee, which would 'engage decisively at long ranges' whilst the carriers kept clear. King and Nimitz were information addressees of the signal and Kinkaid's staff intercepted it and showed it to him.

So, when Halsey signalled that evening that he was proceeding north with three groups 'to attack enemy carrier force at dawn', King, Nimitz and Kinkaid were all reassured that the powerful surface force had been formed and left on guard. None of them dreamed that Halsey's TF 34 remained an intention and not a reality. Even Mitscher, when woken and asked his opinion, said he was sure Halsey had the situation under control and went back to sleep.

Had a supreme commander been appointed for the Pacific, such misunderstandings would have been inconceivable. As it was, although only one destroyer of Nishimura's force survived after battles in the Surigao Strait on 24-25 October, Kurita's force, the other claw of the pincer, was by no means crippled. Flying his flag in *Yamato* (*Atago* had been sunk by the submarine *Darter* on 23 October) Kurita was able to steam through the night unchallenged. Early on the morning of 25 October his capital ships emerged from the San Bernardino Strait. Before them, protected only by a thin screen of light escort carriers under Rear Admiral Clifton F. 'Ziggy' Sprague, were the Leyte troop anchorages.

In spite of an outstandingly gallant defence by Sprague's little carriers and destroyers, the destruction of the invasion force seemed inevitable. Kurita had lost some ships, but he could still have won a great victory when, inexplicably, he broke off the action. He meant merely to reform his ships and return, but he did not do so. Shortly after midday he signalled to Tokyo that he was retiring. The great prize for which so many Japanese men and ships had been sacrificed was lost. The hopes and plans of Toyoda and Ozawa, and of Kurita himself, were brought to nothing.

Kurita had had his flagship sunk under him. He had been under air attack for most of three days. He thought he faced massive counter-attack from Halsey's carriers and from airfields ashore. He had heard the news of the disaster to Nishimura's Southern Force. As Churchill magnanimously wrote, 'Those who have endured a similar ordeal may judge him.'

Unsurprisingly, as 'Ziggy' Sprague fought off Kurita, the ether thickened with ever more frantic appeals for help. Some, from Kinkaid to Halsey, were not even coded, but in plain language. One, from Nimitz to Halsey, was in even plainer language: 'Where is Task Force 34?'

This was to lead to one of the most famous communications *contretemps* of the war. For cryptographic security, every enciphered message had to begin and end with 'padding' which had literally to be nonsense so that it could never be mistaken for part of the message proper, whose start and finish was separated from the padding by double letter groups. Unfortunately, the encoding officer at Pearl Harbor, possibly influenced by unconscious memories of Balaclava (whose anniversary fell on that date, 25 October) used padding with Tennysonian resonances. The message as originally sent was 'Turkey trots to water – FF – Where is, repeat where is, Task Force 34 – JJ – The world wonders'.

In the haste of action, the decoders in *New Jersey* tore off the first padding but, understandably, failed to remove the latter. So the message passed to the flagdeck was 'Where is, repeat where is, Task Force 34 the world wonders?' Mortally insulted (the message was repeated to King and Kinkaid), Halsey took off his cap, smashed it to the deck and jumped on it.

The first of six strikes launched on 25 October reached Ozawa's ships at about 8 am. *Zuikaku*, the last surviving 'villain' of Pearl Harbor, *Zuiho*, *Chitose* and a destroyer were sunk and another carrier, *Chiyoda*, was abandoned (to be sunk by US cruisers the next day). As for Halsey, after that 'Task Force 34' signal he detached one carrier group and most of Lee's TF 34, including *New Jersey*, and went south to help Kinkaid. But they were too late by several hours to intercept Kurita, who was long gone through the San Bernardino by the time they arrived. Ozawa's ships had been only 42 miles away from *New Jersey*'s guns when Halsey broke off. As he said sadly, 'I turned my back on the opportunity I had dreamed of since my days as a cadet'.

Leyte Gulf ended the effectiveness of the Imperial Japanese Navy at sea. In the four days from 23 to 26 October they had lost three battleships, four carriers, ten cruisers and nine destroyers, with numerous other ships badly damaged. The US Navy lost a light fleet carrier, two escort carriers, two destroyers, a destroyer escort and a submarine.

Substantial Japanese units, including six battleships, remained after Leyte, but for the rest of the war the principal enemies at sea were the shore-based Japanese navy and army air forces. This change was underlined in a most ominous manner during the Leyte invasion by the first appearance of organized kamikaze suicide bombers.

For the Eastern Fleet the great actions of the Pacific – Coral Sea, Midway, Guadalcanal, the Philippine Sea, and now Leyte Gulf – had rumbled like distant thunder on the eastern horizon. But from the summer of 1944 onwards it had been common knowledge in the wardrooms and on the messdecks of the fleet that the newest and fastest ships amongst them, with others coming out from the

UK every week, would form a new fleet to steam east and join the Americans in the Pacific.

Admiral Sir Bruce Fraser hoisted his flag as Commander-in-Chief British Pacific Fleet on 22 November, 1944. After carrying out air strikes against oilfields in Sumatra in December and early in January, 1945, the fleet – four large carriers, the battleship *King George V*, four cruisers and ten destroyers – sailed on 16 January and launched two major strikes against oil refineries at Palembang in southern Sumatra on passage to Australia.

Those who were left, to form the renamed East Indies Fleet, naturally felt a somewhat anticlimactic sense of being a 'Second Eleven'. Their tasks were, as before, to deny the Japanese the use of the Indian Ocean and to give close support to the seaward flank of 15th Corps in the new campaign in the Burmese Arakan which had opened in December, 1944.

But by 1945 the Japanese had virtually abandoned the Indian Ocean, at least for the passage of large ships. Ceaseless attacks by Allied aircraft and submarines forced them to use convoys of small ships which crept inshore, hugging the land as closely as possible. These convoys were regularly disclosed by ULTRA and East Indies Fleet destroyers went on anti-shipping sweeps to intercept and sink them.

For immediate operational purposes, some of the most important and prolific sources of intelligence were the 'Y' Groups ashore in *Anderson* and also embarked, in parties of three or four men, in ships down to destroyers. The 'Y' Groups, trained in spoken Japanese, kept radio watches, generally on special sets codenamed 'Headache', to monitor Japanese radio frequencies and give rapid and up-to-date information on the movements and intentions of Japanese surface ships.

By February, 1945, the Japanese empire in the East Indies was beginning to crumble at the edges to such an extent that Japanese garrisons were being withdrawn from outlying islands. The Japanese intended to hold Java, Borneo and Sumatra as long as possible but to mount their main defence in Malaya and Indochina, where troops were to be concentrated by four major evacuation programmes.

The evacuation which most concerned the East Indies Fleet, because it might bring larger Japanese warships into the Indian Ocean, was codenamed SHO (Akiraka), the movement of troops from the Nicobar and Andaman Islands to Singapore. By that stage the two heavy cruisers *Ashigara* and *Haguro*, forming the 5th Cruiser Division, and the old destroyer *Kamikaze* were the only sizeable warships in the 10th Area Fleet, based at Singapore, capable of assisting and protecting SHO (Akiraka).

Radio Intelligence revealed on 12 April that two cruisers of Crudiv 5 and the destroyer *Kamikaze* were to transport troops of 46th Army Division from Batavia to Singapore in two phases, using one cruiser and one destroyer each time, departing from Batavia on 17 and 22 April. *Haguro* had been reported on 22 April carrying troops from Java to Singapore and on 25 April there was evidence that *Ashigara* had arrived in Singapore late on the 24th from Batavia and was due to enter dry dock for repairs from 27 April; it was suggested she had suffered damage due to torpedo attack or possibly damage to a propeller. (For some time Allied intelligence was not sure whether *Haguro* or *Ashigara* was the *Nachi* Class cruiser referred to in these signals.)

SHO (Akiraka) had not been carried out by the time the Allies recaptured Rangoon (Operation DRACULA), with hardly a shot fired, early in May, 1945. The East Indies Fleet went to sea at the end of April, to cover the assault landings, and to provide diversionary bombardments and air strikes on the Nicobars and the Andamans, to confuse the enemy and to prevent air or sea interference with DRACULA.

Traffic analysis still put *Haguro* and *Ashigara* at Singapore and a third heavy cruiser, *Takao*, badly damaged at Leyte Gulf, was just possibly seaworthy again. It was also possible that the Japanese might stage replacement aircraft through the airfields on the islands. (It was not realized at the time that the successes of the 14th Army in Burma had already forced the Japanese to begin evacuating Rangoon.)

Victory in Europe was announced on 8 May. All ships spliced the mainbrace and held services of thanksgiving, and returned to Trincomalee on 9 May to rearm and refuel. The men of the fleet had little time to celebrate. At 10 pm that evening a general alarm was flashed around the harbour: 'All ships addressed . . . ' the signal was classified Top Secret and priority Immediate, ' . . . raise steam for 16 knots by 0600 10 May. Proceed in Groups to be signalled.'

ULTRA had revealed that the Japanese were about to try to put SHO (Akiraka) into effect: 'ULTRA. Comcrudiv 5 in ASHIGARA [sic] + KAMIKAZE departing Singapore X Day with about 650 tons supplies and arrives Port Blair (Andamans) evening X + 2 Day when will load 2 Army battalions for return to Singapore. No 1 KURUSHIO Maru + 1 subchaser departing Singapore Y Day with about 150 tons supplies and arrive Nancowry (Nicobar) Y + 3 Day probably in evening when will load about 450 army personnel for return to

Singapore. Army and Navy air patrols to be provided for above movements. X Day is 10 May and Y Day 11 May.'

At Trincomalee Vice Admiral H.T.C. ('Hookey') Walker, commanding the 3rd Battle Squadron, formed Force 61 with almost every ship in harbour – the battleships *Queen Elizabeth* and the French *Richelieu*, the 21st Aircraft Carrier Squadron, of *Hunter*, *Khedive*, *Emperor* and *Shah*, three cruisers and seven destroyers – which sailed in three groups from 0600 on the 10th onwards. Their object was to intercept the enemy some time on 12 May in an operation later codenamed DUKEDOM.

Haguro sailed from Singapore, escorted by *Kamikaze* and two submarine chasers, on 9 May and was reported and then unsuccessfully attacked in the Malacca Strait by the submarine *Subtle* on the 10th. With this information Walker planned to intercept on the night of the 11th/12th. However, there were delays and in any case Force 61 was sighted. Two ULTRA intercepts on 11 May revealed that the Japanese had flown three special air reconnaissance flights that day. An ULTRA intercept on the 12th read: 'One heavy enemy ship sighted by air recce'. Shortly afterwards a fourth ULTRA intercept showed that the *Nachi* Class cruiser had been ordered to return to Singapore.

Meanwhile, Walker guessed that he had been sighted and hoped that if he kept his ships away unobtrusively to the south the enemy might make another sortie. But he detached the battleship *Richelieu*, the cruiser *Cumberland* and five destroyers of the 26th Flotilla after dusk on the 11th to steam eastwards in case there was still a chance of an interception on the 12th.

Haguro and *Kamikaze* had indeed turned back into the Malacca Strait, where *Subtle* carried out a second unsuccessful attack and had to endure a prolonged and unpleasantly accurate depth charge attack by *Kamikaze*. But from now on *Haguro* was dogged by ULTRA, although a certain amount of communications confusion almost allowed her to escape.

Kurishoyo Maru No. 2, escorted by Submarine Chaser No. 57, left Penang on 12 May and, hidden by bad weather, reached Nancowry safely early on the 14th. *Haguro* and *Kamikaze* had been waiting in the Malacca Strait and, evidently encouraged by *Kurishoyo* Maru's progress, they made a second sortie which was betrayed by an ULTRA intercept received during the morning of the 14th, reporting one heavy cruiser being sent from Singapore to the Andamans, although this heavy cruiser was not necessarily the same *Nachi* Class mentioned in earlier intercepts.

Kurishoyo Maru, also by now betrayed by ULTRA, embarked 450 troops from the Nicobars and sailed for Singapore on the evening of 14 May. She was sighted by Liberators but their report did not reach Walker.

On the evening of 14 May the 'Y' parties began to report radio transmissions from minor surface ship activity around the northern coast and capes of Sumatra. This had been anticipated and a subsidiary operation, codenamed MITRE, for an air and surface sweep in search of such targets, had been planned.

Early on 15 May a message from *Haguro* was decoded stating that she was due to do something (groups corrupt, possibly arrive) at One Fathom Bank [in the Malacca Strait] at 1000 Japanese time (Zero minus nine hours) on 16 May. This appeared to confirm that *Haguro* was about to have another try. By then Walker had *Richelieu*, *Cumberland* and five destroyers of the 26th Flotilla in the Six Degree Channel (between Great Nicobar and Sumatra) and the rest of his ships in support.

In the early hours of 15 May Admiral Walker initiated MITRE and dispatched the 26th Destroyer Flotilla, of *Saumarez* (Captain Manley Power), *Venus*, *Verulam*, *Vigilant* and *Virago*, eastwards to carry it out. During the day *Shah*'s aircraft operating from *Emperor* sighted and reported a large landing craft and a submarine chaser. This was *Kurishoyo* Maru and her escort.

Meanwhile the staff at Colombo had decided that the main object, to prevent the *Nachi* threatening Allied forces at or on their way to Rangoon, had been achieved now that the *Nachi* had retired into the Malacca Strait. A signal cancelling MITRE was sent to Power. He, however, decided that Colombo could not know of the aircraft's reports of targets up ahead and took the Nelsonian view that no officer could do wrong if he continued to pursue the enemy. He reduced speed but held on to the east.

Power was entirely vindicated towards noon, when a second search aircraft from *Emperor* (who had actually been looking for *Kurishoyo* Maru) signalled that they had sighted a cruiser and a destroyer, and had dive-bombed the cruiser. *Haguro* had abandoned her second sortie and was once more making for Singapore. The five destroyers increased speed and steered to cut her off.

After a radar contact obtained at freakishly long range at 10.40 pm that night, the flotilla closed their target and just after 1 am on 16 May engaged *Haguro* and *Kamikaze* in a hectic gun and torpedo night action. *Haguro* was heard to transmit two brief operational dispatches at about 1.30. She sank after several torpedo hits a few minutes after 2 am, in a position some 45 miles south-west of Penang. *Kamikaze* was damaged but escaped to Penang. Of the 26th Flotilla, *Saumarez* was damaged by *Haguro*'s gunfire.

At 1.54 am, when the action was at its height, a H/F D/F operator in *Venus* picked up a Japanese surface unit transmitting on a bearing of 105°, with a ground wave transmission giving a range of less than 15 miles away. The message consisted of 36 words of 4-sign code and was transmitted to Singapore, bearing the highest degree of priority. It was repeated at 2.07 am but at neither time was Singapore heard to give a receipt.

However, *Anderson* picked up fragments of a message from an unknown operator, time of origin some three hours after *Haguro*'s sinking, describing an action fought by *Haguro* and *Kamikaze* against an Allied force of two (possibly cruisers) and a destroyer. The message did not mention that *Haguro* had been sunk, but stated that one of the Japanese ships had received hits in three places, with 32 casualties, and that one of *Haguro*'s guns had been destroyed. This, its own way, was a fairly accurate résumé of the action until the time *Kamikaze* left the scene and it was clearly transmitted by her. *Kamikaze* later came out to pick up about 400 of *Haguro*'s survivors.

The sinking of *Haguro* was a model night destroyer action, made possible by ULTRA and splendidly executed by the 26th Destroyer Flotilla.

Kurishoyo Maru and SC 57 reached Penang safely, but they were again betrayed by ULTRA on 12 June when they were intercepted and sunk thirty miles north of Sabang by the destroyers *Eskimo* and *Nubian*. This was the last surface action in the Indian Ocean brought about by ULTRA and indeed the last of the war for the East Indies Fleet.

XIII

THE SUBMARINE WAR TO THE END

For the US submarines in the Pacific 1944 was the big year. By the beginning of that year, every submarine was fitted with dependable radar and at last had reliable torpedoes. The new Mark 18 electric torpedo was in service, and a new explosive which greatly increased the destructive power of warheads.

The three Pacific submarine commands, based at Pearl Harbor, Brisbane and Fremantle, began 1944 with 75 submarines, nearly all of them fleet boats, most of the old S-Class having been relegated to training duties. There were plenty of targets and the figures of tonnage sunk in 1944 soared, to 548 Marus, of 2,451,914 tons, nearly a third of the ships sunk being tankers.

It was an outstanding achievement by a relatively small submarine force, made possible by ULTRA. So large a part did ULTRA play that it is hard to find a Pacific submarine operation in 1944 not influenced by it. Grateful tribute to ULTRA was paid in 1947 by Vice Admiral Charles Lockwood, ComSubPac from February, 1943, to the end of the war. 'I can vouch,' he said, 'for the very important part which Communication Intelligence played in the success of the submarine campaign. Through intercept, cryptanalysis and translation of Japanese messages, Communications Intelligence supplied the Submarine Force with a continuous flow of information on Japanese naval and merchant shipping, convoy routing and composition, damage sustained from submarine attacks, anti-submarine measures employed or to be employed, effectiveness of our torpedoes, and a wealth of other pertinent intelligence.

'The Submarine Force Operations Officer was designated the Combat Intelligence Officer. He was given access to all of the Communications Intelligence files and through him information was furnished to the Force Commander and thence to the individual submarines concerned. A private telephone was installed between SubPac operations office and the combat intelligence center of JICPOA so that information on convoy routing could be supplied with a minimum of delay. Special internal codes, carried only by submarines, were used for relaying this type of information, so that our own surface ships, though they might be able to decipher the submarine messages, were unable to determine the type of information being supplied. When ComSubPac moved his operational headquarters to Guam a special cryptographic channel was authorized by OpNav to supply this information direct from JICPOA at Pearl Harbor.

'The information furnished made possible the assignment of submarines not only to the most profitable patrol areas but also to specific locations at particular times where contacts were made with convoys of known composition and importance, and frequently with enemy course and speed known exactly. Combatant units of the Japanese Fleet were similarly located on many occasions. During periods, which fortunately were brief, when enemy code changes temporarily cut off the supply of Communication Intelligence, its absence was keenly felt. The curve of enemy contacts and of consequent sinkings almost exactly paralleled the curve of Communication Intelligence available.

'There were many periods when every available submarine on patrol in the Pacific was busy on information supplied by Communication Intelligence. The vast reaches of the Pacific Ocean could not otherwise have been covered so thoroughly unless a far greater number of submarines had been available. In early 1945 it was learned from a Japanese prisoner-of-war that it was a common saying in Singapore that you could walk from that port to Japan on American periscopes. This feeling among the Japanese was undoubtedly created, not by the great number of submarines on patrol, but rather by the fact, thanks to Communication Intelligence, the submarines were always at the same place as Japanese ships.

'The sinkings of Japanese merchant ships resulting from Communication Intelligence ran into hundreds of ships and probably amounted to fifty per cent of the total of all merchantmen sunk by submarines.

'In addition to the direct results there were equally as important indirect results which must be credited to the same source of information. For example: From an analysis of Communication Intelligence extending over a period of many months it was determined that our magnetic torpedo exploders were not functioning properly, and steps were taken to correct the defects.

'Then again, information concerning enemy minefields was so complete that defensive minefields laid down by the enemy served our purpose rather than his. Not only were our submarines able to avoid the areas of danger, but Japanese ships, being required to avoid them as well, were forced into relatively narrow traffic lanes, making it easier for the submarines to locate and attack them. It is impossible to estimate the number of our submarines which were saved and the number of Japanese ships which were lost because of the accurate information about enemy minefields supplied by Communication Intelligence. Also, information concerning names of ships sunk, nature of cargo and number of troops lost was of inestimable value in assessing the damage sustained by the enemy and gauging his capabilities.' (It is clear from Admiral Lockwood's account that the precaution of providing a 'cover story' before ULTRA could be used was virtually discarded.)

Pacific submarines began on 1 January, 1944, when *Herring* (Lt Cdr R. W. Johnson) sank the cargo-aircraft ferry *Nagoya* Maru in the East China Sea, *Puffer* (Lt Cdr F. G. Selby) sank the freighter *Ryuyo* Maru off the coast of Mindanao and *Ray* (Cdr B. J. Harrel) sank the converted gunboat *Okuyo* Maru off Halmahera, making a total of 15,683 Japanese tonnage lost on the first day of the new year.

The first success of January, 1944, credited to ULTRA began on the 9th when submarines on patrol around Truk were warned of a convoy of three tankers and escort vessels. They intercepted on the 14th, when *Scamp* (Cdr W. G. Ebert) sank the *Nippon* Maru and *Guardfish* (Lt Cdr N. G. Ward) sank *Kenyo* Maru while *Albacore* (Cdr J. W. Blanchard) sank the destroyer *Sazanami*.

On 10 January, 1944, ULTRA laid another ambush for *Yamato*, returning to Kure from Truk after having the December damage repaired, and a wolfpack of *Tullibee* (Cdr C. F. Brindupke), *Haddock* (Lt Cdr R. M. Davenport) and *Halibut* (Lt Cdr I. J. Galantin) lay in wait. *Halibut* sighted her but was unable to get into a firing position because of her speed and lost contact. Later, both *Batfish* (Lt Cdr W. R. Merrill) and *Sturgeon* (Lt Cdr C. L. Murphy, Jr) sighted a battleship in the position where *Yamato* was scheduled to be, but she avoided them both by greater speed. But on the same day *Seawolf* (Lt Cdr R. L. Gross) fell upon a convoy west of Okinawa and in four days of attacks sank four Marus totalling 23,355 tons.

Meanwhile, after ULTRA messages, *Thresher* (Lt Cdr D. C. McMillan) sank two ships from a convoy off Luzon on 15 January and two more from a convoy south of Formosa on the 27th; *Tautog*

(Lt Cdr W. B. Sieglaff) hit and damaged the carrier *Shikoku* north of Truk on the 15th; and *Seahorse* (Lt Cdr S. D. Cutter), on patrol off the Palaus, sank two Marus from a convoy on the 21st. *Gar*, also off the Palaus, sank two Marus from a convoy on 20 and 23 January. The same convoy was attacked and followed by *Seahorse*, losing two more Marus on 30 January and 1 February. *Seahorse* then headed for the barn, having sunk 13,716 tons during her patrol.

Submarines sank 50 Marus, of 240,840 tons, during January, 1944, the largest monthly total of the war so far, and setting the tempo for the year.

In February ULTRA revealed the straits to which some Japanese garrisons were reduced because of shipping losses. Even the great stronghold of Rabaul was affected. Of twenty ships bound there in January, seven were sunk on passage, four in harbour and three on the return passage. On 6 February a decrypt of a signal from Eighth Area Army headquarters at Rabaul to Tokyo read: 'Complete suspension of shipping to Rabaul is something that units in this area cannot bear.'

As Admiral Lockwood said, ULTRA often revealed the results of submarine attacks. On 1 March Army headquarters in Manila signalled to Tokyo: 'While returning to Japan, a convoy of six tankers was attacked by enemy submarines on 20 February in the waters NW of the Philippines and five tankers were sunk. The present situation is such that the majority of tankers returning to Japan are being lost.'

The Japanese attributed this state of affairs to the difficulty of preventing espionage in Manila harbour. In fact it was ULTRA which was directing the submarines towards their targets. That tanker convoy was attacked on 19 February by *Jack* who sank four tankers of over 20,000 tons in one day – a record.

However, the signal was correct about the gravity of the tanker situation. In the first eight weeks of 1944 the Japanese lost 21 tankers, almost as many as they had lost in the whole of the previous year. By the end of June, 1944, Japan had lost 43 tankers since the beginning of the year, 27 of them sunk by submarines.

Not only tankers, but troopships were being sunk at a rate which was already making the Japanese Naval Staff uneasy by the end of 1943 when, as one staff officer wrote after the war, 'Everyone aboard a transport or merchant had to be resigned to the likelihood of being sunk in his travels.' In the autumn of 1943 the Japanese carried out Operation TURTLE: the transfer of Second District Army, consisting of seven divisions of the 2nd Army and the 19th

Army, from Manchuria, China, Korea and the Japanese mainland to the Celebes, Morotai, Halmahera and Biak.

About 40 per cent of the TURTLE troop transports were lost to enemy action. One contingent loaded at Pusan, Korea, had the misfortune to have ships sunk under them three times en route – the first near Okinawa, the second off Formosa and the third near New Guinea. Only about half of their original strength remained when these troops finally landed in New Guinea, and even then they were without weapons. Many had no shoes and large numbers of them were ill.

On 29 February, south-east of Okinawa, the veteran submarine *Trout* (Lt Cdr A. H. Clark) now on her eleventh war patrol, attacked a fast troop convoy, Eastern Matsu No. 1, carrying troops from Korea to reinforce Saipan and Guam. *Trout* damaged the 11,500 ton *Aki* Maru and sank the 9,245 ton *Sakito* Maru which had 4,124 troops and a crew of 105 on board. Of these over 2,500 were drowned. But the escorts counter-attacked and sank *Trout*.

A decrypt of a message of 1 February, 1944, from the Chief of Staff of the Eighth Area Army to the Eighteenth Army, gave full details of naval convoy traffic and supply schedules from Palau to Rabaul, New Britain and Wewak, New Guinea, including lists of supplies, cargoes, personnel carried, the numbers and names of ships in a convoy and the strength of the escort and, most important of all, arrival times for five convoys to Wewak between early February and early March, 1944.

On 26 February the four ships of Wewak Convoy No. 20, which had three escorts and 30 to 80 fighters providing air cover, was attacked by *Gato* (Lt Cdr R. J. Foley) who sank *Daigen* Maru No. 3, with the loss of 400 troops of the 66th Infantry Regiment, 51st Division. On 29th Hollandia Convoy No. 6, carrying the Sixth South Seas Detachment left Palau for Hollandia as previously disclosed by ULTRA. Thus forewarned, *Peto* (Lt Cdr P. Van Leunen) attacked the convoy on 4 March and sank *Kayo* Maru with the loss of 40 soldiers including the Detachment commander. Later ULTRA revealed that between 29 February and 20 March twelve Marus were lost from convoys to Wewak through Allied naval or air action.

Acting on ULTRA, *Sandlance* (Lt Cdr M. E. Garrison) on her maiden war patrol attacked and sank the light cruiser *Tatsuta* and one Maru from a convoy carrying reinforcements to the Marianas on 13 March.

In March ULTRA revealed that the Japanese had virtually abandoned the use of surface vessels to supply Rabaul. On the night of 23 March *Tunny* (Cdr J. A. Scott) was on lifeguard duty, ready to pick up downed aviators during a Fast Carrier strike on the Palaus, when she received an ULTRA revealing information about a Japanese submarine on a supply run to Rabaul. Lying in wait along the target's predicted course, *Tunny* picked up a radar contact and fired four torpedoes, sinking *I-42*.

These shocks of early 1944 caused the Japanese Naval General Staff to consider the question of convoy seriously for the first time. Troopships had always been convoyed but the Japanese had so far only tinkered with the problem of general convoy for all ships. Only as recently as 15 November, 1943, had they set up the sonorously named Grand Escort Command Headquarters, with a very senior Admiral, Koshiro Oikawa, as C-in-C. The Japanese Navy was reorganized into three main commands: the Combined Fleet, the China District Fleet and the Combined Convoy Escort Fleet.

Oikawa was responsible for the protection of shipping, convoy control and routeing, and anti-submarine warfare everywhere except between ports along the Chinese coast and on such local routes as between Truk and the Marshalls, and on the fringes of the Japanese Empire, south of the Philippines and west of Singapore.

It was a huge task and at that stage of the war virtually impossible to achieve. Oikawa, a man of over sixty, was short of everything – trained officers and men, ships, aircraft, tactics, radar, communications personnel and equipment, competent staff, ideas and, above all, time. After the disasters of early 1944 the General Staff demanded 'a study meeting before the Emperor concerning the convoy escort situation'. Oikawa's staff had the task of assembling the humiliating facts for the meeting.

Clearly loss of face had much more effect on the Navy than the loss of ships, for in March, 1944, the Japanese finally instituted what they called 'a large convoy system' (although to the Allies, accustomed to running convoys of seventy or eighty ships across the Atlantic, Japanese convoys of only five to fifteen ships hardly seemed large). An Escort of Convoy Headquarters was set up, and despite all the difficulties and the shortages, and the sheer lack of practice and expertise, convoy at once began to save ships. It was soon clear that sinkings of independents were two and a half times those of convoyed ships. Furthermore, the escorts were hitting back. US submarines lost more of their number to convoy escorts than to patrols, mines, aircraft or indeed any other single cause.

However, the combination of experienced and determined submarine captains and accurate information from ULTRA continued to decimate Japanese convoys. In April, 1944, the Japanese kept up their attempts to reinforce the Marianas and Carolines by fast troop convoys. On 3 April *Pollack* (Lt Cdr B. E. Lewellen) sank one of seven transports from convoy Matsu No. 4, on its way from Japan to the Marianas and Truk.

The next convoy, Matsu No. 5, landed its troops safely in the Palaus on 20 April and its four large transports, escorted by the destroyer *Hatakaze* and three frigates, started on their return journey. But *Trigger* (Lt Cdr F. J. Harlfinger) was waiting in their path. Harlfinger made three attacks on the night of the 26th, firing all but one of his torpedoes, and hitting the 12,000-ton ex-N.Y.K. liner *Miike* Maru, which burned for three days and then sank, and the 9,000-ton former Mitsui liner *Asosan* Maru, which was badly damaged but was eventually salvaged.

The Japanese were also withdrawing troops from Manchuria to reinforce the hard-pressed 18th Army on the Vogelkop in New Guinea. In April they assembled a convoy of nine transports and a dozen escorts, called 'Take Ichi' (known to the Allies as Bamboo No. 1). Commanded by Admiral Kajioka (the officer who was to have led the Japanese invasion force into Port Moresby back in 1942), 'Take Ichi' sailed from Shanghai on 17 April.

Kajioka flew his flag in the aged coal-burning minelayer *Shirataka* whose towering pall of black smoke guided *Jack*, already waiting north of Luzon, towards the convoy on 26 April, sinking the transport *Yoshida* Maru No. 1, who took with her an entire infantry regiment.

Traffic analysis tracked 'Take Ichi' to Manila where, before the convoy left on 1 May, ULTRA had established that it was carrying 12,874 men of the 32nd Division and 8,170 of the 35th, with much stores and equipment (which ULTRA revealed in detail). ULTRA also revealed the convoy's scheduled noon positions each day from 2 to 9 May; its alternative route, which was only to be followed on special instructions; the precise point where the convoy was to divide into two groups on 7 May and the ultimate destinations of both groups.

Not surprisingly, given such wealth of information from ULTRA, 'Take Ichi' was ambushed by *Gurnard* (Cdr C. H. Andrews) on 6 May while it was crossing the Celebes Sea and three more transports, totalling almost 20,000 tons, were sunk. A later decrypt gave details of how and where the convoy was attacked, the ships lost, the thousands of soldiers drowned and hundreds of tons of equipment lost, and the convoy's rerouteing, because of the risk of further losses to submarines. The surviving troops were disembarked in Halmahera, in the Moluccas, far from their destination. Very few of them ever reached New Guinea in time to be of any use in the campaign there.

On the same day, off North Borneo, *Crevalle* (Lt Cdr F. D. Walker Jr) sank the giant 16,600 ton tanker converted from a whale factory ship, *Nisshin* Maru. Eighteen days later, off the southern tip of Mindanao, *Gurnard* sank another tanker, the 10,090 ton *Tatekawa* Maru.

It may be wondered why, when so few attempts appear to have been made to account for a submarine's attack by a 'cover story', the Japanese never realized that the presence of so many enemy submarines wherever so many of their own ships went could not *all* be due to coincidence or intelligent guessing by the enemy. There *must* be some other factor working in the enemy's favour.

It is incredible that seemingly no Japanese staff officer ever calculated that to achieve such numbers of sinkings over an ocean as big as the Pacific entirely by good luck or good judgement would require a submarine fleet so large as to be beyond even the United States' resources. The question could have been approached in another way, by making a shrewd estimate of the number of submarines in the US Pacific Fleet and then calculating how that number could possibly make so many successful attacks in so many different places. Either way, it should have been apparent that there was a basic improbability in the figures.

US submarines responded to the challenge of improved Japanese convoy and escort with wolf-pack tactics. Three or four submarines, with picturesque nicknames based on their senior officer's name – the 'Mickey Finns', 'Wogan's Wolves', 'Coye's Coyotes', (incidentally showing how many successful submarine commanders were Irish-Americans) – would operate together, to detect, follow and attack their targets, using good R/T communication between boats and excellent surface radar sets. The curve of Japanese shipping losses, which had dipped slightly in March and April, 1944, soared again in May to its highest figure of the war so far: 63 Marus, of 264,000 tons.

ULTRA-inspired submarine attacks affected the campaign on Saipan as well as in New Guinea. An ULTRA decrypt enabled Captain Leon N. Blair's 'Blair's Blasters', of *Shark II* (Lt Cdr E. N. Blakely), *Pintado* (Lt Cdr B. A. Clarey) and *Pilotfish* (Lt Cdr R. H. Close) to intercept the Saipan-bound Convoy No. 3530, of seven transports and freighters carrying 7,200 men (many of the 118th Infantry Regiment) and 22 tanks on the morning of 4 June.

In a three-day pursuit *Shark II* first sank the 6,900-ton transport *Katsukawa* Maru, with 2,800 soldiers on board and next day, the 5th, a 3,000-ton freighter and a 7,000-ton transport *Takaoka* Maru with 3,000 troops and eleven tanks. On 6 June *Pintado* sank a 2,800-ton freighter and the 5,600-ton transport *Havre* Maru, with 1,120 soldiers and the other eleven tanks. The escorts rescued many of the soldiers and landed them on Saipan, but, of course, without their weapons and the tanks. Thousands of tons of construction equipment were also lost. All these losses made the eventual capture of Saipan later in the month that much less difficult.

In August, 1944, US submarines moved to a base at Saipan, 3,600 miles nearer the action than Pearl Harbor, and were able to stay much longer on patrol. Japanese convoys were soon forced to leave the eastern side of the East China Sea and hug the Chinese coast. The stretch of the East China Sea, from Luzon Strait across to Formosa and the Chinese coast, was named 'Convoy College', where the 'wolf packs', assisted by ever more detailed ULTRA, were generally too much for the convoy escorts.

Commander 'Red' Ramage, in *Parche*, for example, with *Steelhead* (Lt Cdr D. L. Welchel) and *Hammerhead* (Lt Cdr F. T. Smith), attacked a convoy in the Luzon Strait on 30-31 July and sank a tanker, two transports, and two passenger-cargo Marus, for a total score of 39,000 tons. Another pack, 'Donk's Devils', under Cdr G. R. Donaho in *Picuda*, with *Redfish* (Lt Cdr L. D. McGregor) and *Spadefish* (Lt Cdr G. W. Underwood), sank four ships in one convoy on 25 August and finished their patrols with a total of 64,456 tons sunk.

On 3 August, 1944, Oikawa was appointed Chief of the Naval General Staff, and Grand Escort Command was amalgamated with the Combined Fleet. Any hopes of a successful anti-submarine campaign around the convoys promptly vanished. Even the 901st Naval Air Group, who had been specially formed for anti-submarine duties and who had actually acquired some expertise in radar operations against submarines, was thrown away as a reconnaissance unit for the Combined Fleet in air battles with TF 38 off Formosa in October, 1944.

Grand Escort Command was defunct in everything but name, and the only question now remaining was how quickly US submarines could finish off the rest of Japan's merchant marine. In October, 1944, sixty-eight submarines sank 320,906 tons of Japanese shipping, the highest monthly total of the war. In November the figure dropped to 214,506 tons, and there began to be a noticeable shortage of targets.

On 14 November, 1944, a message from the First Transport Staff at Moji in Japan to air force units concerned was decrypted, requesting air escort for two convoys, Hi-81 and Mi-27, transporting the 23rd Infantry Division from Manchuria to Luzon. The message revealed that Hi-81, of seven transports and an oiler, escorted by six destroyers and an escort carrier, was due to leave Mutsure, on the seaward side of the narrow Shimonoseki Strait between Honshu and Kyushu on the 15th, and the convoy's route from the 15th to the 22nd was also given.

Hi-81 had hardly cleared the land when it was attacked by *Queenfish* (Cdr C. E. Loughlin), one of 'Loughlin's Loopers', who sank the 9,000-ton aircraft ferry *Akitsu* Maru, taking two battalions and the divisional artillery to the bottom of the East China Sea. On the 17th Hi-81 reported that it had been sighted by a B-29 and there was a strong indication that Mi-27 had also been sighted (this B-29 provided the ULTRA 'cover story' to account for the presence of the submarines).

On the same day, the 17th, the 9,500-ton passenger-cargo ship *Mayazan* Maru was sunk by another 'Looper', *Picuda* (Lt Cdr E. T. Shephard), who also damaged the oiler. A later decrypt gave the final score for both convoys as six ships sunk, one disabled and one ship on fire. Diaries of two survivors, picked up in Luzon, confirmed the damage done – and added one aircraft carrier also sunk.

The carrier was the 21,000-ton ex-German liner *Scharnhorst* which, as ULTRA had been reporting periodically since December, 1943, the Japanese had converted into a carrier and renamed *Jinyo*.

While *Picuda* had been attacking, *Spadefish* (Cdr G. W. Underwood), of 'Underwood's Urchins', had also sighted five large Marus of Hi-81 and a carrier, escorted by destroyers and subchasers. Underwood decided to let the convoy run over him and make a night surface attack. Just before midnight he fired six torpedoes from his bow tubes at the carrier and four from his stern tubes at a tanker. Four bow torpedoes hit. *Jinyo* burst into flames and settled by the stern. As Underwood watched, aircraft began sliding off *Jinyo*'s flight deck. Her bows were last seen pointing at the sky.

ULTRA assisted in submarine attacks on two more Japanese carriers in December, 1944. On the 8th *Redfish* (Cdr L. D. McGregor) lay in wait off Nagasaki for a reported Japanese squadron of a battleship, a carrier and three destroyers. He first detected fast zigzagging targets that evening and tracked them until they made a lucky zig in *Redfish*'s direction at about 1.30 am on the 9th, when he scored two torpedo hits on the 24,000-ton carrier *Junyo*, sometimes mistakenly called *Hayataka*. Converted from the N.Y.K. liner *Kashiwara* Maru, *Junyo* was a veteran; her aircraft had bombed Dutch Harbour in the Aleutians in 1942 and damaged *South Dakota* at Santa Cruz, and she was herself damaged in the Philippine Sea. *Sea Devil* (Cdr R. E. Styles), operating in the same area, also hit *Junyo* with one torpedo. She was not sunk but was disabled and put out of the war.

After MacArthur's forces landed on the Philippine island of Mindoro on 15 December the Japanese decided to bombard the American beachhead with a scratch force, the most the Japanese Navy could muster, of two cruisers and six destroyers which sailed from Camranh Bay in Indochina on the 16th. These were reported by ULTRA, as were four unidentified units which left Kyushu on the 17th. Traffic analysis identified one of the four as the new 18,000-ton aircraft carrier *Unryu*. She and three escorting destroyers were hurrying south to give air cover to the Mindoro bombarding force but, forewarned by ULTRA, *Redfish* lay in their path.

On the afternoon of 19 December, in the East China Sea, Cdr McGregor first sighted an aircraft, which bombed him, and then ships' masts which he identified as those of destroyers and, behind them, a carrier. He fired four torpedoes, of which one hit the carrier and brought it to a stop, dead in the water, and with a heavy list. *Redfish*'s tubes' crew reloaded and McGregor fired a fifth torpedo which hit abreast *Unryu*'s island. The carrier disintegrated before McGregor's eyes.

The destroyers retaliated with a determined and unpleasantly accurate depth-charge attack. *Redfish* lay on the sea bottom, surfaced after dark and escaped.

ULTRA betrayed not only convoys but single blockade runners. The fate of *I-29* was a perfect ULTRA *coup*. *I-29*, named *Matsu*, was the submarine which rendezvoused with a German U-boat off Madagascar in April, 1943, embarked Subhas Chandra Bose, the leader of the movement for Indian independence and self-styled C-in-C of the Indian National Army, and took him to Penang.

I-29 (Cdr T. Kinashi) left Penang, bound for Europe, early in November, 1943, and sailed from Lorient, bound for Japan, on 16 April, 1944. Among the passengers were four German technicians and thirteen Japanese Army, Navy and civilian personnel. The cargo included German anti-submarine counter-measure equipment, acoustic and magnetic torpedoes, radar apparatus, plans for the latest high-submerged-speed submarines, and influenza virus.

I-29's passage was traced through intercepted signals from Berlin, and a Singapore broadcast in diplomatic code, addressed to *I-29* only on 3 July, indicated its presence in the Indian Ocean. An ULTRA from *Anderson* on 11 July read: 'Friendly sub [identified as probably *I-29*] scheduled to pass through Sunda Strait on morning of 12 July, and arrive at eastern entrance to Singapore at 1200 on 14th.' It was later confirmed by ULTRA that *I-29* had indeed arrived that day.

On 17 July, 1944, a decrypted message from Berlin to Tokyo listed *I-29*'s cargo in detail: five 'special weapons', various radar apparatus, 20 Enigma coding machines, ordnance parts, rocket-type launching apparatus, bomb sight plans, pressure cabin parts and plans, parts of a British Mosquito plane, and atabrine ampoules and tablets. Two days later, in a decrypted message, Berlin congratulated Tokyo: 'It is indeed gratifying to learn that the MATSU has arrived safely at Singapore with her passengers and cargo. We pray for her safe voyage to Japan.'

But on 20 July Kinashi broadcast a fatal signal giving full details of his route to Japan: leaving Singapore at 1500 on the 22nd, arriving Kure at 1000 on 30 July, and giving his noon position for the 26th as the Balintang Channel [between Formosa and Luzon]. CincPac's Bulletin for 24 July read: '*I-29* recently arrived Singapore from Europe carrying samples and plans of many recent German developments in fields of radar, communications, gunnery, aeronautics and medicine. Left Singapore 22 July en route Kure. Believe very important cargo very likely still aboard. Will pass through posit 15 N., 117 E., at 251400 and through Balintang Channel at 261200, speed 17 arriving western channel of Bungo Channel at 291000.'

On 25 July *I-29* signalled that a surfaced enemy submarine had been sighted (possibly the 'cover story') and gave the position, about 300 miles west of Manila. On the 26th *Sawfish* (Cdr A. B. Banister, leader of 'Banister's Beagles') signalled: 'He did not pass. At 0755Z [1655 local time] in posit 20-12 N., 121-55 E. [Balintang Channel] put three fish into Nip sub which disintegrated in a cloud of smoke and fire.'

On 7 August a mournful Tokyo broadcast to Berlin was intercepted: 'All her passengers had proceeded to Tokyo from Singapore by plane, but her cargo had been left aboard. Though it is indeed regrettable, we can no longer hope for her safety. Despite the fact that we received, through your great efforts and the understanding cooperation of the

Germans, many articles which were to strengthen the nation's capacity to prosecute the war, our inability to utilize them owing to the loss of the ill-fated ship is truly unfortunate and will have a great effect throughout the Imperial Army and Navy.'

The most remarkable submarine-v-submarine encounter set up by ULTRA took place in February, 1945. By that time the Japanese air force in the Philippines had been virtually destroyed and numbers of aircraft-less pilots and ground crews were trapped in northern Luzon. Four Japanese submarines were ordered to pick up these redundant aircrews at Aparri, on the north coast of Luzon, and take them to Formosa.

Indications of Japanese intentions were included in CincPac's Bulletin for 6 February: 'This is ULTRA. Believe sub RO-46 will attempt evacuate personnel from N. Luzon 8th between 2030 and 2130. Loading point 1000 m. west of Batulinao Point. Will be postponed one day if difficulty encountered.'

An ULTRA ambush was laid. There were several submarines in the area but the main chances fell to Cdr J. K. Fyfe in *Batfish*, who took them all. Late in the evening of 9 February, on patrol off northern Luzon, *Batfish* picked up radar emissions from a surfaced submarine. Fyfe decided to attack on the surface but missed with four torpedoes. He made a fast 'end-around' approach and just after midnight on the 10th attacked again with three torpedoes, one of which hit and sank *RO-55*.

On the following night radar signals were again detected and just as Fyfe was preparing to fire the target submerged. But it was heard surfacing again half an hour later. Fyfe made a dived attack, firing by radar, and one of his four torpedoes sank *RO-112*.

Two nights later it all happened again, with almost eerie similarity: radar contact, target dived, then surfaced, dived attack, firing by radar, and one hit which sank *RO-113*. *Batfish* had sunk three Japanese submarines in four nights, all within a few miles of each other. It was a feat unequalled by any other Allied submarine. (*RO-46* was delayed but did reach Takao in Formosa with her evacuees on 12 February.)

ULTRA also played an important part in British submarine v. submarine actions. For instance, on 13 November, 1943, HMS *Taurus* (Lt Cdr M.R.G. Wingfield) was on patrol in the Malacca Strait when she was ordered to a position near the entrance to the swept channel leading into Penang, and was informed that a U-boat would arrive there about dawn. The signal also gave the U-boat's course and speed.

Taurus was on the surface just before dawn when Wingfield sighted his target approaching. As the light improved rapidly, he dived. He could see nothing through the periscope and so attacked relying entirely on sonar. Foolishly, the target was not zigzagging. One of a salvo of six torpedoes hit and sank *I-34*.

Almost a year later, in the same waters, ULTRA provided a similar target for HMS *Trenchant* (Cdr A. R. Hezlet). On 22 September, 1944, patrolling off the north coast of Sumatra, *Trenchant* was suddenly ordered north of Penang to intercept a German U-boat. It was clear to Hezlet (who suspected the existence of ULTRA although he was supposed to be ignorant of it) that the signal ordering the U-boat's rendezvous with its Japanese escort had been 'unbuttoned'. *Trenchant* crossed the Malacca Strait at full speed on the surface all night and next morning intercepted and sank *U-859* in the exact place and at the precise time predicted.

ULTRA could set up targets, but the submarines still had to sink them. On 9 February, 1945, CincPac's Bulletin mentioned 'Fragmentary evidence 8th Feb that Cardiv 4 [the hybrid battleship/carriers *Ise* and *Hyuga*] probably will carry out some sort of transportation operation in near future. In connection this operation 4 medium bombers to be stationed presumably for cover or special search, 2 at Singapore and 2 at Saigon. Estimate this movement will be northward through S China Sea from Singapore – Lingga area.'

An ULTRA early on the 10th revealed 'Cardiv 4 + CH Ashigara and 3 destroyers departing Singapore Straits 102100 transporting avgas and other critical materials to Japan. Due arrive Moji afternoon 19 Feb via route off Indochina and through Formosa Strait. At 131100 will be in 12N 111-30E. At 141000 in 17-10N 110-50E.' A second ULTRA later that evening confirmed that the ships had sailed.

With such warning, Admiral James Fife, who had relieved Christie as ComSubSoWesPac on 30 December, 1944, alerted every submarine in the South China Sea. Shortly after noon on 11 February, east of the Anamba Islands, Lt Cdr H. S. Mackenzie in HMS *Tantalus* sighted the fighting tops of two capital ships and the superstructure of a third ship: *Ise* and *Hyuga* and one of their escorts. Mackenzie tried desperately to get ahead of his targets, but he was hampered by the air escort, detected, bombed, forced to go deep and was unable to intercept.

Two US submarines, *Blackfin* and *Charr*, sighted the group next day but were unable to attack. On 13 February *Blower* (Cdr J. H. Campbell) fired six torpedoes at a cruiser and a battleship which overlapped, and claimed two hits. Half an hour later *Bergall*

(Cdr J. M. Hyde) also fired six torpedoes and believed he had one hit. However, no ship was damaged and by a combination of good luck and bad weather *Ise* and *Hyuga* reached Moji on 19 February.

The two hybrids had escaped, but the 5,400-ton cruiser *Isudzu* was not so lucky. Her route across the Flores Sea in April, 1945, was disclosed by ULTRA to submarines waiting to waylay her. On the 4th HMS *Spark* (Lt D. G. Kent) fired four torpedoes at long range in a flat calm sea and missed, but passed an enemy sighting report to USS *Besugo* (Cdr H. E. Miller) and *Gabilan* (Cdr W. B. Parham). *Besugo* sank one of three small escorts on the 6th and *Gabilan* torpedoed *Isudzu* early the next day. *Charr* (Cdr F. D. Boyle) saw the explosion, closed the target and hit *Isudzu* with three torpedoes. *Spark*, hastening towards the scene, was in time to see *Isudzu* sink.

The two *Nachi* Class cruisers, *Ashigara* and *Haguro*, and the destroyer *Kamikaze* were now the only operational warships of any size left in the Tenth Area Fleet at Singapore (the cruisers *Myoko* and *Takao* were in Singapore harbour, but both were badly damaged).

ULTRA delivered *Haguro* up to her fate in May, and in June did the same for *Ashigara*.

Ashigara's docking problems had already appeared in CincPac Bulletins. At the end of April her Captain reported that 'hull, rudder and propellers were OK but asdic (dome?) was cut off'. He considered he must have scraped a wreck. He requested 'sweeping and examination of his proposed route'. The ULTRA signal concluded: 'Route to be (as before?) and A/S precautions will be carried out'.

Early in June, 1945, there was evidence that *Ashigara* and *Kamikaze* were about to take part in transporting troops of the 48th Division from Batavia to Singapore. On the 3rd an ULTRA stated: 'CC *Ashigara* and DD *Kamikaze* departing Singapore 030900 for Batavia. This is ULTRA. Depart Batavia 070900 on troop transport mission probably to Singapore. Will act en route as target ships for training of army torpedo plane unit based at Lingga.'

It was another opportunity for an ULTRA ambush and Fife disposed his submarines accordingly. On 5 June Hezlet, in *Trenchant* on patrol off the Malayan coast, heard *Bluejack* and *Chubb* report a Japanese cruiser and a destroyer entering Batavia. He guessed that they would be returning to Singapore and asked permission to patrol the northern entrance to the Banka Strait on the east coast of Sumatra. Fife agreed reluctantly: the Strait was confined water with shoals, strong tidal currents and an Allied minefield. He would never have *ordered* a submarine to patrol there.

On the 7th *Trenchant* met HMS *Stygian* (Lt G. S. Clarabut) who agreed that Hezlet should have the 'inner berth'. Early on 8 June Hezlet received *Bluejack*'s signal that the enemy cruiser and destroyer had left Batavia, northbound, on the 7th. Soon afterwards Hezlet sighted *Kamikaze*, who had accompanied *Haguro* on her last voyage, heading up the Strait. After a brush with *Trenchant*, *Kamikaze* was distracted by *Stygian* who was the perfect 'catspaw', keeping *Kamikaze* occupied while Hezlet dealt with *Ashigara*.

Hezlet sighted *Ashigara* steaming north up the Strait just before noon on the 8th. An unexpected choice of course by the cruiser left Hezlet with a difficult shot from abaft the beam, but he fired a salvo of eight torpedoes and secured five hits. *Ashigara* vanished in a cloud of smoke and steam. As before with *Haguro*, *Kamikaze* came back to pick up survivors.

By the spring of 1945 there was only one stretch of water where Japanese ships could still move free of submarine attack – the Sea of Japan itself. In June even this last resort was penetrated, in Operation BARNEY, when 'Hydeman's Hellcats', a wolf-pack of nine submarines led by Cdr E. T. Hydeman in *Sea Dog*, passed through the Tsushima Straits on the night of 6/7 June and, in eleven days, sank twenty-seven merchant ships and the submarine *I-122*, for a total of 57,000 tons.

From then on targets dwindled so much that more submarines were devoted to life-saving than ship-sinking, providing lifeguard patrols for ditched airmen, mostly B-29 crews. But there were still a few opportunities for ULTRA. In June the Japanese had become alarmed enough about the possibility that their codes had been broken that they sent new code-books to Singapore in the submarine *I-351*. CincPac's ULTRA Bulletin for the 14th noted that 'Sub I-351 scheduled depart Sasebo about 19 June en route Singapore transporting AA ammo and cryptographic publications. Estimate will transport Avgas and other strategic materials on return trip to Japan.'

I-351 was in the news again, in the ULTRA Bulletin for 22 June: 'Enemy now using 68% avgas 32% alcohol. I-351 depart Sasebo 221400 for Singapore. May be off China Coast 28-20N at noon 25th.' *I-351* was not intercepted on that voyage but its time was running out. In July an ambush was laid. A line of seven submarines was stationed across the South China Sea.

Early on 14 July *Bluefish* (Lt Cdr G. W. Forbes), on patrol northeast of Great Natoena Island, off the coast of Borneo, received a contact report from the next submarine, *Blower*. Early on the 15th Forbes heard explosions and *Blower* said she had attacked something. An hour later Forbes identified a Japanese submarine, zigzagging on the surface, and scored two hits on it. CincPac's ULTRA Bulletin of 15 July said: 'Estimate sub reported sunk by Bluefish morning July 15th off N. W. Borneo probably I-351 returning Japan from Singapore with Avgas and other strategic materials.' That was the end of *I-351*.

ULTRA had served the submarines well. It fell to a submariner to do a service for ULTRA. One of the US submarines strategically disposed for the invasion of the Gilberts in November, 1943, was *Sculpin* (Cdr F. Connaway), on patrol between Truk and Ponape. Also in *Sculpin* was Captain John P. Cromwell, Commander, Submarine Division 43, who was on board so that he could, on orders from Admiral Lockwood, form a wolf-pack to coordinate attacks by several submarines should the Japanese fleet sally out from Truk.

On about 16 November FRUPAC decrypted a message giving the route of an important convoy passing through *Sculpin*'s area and the information was sent to her. On the 19th a Japanese ship transmitted a short-form message reporting a submarine attack in about the position where *Sculpin* should have met the convoy. Eight hours later the destroyer *Yamagumo* reported sinking a submarine in the same area. Nothing more was ever heard from *Sculpin*. The US Navy announced her loss on 30 December, 1943.

After the war it was learned from the *Sculpin* survivors who returned from Japanese prisoner-of-war camps that *Yamagumo* had forced *Sculpin* to the surface with a depth-charge attack and then sank her with gunfire. Forty-two of *Sculpin*'s crew were picked up but Cromwell chose to stay on board and ride *Sculpin* down in her last dive.

Cromwell was awarded the Congressional Medal of Honour for sacrificing his life to safeguard the secrets of the Gilberts invasion. But, as Cromwell's great friend Holmes pointed out, these were secrets which would have been of no use to the Japanese in a few days' time. The real reason, as Holmes said, was that, 'Cromwell knew too much about the intimate connection between submarine operations and radio intelligence. He chose to die to protect the ULTRA secret.'

XIV

KAMIKAZES OFF OKINAWA

IN 1945 the naval use of ULTRA in the Pacific was directed almost entirely to the war over and under the sea. Surface ship-to-ship confrontations were no more. ULTRA continued to reveal the composition, departures and sailing routes of the ever-decreasing number of Japanese convoys, the whereabouts and intentions of Japanese submarines, and the design and deployment of special attack weapons – especially kamikaze aircraft, which the Japanese began to use in large numbers in lieu of a fleet at sea.

The Third Fleet returned to Ulithi for rest and recreation on 25 January, 1945. The fleet had been at sea continuously, except for short periods, for the previous eighty-four days. They claimed to have destroyed over 7,000 Japanese aircraft, sunk over ninety Japanese warships of various kinds, and nearly 600 merchant ships of over a million tons.

At Ulithi Spruance relieved Halsey, the fleet became once more the Fifth Fleet and the Fast Carrier Task Force TF 58 again. While Kinkaid's Seventh Fleet ships (minus some Fifth Fleet ships which had been gently and tactfully disentangled by Nimitz, now based at Guam, who needed them for Iwo and Okinawa) went south with MacArthur's South-West Pacific Area force to attack islands in the southern Philippines and, ultimately, in Borneo, the Fifth Fleet sailed from Ulithi on 10 February for a series of strikes against the Japanese mainland – the first since General Doolittle's, what seemed several centuries earlier – as preliminaries to Operation DETACHMENT, the occupation of Iwo Jima.

Iwo Jima, an island in the Volcano group, 625 miles north of Saipan and 660 miles south of Tokyo, could have been taken virtually unopposed in September, 1944. Even in January, 1945, the task would not have been so difficult. But Japanese resistance in the

Philippines was so fierce (Yamashita, the army commander, and the remaining 50,000 of his troops on Luzon did not surrender until 15 August, 1945) that the assault on Iwo Jima could not be launched until 19 February. By that time the island commander, Lieutenant General Tadamichi Kuribayashi, had made Iwo into a formidable fortress, in which the natural qualities of the terrain were brilliantly allied to the defensive ingenuity and fanatical resistance of the Japanese garrison.

Iwo Jima was subjected to the heaviest, most prolonged and, ultimately, least effective air and naval bombardment of any Pacific island. Bombing raids began in August, 1944, and continued in September, October and December. Heavy cruisers bombarded late in December and early in January. The nearby islands of Chichi and Haha Jima were also pounded to prevent reinforcements being staged through them. Iwo Jima itself was bombed day and night for two weeks from 31 January, 1945. By D-Day, 19 February, an estimated 6,800 tons of bombs and 22,000 rounds of shell from 16-inch to 5-inch had landed on the island.

Unfortunately it was all to no avail. As 'Howlin' Mad' Smith said when he first saw Iwo, 'This is our toughest yet'. The labyrinth of artillery, mortar and machine-gun positions, connected by underground tunnels and passages, could not be neutralized by bombardment, no matter how heavy. They were virtually impossible to spot and were only revealed when a direct hit physically blew away the volcanic sand of the island and the protective camouflage erected by the Japanese.

For DETACHMENT five Radio Intelligence Units were embarked: in Spruance's flagship *Indianapolis*, in Mitscher's flagship *Bunker Hill* (included in TG 58.3), and in three of the four Task Group flagships *Hornet* (TG 58.1), *Yorktown* (TG 58.4) and *Enterprise* (TG 58.5, the Night Group). Royal Navy officers were also embarked, as observers, in *Bunker Hill* and *Hornet*.

The RI Units monitored Japanese air and picket boat traffic from 16 February when the first air strikes were made against targets in the Tokyo area. Enemy reaction was surprisingly light until 21 February when a large group of 'bogies' was detected on the radar screens and transmissions were heard 'with menacing signal strength'. Thirty-two aircraft from Katori in Japan, who had refuelled at Hachijo Jima, penetrated the CAP screen, hit and sank the escort carrier *Bismarck Sea* and damaged five other ships, including the carrier *Saratoga*. This was the only intervention by kamikazes at Iwo Jima.

The Japanese Navy's only contribution to the defence of Iwo Jima was made by submarines carrying 'kaiten' (meaning 'the turn towards heaven') human torpedoes. A 'kaiten' had sunk a tanker in Ulithi lagoon in November, 1944, but this was their sole success.

Decrypts had already revealed the possibility of 'kaiten' attacks on ships in the Iwo Jima area. When the main Allied bombardment of Iwo began in February the Chibaya 'kaiten' unit was formed, with the submarines *I-368*, *I-370* and *I-44* which sailed from Kure for Iwo Jima on 22 and 23 February. But *I-370* was sunk by the destroyer escort *Finnegan* off Iwo on 26 February and *I-368* by aircraft from the escort carrier *Anzio*, also off Iwo, a day later. *I-44* struggled back to Japan after being kept down by destroyers for over 48 hours and almost suffocating her crew.

After this débâcle, a second 'kaiten' unit, Kamitake, was formed, of *I-58* and *I-36*. *I-36* left Kure on 2 March but had to turn back almost at once. *I-58*, which had left a day earlier, reached Iwo Jima but was constantly harassed by anti-submarine craft and was recalled on 9 March. So ended the Japanese Navy's part at Iwo Jima.

The struggle for Iwo Jima between the US Marines and the defending Japanese became one of the legends of the Second World War. The Marines had to take the island literally yard by yard. As Iwo was only 4½ miles long by 2½ wide at its widest point, the Marines could be assisted at every point by some of the most intense, sustained and accurate naval bombardment of the war.

General Kuribayasha knew very well that Iwo Jima was sealed off from all reinforcement and he could expect no help from the Japanese Navy. But he husbanded and deployed his garrison with such skill that he inflicted on the US Marines and Navy casualties of 5,931 men killed or died of wounds and another 17,272 wounded. Of his own garrison of 22,000 men, only 216 were taken prisoner. Kuribayasha was not among them.

The airfields on the island were at once taken in hand by the Seabees (Construction Battalions) and by the end of the war some 2,400 B-29 landings had been made there, with many more long-range fighter sorties by Mustangs, who would not otherwise have had the range to accompany the B-29s to Japan. Iwo's main use therefore was as an emergency landing field for B-29s which otherwise would probably have been lost. As one B-29 pilot said, 'Whenever I land on this island, I thank God and the men who fought for it.'

Iwo Jima was declared secured on 16 March, 1945 (although, surprisingly, as many as 867 more Japanese surrendered in April and May, and isolated parties held out even longer). By that date, the battle had moved westwards where Operation ICEBERG, the invasion of Okinawa, the largest island in the Ryukyus and only 350 miles from metropolitan Japan, was under way.

TF 58 began the strategic isolation of Okinawa with strikes at airfields in Kyushu and Honshu, and at shipping in the Inland Sea, on 18 and 19 March. The Japanese retaliated with more suicide attacks. *Enterprise*, *Yorktown* and *Wasp* were all hit and *Franklin*, hit for the third time, was very badly damaged and nearly 800 of her ship's company were killed. With superb firefighting and damage control, *Franklin* survived and reached the United States.

The Ryukyus had been closed to outsiders for many years before the war and accurate intelligence about Okinawa was scanty at first. But over the months preceding ICEBERG, JICPOA accumulated a volume of intelligence information which, according to Holmes, weighed 127 tons when it was finally distributed to all units.

By March, 1945, the Japanese had nearly 6,000 aircraft assigned to the defence of the approaches to Japan, most based in Japan and Formosa, and about 4,000 of them kamikazes. The 10th Air Fleet, based in Kyushu, had some 2,000 aircraft, of which 1,300 were in training, but were to be ready for combat by 30 April.

It was believed that the Japanese had about 50,000 troops on Okinawa, but in fact it was defended by two divisions and one brigade, some 70,000 men, of the Japanese 32nd Army, under another very able field commander, Lieutenant General Mitsuru Ushijima. With additional naval and native Okinawan personnel, the total garrison was nearly 100,000 men, most of them concentrated in the southern stronghold of Shuri, the ancient capital of Okinawa.

The task of taking Okinawa was given to the US 10th Army, newly formed but with two veteran corps: the 24th (Major General John R. Hodge) had captured Leyte, and the 3rd Amphibious Marine Corps (Major General Roy S. Geiger USMC) had taken Guam and Peleliu. Its total strength was some 182,000 men, although more than half a million men were to be engaged on Okinawa before the end. Richmond Kelly Turner was in command of the Joint Expeditionary Force, which sailed from eleven different ports, from Seattle to Ulithi, and from Pearl Harbor to Noumea, in 430 troopships, which were only part of a total invasion fleet of 1,457 ships.

The Japanese had transferred their 9th Division from Okinawa to Formosa (which had indeed once been a planned Allied objective) late in 1944 and did not have enough troops to defend all the out-lying islands. On 26 March the 77th Infantry Division landed almost unopposed on the Kerama Retto, a group of small islands fifteen miles west of southern Okinawa. Some 250 suicide motorboats, which were to have been the main component of the Japanese Navy's defence of Okinawa, were captured. More importantly, the islands made an excellent logistic base, with an anchorage in the immediate operating area. Fleet tenders, oilers and repair ships of Service Squadron 10 had gratefully occupied it within four days. (By contrast, when the 77th landed on 16th April at Ie Shima, an island which had appeared deserted, not responding to any kind of stimuli from air or sea, they had to kill over 3,000 concealed Japanese before securing the airfield.)

L-Day was 1 April, Easter Sunday. Preliminary air and sea bombardments began during the five previous days of Holy Week. The Japanese struck back with more kamikaze attacks; one damaged *Indianapolis*, Spruance's flagship, so that he had to shift his flag to the battleship *New Mexico*. This was a foretaste of things to come.

For ICEBERG there were six RI units, in *Indianapolis* (transferring with Spruance to *New Mexico* and later to *Missouri*), *Bunker Hill*, *Hornet* (TG 58.1), *Enterprise* (TG 58.3), *Yorktown* (TG 58.4) and, for the first time, in the headquarters ship *Eldorado*, flagship of Admiral Turner, commanding TF 51, the Joint Expeditionary Force. There were Royal Naval observers in *Bunker Hill* and *Yorktown*.

The struggle for Okinawa was crucial for Japan and such was the desperate position the country was in that there was at times a general relaxation of communication security. The RI Units derived much intelligence which would not have been possible had the enemy adhered strictly to security regulations.

The landings on 1 April took place with unexpectedly little opposition, Ushijima having decided to conserve his strength and engage his enemy inland, where they would not have naval gunfire support. But the radio listeners around the Pacific soon picked up indications of Japanese plans to repel the invaders. The Allies had learned from previous operations that it usually took the Japanese about four days to mount a counter-attack after a landing, so L + 4 would be the danger day. An ULTRA message of 4 April reported: 'Evidence afternoon 3rd that X-Day for Kikusui No. 1 will be 5th.' A further ULTRA a day later amended: 'X-Day may be 6 rather than 5 April.'

The Japanese launched the first of ten massed kamikaze attacks in their picturesquely-named *Kikusui* or 'floating chrysanthemum' campaign, as forecast, on X Day, 6 April. The attacks began at about 3 pm and lasted intermittently for two days. Some 660 aircraft were involved, 355 of them suiciders of the *tokko tai* 'special attack force' (230 were Navy pilots and 125 Army).

The attackers lost some 380 aircraft, either crashed or shot down by fighters from TF 58 and 51 or by anti-aircraft fire, but sheer weight of numbers overwhelmed the defence. The initial blow fell upon the radar picket destroyers. *Bush* and *Calhoun* were sunk. Two ammunition supply ships were sunk in the Kerama anchorage, leaving 10th Army short of certain types of mortar ammunition for most of the campaign. In all six ships were sunk and twenty-one damaged including the carrier *Hancock*, who was knocked out of the battle line.

As the *Kikusui* aircraft were attacking the fleet, another special attack force was putting to sea. On 5 April the C-in-C Combined Fleet, Admiral Toyoda, had signalled to his fleet: 'I order the Special Sea Attack Force to carry out on Okinawa the most tragic and heroic attack of the war'. An ULTRA message of 6 April, timed at 2010, was repeated in CincPac's Bulletin for that day: 'Commander 2nd Fleet in YAMATO along with one light cruiser believed either YAHAGI or SAKAWA plus eight destroyers sortied from Bungo Channel at 061800. At 0400 (?) the 7th in Van Diemens Straits (?). At 1000 in 31-12N 128-15E. At (2200?) in 28-12N 126-(56?)E, arriving off Okinawa 080500. Nil evidence any other surface forces proceeding to Okinawa however possibility such an eventuality should not be disregarded.'

Practically all of this information had been derived from JN-25. A new basic code book for the system came into effect on 1 February, 1945. The cipher was changed on the first of each month. But by that stage of the war, Japanese ciphers were being broken at speed, even though their complexity had increased. The new cipher introduced on 1 April was solved the next day and from 3 April onwards it was read currently.

The first inkling of *Yamato*'s sortie came from a decrypt early on 6 April requesting fuel oil to be supplied at once in connection with 'the 2nd Fleet sortie'. Later that day another decrypt of a Japanese message timed at 1305 gave the exact route and schedule of the enemy surface force from Bungo Channel to Okinawa.

The Surface Special Attack Force, commanded by Vice Admiral Seiichi Ito, of the giant battleship *Yamato* (Rear Admiral Kosaku Ariga), the light cruiser *Yahagi* (Rear Admiral Keizo Komura), and the destroyers *Fuyutsuki, Suzutsuki, Isokaze, Hamakaze, Yukikaze, Asashimo, Kasumi* and *Hatsushimo* sailed from Tokuyama in the Inland

Sea at 1520 on 6 April and was sighted by a B-29. After clearing the Bungo Channel at 2000 it was sighted again and reported by the submarines *Hackleback* and *Threadfin* (both specially in position and alerted by ULTRA).

The ships, with their magazines crammed full of ammunition and with 7,000 tons of fuel embarked, all that had been allotted to the Navy for the defence of Okinawa, were sailing on a kamikaze sortie on an Homeric scale, in aid of the soldiers on Okinawa. After firing their last shells at the American fleet, the ships were to be beached and their ship's companies were to join Ushijima.

Ito's ships were shadowed by two Mariner amphibians from Kerama Retto as they rounded the southern tip of Kyushu. They were sighted, zigzagging and making frequent changes of course south-west of Kyushu, by an aircraft from *Essex* on the morning of the 7th. Turner's battleships moved out to prevent *Yamato* reaching the landing beaches, although their 16-inch would have been outranged by *Yamato*'s monster 18.1-inch guns.

But in any case TF 58's aircrews were not to be denied such a target. At 1000 TGs 58.1 and 58.3 began launching strikes of 280 aircraft, 98 of them torpedo-bombers, from a position off the Amami Gunto, some 250 miles south-east of *Yamato*. The first attack developed just after 12.30. The Japanese had chosen to send all their aircraft to attack the American fleet and *Yamato* had no air cover. Her predicament oddly resembled that of *Prince of Wales* and *Repulse* years before. Yamamoto, when asked how aircraft could possibly sink huge battleships, had replied, 'With torpedo-bombers. The fiercest serpent can be overcome by a swarm of ants.'

So it proved. The first strike hit *Yamato* with two bombs and one torpedo, sank *Hamakaze* and brought *Yahagi* to a dead stop in the water with one bomb and one torpedo hit. A second strike of 100 aircraft sank *Isokaze*, *Asashimo* and *Kasumi* and hit *Yamato* with three more bombs and nine more torpedoes.

Yamato, one of the most beautiful battleships ever built, whose very name was an ancient and sacred one for Japan herself, sank at 2.23 pm. With her went Admiral Ito and all but 269 of her company of over 2,700 men. *Yahagi* also sank after no less than twelve bomb and seven torpedo hits. The four surviving destroyers, three badly damaged, returned to Japan. The total Japanese Navy casualties were 3,665 dead. Of the 386 US aircraft taking part, ten were lost, and twelve aircrew. This Battle of the East China Sea was the Imperial Japanese Navy's last spasm of activity at sea.

Kamikaze attacks by single or small groups of aircraft took place almost every day, but the next organized *Kikusui* (again revealed beforehand by ULTRA) was by 185 aircraft on 12/13 April and included a new weapon, the Ohka, or Cherry Blossom, which was a small single-seater wooden aircraft, rocket-powered. It was in effect a piloted 4,000-lb bomb, carried to its target area under the belly of a parent bomber and released to plunge towards its target, blasting itself earthwards with its three rockets. The Allies called it *Baka* (foolish) but, with its range of twenty miles from 20,000 feet, it sank one destroyer, *Mannert L. Abele*, and damaged several other ships.

Although the *Kikusuis* suffered terrible losses, of between 60 and 90 per cent of the aircraft taking part, so that successive *Kikusui* waves contained fewer and fewer aircraft, they continued to batter the ships off Okinawa. ULTRA continued to give warnings. Current issues of the Japanese aircraft code were periodically recovered during the Okinawa campaign, enabling the RI Units to read much of the coded traffic, as well as the many messages in plain language.

But in spite of this invaluable help from radio intelligence, and in spite of radar pickets' warnings, doubled and redoubled anti-aircraft armament, extensive use of close-proximity shell fuses, ever more skilful fighter direction and ever braver and more devoted fighter CAPs, the Divine Wind, as the Americans said, kept on coming. Kamikazes hit *New Mexico*, *Maryland* and *Tennessee*, *Bunker Hill*, *Enterprise* and *Intrepid* (again) and a long list of minor warships and landing craft. By mid-May TF 58 had to be reorganized in three groups because there were no longer enough carriers for four.

South of Okinawa, off the Sakishima Gunto, the carriers of the Royal Navy were also suffering kamikaze attack. After a long period of political negotiation and some disagreements, the British Pacific Fleet had finally sailed from Manus in the Admiralty Islands on 18 March, 1945, to serve under Spruance and Nimitz.

Admiral King, no Anglophile, feared that a British fleet in the Pacific would drain away American logistical resources and insisted that the British be 'self-sufficient'. The Royal Navy did manage to assemble a motley fleet train of tankers, store and repair ships, but their performance, although a triumph of morale over *materiel*, would not have been enough without the magnificent 'can do' spirit of the Americans in the Pacific, from Nimitz downwards, who interpreted 'self-sufficiency' in an astonishingly generous way.

In intelligence the Americans were just as lavish. Nimitz ordered that British forces were to be provided with intelligence material by

JICPOA on exactly the same level as American forces. A Lieutenant Commander RN came to Pearl Harbor early in 1945 to arrange matters with JICPOA. Current intelligence was no problem, just a question of adding British ships to the distribution list. But old material was another matter. 'JICPOA had already issued 200 or 300 bulletins,' said Holmes, 'in addition to CincPac-CincPOA's weekly intelligence and maps, charts, and aerial photographs. We took the British intelligence officer into our stockroom to select what he wanted. He wanted nearly everything. When it was added up, and each item was multiplied by the number to be distributed to each unit, there were two plane-loads of intelligence material to be transported to Sydney.'

The British Pacific Fleet also had its RI Units, or 'Y' Groups, one in *King George V*, flagship of Vice Admiral Sir Bernard Rawlings who commanded the fleet at sea (the C-in-C Admiral Sir Bruce Fraser had his headquarters in Sydney), and a second in *Indomitable*, flagship of Rear Admiral Sir Philip Vian, who commanded the carrier squadron. The RI Units consisted of two officers, who were Japanese speakers, and nine intercept operators (who were trained only in hand-copying, and had no knowledge of or training in call types or idents, or in inference work).

The fleet fuelled at Ulithi and sailed for Operation ICEBERG on 23 March. Although its strength of two battleships, four carriers with 218 aircraft, four cruisers and destroyer escort was no greater than the average US task group, the British Pacific Fleet assumed the designation of a full task force, TF 57, on leaving Ulithi.

In ICEBERG, TF 57 had the unglamorous and secondary task of neutralizing by bombing and bombardment the airfields on the Sakishima Gunto, to prevent the Japanese staging reinforcement aircraft through the islands, which ran like a chain of stepping stones from Formosa to Okinawa.

Off the Sakishima Gunto, TF 57 stood no chance of glory and every chance of being attacked, and indeed all four carriers suffered kamikaze hits. They were not so heavily armed with AA guns as the American carriers and, in American eyes, 'were not able to look after themselves'. However, they had armoured flight decks which enabled them to operate aircraft within hours (once within ninety minutes) of a kamikaze strike.

TF 57's main effort was against the two islands of Ishigaki and Miyako. Intercepted signals from both islands revealed TF 57's progress in neutralizing the airfields. CincPac's Bulletin on L-Day, 1 April

(TF 57 having begun their strikes on 26 March) noted that 'Ishigaki was prominent in traffic suggesting its use as a staging point for planes based Formosa'. But by 21 April CincPac's Bulletin mentioned 'Ishigaki and Miyako again prominent although some evidence their usefulness as staging points greatly curtailed'.

In May Ishigaki was reporting a shortage of anti-aircraft ammunition and by the 8th ULTRA revealed evidence that the Japanese were planning an 'urgent transportation operation to Ishigaki soon probably from Keelung employing at least 2 sub-chasers'. There is no evidence that the operation was carried out.

Decrypts revealed details of a particular day's operations. On 9 May TF 57 launched several strikes against both islands. Miyakojima Guard Division reported to Takao Guard District and Sasebo Naval District Intelligence that, 'On May 9 a total of 57 planes [English planes] attack. At 1138 25 planes and at 1645, 21 planes made one bombing run each, chiefly against Army and Navy airfields. Others in formation of one to four planes made 4 patrols staying in air for roughly an hour. 1 direct hit on a searchlight unit wrecking 1 searchlight and 1 generator. 1 man slightly wounded.'

During that day one Corsair from *Victorious* failed to return from a strike and its pilot, Lt D. Cameron of 1834 Sqn, was captured. ULTRA soon revealed the results of his interrogation by the Japanese: 'examination of (pilot? prisoner?) of plane shot down 9 May [British F4U]. Striking Force Organization. Three standard type carriers [Victorious class?, Corsairs and Avenger planes] 3 converted carriers, 2 battleships, 12 destroyers.

'Part 2. Admiral Fraser is commander [of the task force?].

'Part 3. Sortied 28 April from Ulithi, appeared in neighborhood of Miyako 2 May.

'Part 4. Attack objective blank airfields and ammo dumps.

'Part 5. Operation of the British striking force is unskilful when compared to the American.'

During May the land battle for Okinawa fell seriously behind schedule. The further south 10th Army went the stiffer the enemy resistance. After two futile and abortive counter-offensives, Ushijima adopted a policy of attrition, to make the Americans pay for every knob and knoll of territory. Such delaying tactics, and intelligent use of mutually supporting defensive positions with interleaving arcs of fire, coupled with heavy rainfall over the whole battle front which converted the killing grounds into quagmires, brought 10th Army's offensive almost to a halt.

This stubborn Japanese resistance on land directly affected Allied losses at sea. There were not enough airfields on Okinawa to give 10th Army complete air cover, and the balance had to be made up from the carriers. TF 58 was thus forced to stay offshore, within range of an effective and suicidally inclined shore-based enemy air force, for many weeks.

Mitscher had no desire for a war of attrition. TF 58 was not designed or intended for this role and he was anxious to get away. When the *Kikusui* attacks began to dwindle, Mitscher suggested that land-based air forces, with B-29 raids from the Marianas, could now handle the situation ashore. Spruance, cautious and shrewd as ever, rejected the proposal. It was as well he did, for the kamikazes were by no means finished.

The last *Kikusui* waves, the ninth and tenth, of fifty and forty-five aircraft respectively, were launched on 3–7 and 21–22 June. By that time the flying skill of the pilots, never very high, had sunk until many of the kamikazes were being flown by raw recruits, farm labourers and university students, who could barely hold their machines in the sky, let alone navigate or take evasive action. Towards the end, when the Japanese were husbanding their aircraft for the attack they knew must come against Japan herself, the kamikazes included many obsolete trainers and slow seaplanes. The main bodies had to conform to their low speeds, which made them, too, easier to intercept. The kamikazes were shepherded, 'herded' would perhaps be a better word, by so-called 'Gestapo' aircraft, whose experienced pilots directed the kamikazes on to their targets, giving them precise radio instructions, often in plain language, which were intercepted by the RI Units.

Organized Japanese resistance on Okinawa began to crumble in June and the island was declared secured on the 21st. Ushijima committed *seppuku* (ceremonial suicide) that evening. His army were killed or taken prisoner to the last man. The kamikazes had flown 1,809 sorties and lost 930 aircraft. They sank seventeen ships and damaged 198, including twelve carriers and ten battleships.

Meanwhile, in the Singapore area, the destroyer *Kamikaze* was fast becoming the Jonah of the Japanese Navy. She had accompanied *Haguro* and *Ashigara*, both dogged by ULTRA, on their last voyages and her very presence as escort was a certain omen of disaster. Her next sailing, to take part in Operation CHI, the movement of troops from Singapore to Indochina, was revealed by an ULTRA decrypt on 12 June: 'One probable tanker escorted by destroyer *Kamikaze* and one minesweeper departed Singapore 121100 arriving north side Fukwok Islands (10-23N 103-53E) at 171200.'

Kamikaze was heard originating at least five short operational signals in the late afternoon of 15 June, suggesting air or submarine attack. In fact, she and her convoy were bombed by USAAF B-24 Liberators off the south-east coast of Malaya and the tanker, the 10,238-ton *Toho Maru*, was sunk. The indestructible *Kamikaze* escaped with minor damage and picked up two hundred of *Toho* Maru's survivors.

Kamikaze's name continued to appear in decrypts, as ULTRA followed her subsequent progress, like a kind of Japanese Flying Dutchman, around the waters of South-East Asia until the end of the war. She was mentioned in CincPac's Bulletin as late as 15 August, the day the war ended, as having with three other ships embarked one company of a Japanese landing force and taken them to Jemaka Island (2-45N 105-47E) [one of the Anambas Islands in the South China Sea] on the morning of the 12th because of a mistaken report of a landing there by 500 Blue troops from submarines on the afternoon of 10 August. She survived the war, only to run aground while carrying out repatriation duties on 7 June, 1946, near Omae Zaki, on the southern coast of Honshu. Salvage work on her was abandoned.

XV

THE SURRENDER OF JAPAN

IT only remained now to invade metropolitan Japan. On 28 June, 1945, CincPac issued a timely warning, which amounted to a restatement of policy on the use and the value of ULTRA in the final stages of the war at sea. It was from CincPac's Advance Headquarters, addressed to all holders of Crypto Channel 35-S, and it quoted from Cominch's ULTRA weekly summary: 'A recent Japanese Navy despatch reporting the failure of an operation for reinforcement of several islands north of Okinawa attributed the success of Allied operational tactics to the apparent interception of Japanese messages concerning details of the transportation involved.

'Though this message may merely represent an excuse on the part of the commander concerned, it fixes attention on the recurrent suspicion in the Japanese mind that his traffic is being read. As the war has moved closer to Japan and as Japanese offensive capabilities have greatly decreased, the emphasis in value of Ultra intelligence has gradually shifted from tactical to strategic considerations. The long-range worth to our forces of vital information currently being obtained on Japan's anti-invasion plans, military and economic means, and dispositions now far outweighs any advantage to be gained through the use of Ultra intelligence in small-scale encounters, and calls for ever closer scrutiny of operational plans primarily based on advance information derived from this source.'

By all rational parameters of measurement, Japan was now beaten, but it remained to force her rulers to admit defeat, and it would require a colossal weapon, tinged with the awe of the supernatural, to bring that about. In the meantime, the Chiefs of Staff's planners went ahead with Operation OLYMPIC, the invasion of Kyushu set for November, 1945, and for Operation CORONET, the crowning blow, the invasion of Honshu and the attack on the Tokyo plain, in the following March, 1946. With the example of the resistance the Japanese had already put up on the Pacific islands before them, the Chiefs of Staff sombrely anticipated Allied casualties of over a million for OLYMPIC alone.

Halsey had relieved Spruance as fleet commander on 27 May, 1945, while Vice Admiral J. S. McCain relieved Mitscher in command of the carriers, for the final stages of the Okinawa campaign. It was Halsey who led the Third Fleet to sea from Leyte on 1 July to begin the 'Victory Cruise' (although nobody could have guessed that at the time) for the final round of operations in the war at sea against Japan.

TF 38, deployed in three groups, had ten fleet and six light carriers, mounting 1,191 aircraft, eight battleships, nineteen cruisers and over sixty destroyers. This huge striking force began operations off the Japanese mainland on 10 July, with exploratory strikes against airfields on the Tokyo plain.

The fleet's tasks were now to reduce the Japanese naval and Army air forces; to attack strategic targets on the Japanese mainland; and to test the strength of Japanese defences in northern Honshu and in Hokkaido, which were both beyond normal reconnaissance range of aircraft from the Marianas (the areas could have been covered by B-29s from Okinawa, but the first operational B-29 sortie over Japan did not take place until the evening before the end of the war). During the coming operations the Third Fleet's tasks were amended to include the destruction of the remnants of the Japanese Navy and merchant fleet – possibly because Nimitz's staff knew that Halsey would go for Japanese shipping anyway, whether programmed or not.

TF 38 was joined on 16 July, some 300 miles east of Japan, by TF 37, the British Pacific Fleet, with four carriers and 255 aircraft, the battleship *King George V*, six cruisers and fifteen destroyers. Admiral King had once stipulated that the BPF should be at seven days' notice to join MacArthur's South-West Pacific Area, but this was long forgotten and TF 37 took up an honoured position on the right of TF 38's line.

Halsey was able to call upon a varied arsenal of weapons: air strikes with guns, bombs and torpedoes, battleship and cruiser bombardments (in which the Royal Navy ships joined), surface sweeps by cruisers and destroyers, radio deception, submarine operations, and mining by sea and air.

He also had the usual assistance of the RI Units, embarked in his flagship, the battleship *Missouri*, in McCain's flagship, the carrier *Shangri-La*, and in *Bennington* (TG 38.1), *Randolph* (TG 38.3) and

Yorktown (TG 38.4). 'Y' Groups were in *King George V*, *Indefatigable* and *Formidable*. But almost all the information they provided was negative. There was very little traffic to listen to. Opposition at sea was non-existent and surprisingly light in the air. The Japanese were once again hoarding their strength against the moment the Allies set foot on Japanese soil. In fact, TF 38's main adversary was the weather, which prevented flying operations on several days.

Halsey's strikes and bombardments ranged from Muroran in Hokkaido in the north, all down the coast of Japan to Matsuyama in Shikoku in the south, while his attendant train of large fast tankers and store ships gave him an astounding mobility which the British ships, with their own makeshift fleet train, could only ruefully admire. In the event, the British Pacific Fleet was stretched too far, and many of its ships were denied what they considered to be their proper place at the end by a shortage of fuel.

The surviving heavy ships of the Japanese Navy were all immobilized in harbour by lack of fuel and were lying, heavily camouflaged and relegated to the status of floating anti-aircraft batteries, the battleship *Nagato* at Yokosuka, and the rest at Kure, on the Inland Sea. In three days of strikes TF 38's aircraft sank or badly damaged them all, in a final revenge for Pearl Harbor: *Nagato*, the battleship *Haruna*, the hybrids *Ise* and *Hyuga*, the carriers *Amagi*, *Katsuragi*, and *Ryuho*, the cruisers *Tone*, *Aoba*, *Kitagami*, *Iwate*, *Izumo* and *Oyodo*, and many other smaller warships.

Somewhat ungenerously, the Americans excluded the British air groups from these attacks, allotting them secondary targets elsewhere on those strike days (although British aircraft did sink the carrier *Kaiyo* at Beppu). Halsey later said that he had reluctantly agreed to his staff's insistence that he should forestall any possible post-war British claim that they had delivered even the least part of the final blows which demolished the remains of Japanese sea-power.

The final blow against the US Navy was struck by Japanese submarines. *I-53* and *I-58*, of Submarine Division 15, both carrying 'kaitens', sailed from Kure on 16 July. A 'kaiten' from *I-53* hit and sank the destroyer escort *Underhill* about 250 miles east of Cape Engano, a northerly point of Luzon, on 24 July. *I-58* launched two 'kaitens' at a tanker and heard explosions but no US tanker was lost that day. But on the night of 29 July, some 300 miles north-east of the Philippines, *I-58* sighted and attacked the heavy cruiser *Indianapolis* which had carried top-secret material for the atomic bomb from San Francisco to Tinian and was then on passage from Guam to Leyte.

Indianapolis was unescorted and not zigzagging when she was hit by two torpedoes of six fired by *I-58* at 11.50 pm and sank about fifteen minutes later. Between 800 and 850 of her complement of 1,199 men survived the attack, though many were burned or wounded. At daylight they expected to be seen and picked up. But nobody came. A decrypt several days before had revealed that *I-58* was on patrol in the Philippine Sea and *I-53*'s success confirmed a submarine's presence there. But because the information came from ULTRA it had a very limited distribution. Certainly *Indianapolis*'s captain was never informed. In any case, there had been so little recent Japanese submarine activity in the Philippine Sea that the danger seems to have been discounted.

FRUPAC intercepted a signal from *I-58* that it had sunk 'a battleship of the *Idaho* Class' shortly after *Indianapolis* was torpedoed. The message was decrypted and passed to CincPac about sixteen hours after the sinking. But nobody linked the position given in *I-58*'s signal with *Indianapolis*'s position. Quite possibly nobody had those two essential bits of information.

This combination of evil circumstances was compounded by garbled radio messages, a failure to receive *Indianapolis*'s own SOS signals, the unwillingness of Army search aircraft to interfere in what they imagined was Navy business, the dismissal of *I-58*'s signal of triumph as just another of the frequent false sinking claims by the Japanese, and a general assumption by sea commands in the area that *Indianapolis* had gone somewhere else and was no business of theirs, and that everything was in order and proceeding according to routine.

The upshot was that *Indianapolis*'s absence was not noticed at Leyte, and it was three and a half days before help arrived, at 3.30 pm on 2 August. By that time nearly 500 more men had died of thirst, exposure, wounds or shark attack. Only 316 of *Indianapolis*'s people survived, including her captain, Captain C. B. McVay, who was censured by court-martial, and ordered to lose seniority (later restored to him). The politicians' handling of the whole affair caused a great deal of resentment in the US Navy. But the necessary secrecy in handling ULTRA material had undoubtedly also played a part in the tragedy.

With the news of the first atomic bomb attack on Hiroshima on 6 August, 1945, the men in the fleets metaphorically lifted their heads from the business of war to sniff, for the first time, the faint smell of possible peace. But strikes carried on even after the second bomb on Nagasaki on the 9th.

224

The Imperial Japanese Navy remained as defiant as ever, as CincPac's Bulletin for 14 August warned: 'Afternoon of 13th Commander 10th Area Fleet (Singapore Area) advised by U/K command: "All Japan placed under alert for Operation Homeland this date. This is ULTRA. The attacking enemy is impatiently trying to end the war quickly and is forcing an invasion-like offensive which is of [blank] type. Rumors are spreading about at unbelievable rate. All naval personnel must conduct themselves loyally and maintain traditions of the service. Enemy must not be permitted to take advantage of us and we must strengthen our loyalty and determination to that end. All hands will strive to increase war preparations and leave nothing undone towards overthrowing the enemy." '

Even after hostilities had been officially declared over, Halsey warned his ships to stay on their guard, because it was possible that the enemy might still attack: 'Any ex-enemy aircraft attacking the fleet,' he signalled, 'is to be shot down in a friendly manner.' It was as well he did so, for the very last kamikazes of the war made their attacks as peace was being proclaimed.

CincPac's Bulletins continued to record the steady decrease in the volume of Japanese cryptographic signal activity. It was like a wasp's nest dying at the approach of winter. On 1 September, 'less than 20 messages encrypted out of total of about 700 received.' On the 11th, 'Only one current despatch enciphered.' On the 16th, 'All traffic Japanese naval circuits 16th was in plain language. Volume of traffic continues to decline.'

On 23 September, 1945, the CincPac Bulletins themselves came to an end: 'With this despatch publication of CincPac daily Ultra bulletin ceases. Intelligence received from Ultra sources will be disseminated hereafter by special despatches in this system to appropriate addressees as occasion demands.'

With that the ULTRA war in the Pacific came to an end.

SOURCES

BOOKS:

APPLEMAN, Roy E., BURNS, James M., GUGLER, Russell H., and STEVENS, John, *Okinawa*: The Last Battle, Historical Division, Dept. of the Army, US Government, Washington DC, 1948

BALLARD, Geoffrey St. Vincent, *On Ultra Active Service*: The Story of Australia's Signals Intelligence Operations during World War II, Spectrum Publications, Richmond, Victoria, Australia, 1991

BERGAMINI, David, *Japan's Imperial Conspiracy*: How Emperor Hirohito led Japan into war against the West, Heinemann, London, 1971

CARPENTER, Dorr, and POLMAR, Norman, *Submarines of the Imperial Japanese Navy*, Conway Maritime Press, London, 1986

CARRUTHERS, Steven L., *Australia Under Siege*: Japanese Submarine Raiders 1942, Solus Books, Melbourne, 1982

DREA, Edward J., 'Ultra Intelligence and General MacArthur's Leap to Hollandia, January–April 1944', in *Intelligence and Military Operations*, edited by Michael I. Handel, Frank Cass, London, 1990

FRANK, Richard B., *Guadalcanal*, Random House, New York, 1990

GALANTIN, Admiral I.J., U.S.N.(Ret.), *Take Her Deep!*: A Submarine Against Japan in World War II, Unwin Hyman, London, 1988

HANDEL, Michael I., *War Strategy and Intelligence*, Frank Cass, London, 1989

HERBIG, Katherine L., 'American Strategic Deception in the Pacific, 1942–44', in *Strategic and Operational Deception in the Second World War*, edited by Michael I. Handel, Frank Cass, London, 1987

HOLMES, W.J., *Double-edged Secrets*: U.S. Naval Intelligence Operations in the Pacific during World War II, USNI, Annapolis,

Maryland, 1979

Japanese Naval Vessels of World War Two: as seen by U.S. Naval Intelligence, Arms and Armour Press, Poole, Dorset, 1987 (first published by US Division of Naval Intelligence, 1942–44)

KAHN, David, *The Codebreakers:* The Story of Secret Writing, Macmillan, New York, 1967.

KURZMAN, Dan, *Fatal Voyage*: The Sinking of the USS *Indianapolis*, Pocket Books, New York, 1990

LAYTON, Rear Admiral Edwin T., with PINEAU, Captain Roger, U.S.N.R. (Ret.) and COSTELLO, John, *'And I Was There'*; Pearl Harbor and Midway – Breaking the Secrets, William Morrow, New York, 1985

LECH, Raymond B., *All The Drowned Sailors* (USS *Indianapolis*), Military Heritage Press, New York, 1982

LEWIN, Ronald, *The Other Ultra*: Codes, Ciphers and the Defeat of Japan, Hutchinson, London, 1982

LUNDSTROM, John B., *The First South Pacific Campaign*: Pacific Fleet Strategy December 1941–June 1942, Naval Institute Press, Annapolis, Maryland, 1976

MARDER, Arthur J., JACOBSEN, Mark, and HORSFIELD, John, *Old Friends New Enemies*: The Royal Navy and the Imperial Japanese Navy, Volume II: The Pacific War 1942–1945, Oxford University Press, 1990

MILLOT, Bernard, *Divine Thunder*: The Life and Death of the Kamikazes, Macdonald, London, 1971

MINSHALL, Merlin, *Guilt Edged*, Bachman and Turner, London, 1975

MOCHITSURA HASHIMOTO, *Sunk*: The Story of the Japanese Submarine Fleet 1942–1945, Panther Books, London, 1954

MORISON, Samuel Eliot, *History of United States Naval Operations in World War II*

Vol.III: *The Rising Sun in the Pacific, 1931–April 1942*. Oxford University Press, 1948

Vol.IV: *Coral Sea, Midway and Submarine Actions, May 1942–August 1942*, Oxford University Press, 1949

Vol.V: *The Struggle for Guadalcanal, August 1942–February 1943*, Oxford University Press, 1949

Vol.VI: *Breaking the Bismarcks Barrier, 22 July 1942–1 May 1944*, Oxford University Press, 1950

Vol.VII: *Aleutians, Gilberts and Marshalls, June 1942–April 1944*, Little, Brown & Company, Boston, 1951

Vol.VIII: *New Guinea and the Marianas, March 1944–August 1944*, Oxford University Press, 1953

Vol. XII: *Leyte, June 1944–January 1945*, Little, Brown & Company, Boston, 1958

Vol. XIII: *The Liberation of the Philippines: Luzon, Mindanao, the Visayas, 1944–1945*, Oxford University Press, 1959

Vol. XIV: *Victory in the Pacific, 1945*, Little, Brown & Company, Boston, 1960

Operational History of Japanese Naval Communications: December 1941–August 1945, Aegean Press, Laguna Hills, California, USA, 1985

PINEAU, Roger, 'Captain Joseph Rochefort US Navy', in *Men of War*: Great Naval Leaders of World War II, edited by Stephen Howarth, Weidenfeld and Nicolson, London, 1992

POTTER, E.B., *Admiral Arleigh Burke*, Random House, New York, 1990

Bull Halsey, US Naval Institute, Annapolis, Maryland, (Rev. Ed.) 1988

Nimitz, US Naval Institute Press, Annapolis, Maryland, 1976

POTTER, John Deane, *Admiral of the Pacific: The Life of Yamamoto*, Heinemann, London 1965

ROSCOE, Theodore, *United States Destroyer Operations in World War II*, Naval Institute Press, Annapolis, Maryland, 1953

United States Submarine Operations in World War II, Naval Institute Press, Annapolis, Maryland, 1949

RUSBRIDGER, James, and NAVE, Eric, *Betrayal at Pearl Harbor*: How Churchill Lured Roosevelt into War, Michael O'Mara Books, London, 1991

SHIZUO, Fukui, Lt Cdr., *The Japanese Navy at the End of WW2*, We, Inc., Old Greenwich, Conn. 1947 (Facsimile reprint, United States Naval Institute, Annapolis, Maryland, 1991)

SPURR, Russell, *A Glorious Way to Die*: The Kamikaze Mission of the Battleship Yamato, April 1945, Sidgwick & Jackson, London, 1982

STRIPP, Alan, *Codebreaker in the Far East*, Frank Cass, London, 1989

WINTON, John, *Convoy*: The Defence of Sea Trade 1890–1990, Michael Joseph, London, 1983

Sink the Haguro!: The Last Destroyer Action of the Second World War, Seeley, Service & Co., London, 1979

The Forgotten Fleet, Michael Joseph, London, 1969

War in the Pacific: Pearl Harbor to Tokyo Bay, Sidgwick & Jackson, London, 1978
ZENJI ORITA, and HARRINGTON, Joseph D., *I-Boat Captain*, Major Books, Canoga Park, Calif., 1976

LETTERS:

DENHAM, Hugh, Letter of 23 November 1991
HANSON, Colin, Letters of 16 October, 7 November 1991, 27 January, 10 February 1992
HEZLET, Vice Admiral Sir Arthur, Letter of 3 February 1992
JAYNES, Vic, Letter of 25 October 1991
SEARLE, Rear Admiral Malcolm, Letter of 21 May 1990
STEVENS, Lt Cdr David, Letters of 27 November 1991, 14 January 1992

MAGAZINE ARTICLES:

BALL, Desmond J., 'Allied Intelligence Cooperation Involving Australia During World War II', *Australian Outlook*, Vol. 32 No. 3, December 1978
BOYD, Carl, 'American Naval Intelligence of Japanese Submarine Operations Early in the Pacific War', *Journal of Military History 53*, April 1989
COCHRAN, Alexander S., Jr., 'MAGIC, ULTRA and the Second World War: Literature, Sources, and Outlook', *Military Affairs*, Vol. XLVI, No.2, April 1982
COLWELL, Rear Admiral Robert N., USNR (Ret.), 'Intelligence and the Okinawa Battle', *Naval War Review*, Vol.XXXVIII, No.2 March/April 1985
DEUTSCH, Harold C., 'Clients of ULTRA: American Captains', *Parameter*, Vol.XV No.2, Summer 1985
DREA, Edward J., 'Ultra and the American War Against Japan: A Note on Sources', *Intelligence and National Security*, Vol.3, No.1, January 1988
GOREN, Dina, 'Communication Intelligence and the Freedom of the Press. The Chicago Tribune's Battle of Midway Dispatch and the Breaking of the Japanese Naval Code', *Journal of Contemporary History*, Vol.16 (1981)

HORNER, David, 'Australia and Allied Intelligence in the Pacific in the Second World War', The Australian National University, Research School of Pacific Studies, Department of International Relations, Work-in-Progress Seminar, 2 October 1980

HORNER, D.M., 'Special Intelligence in the South-West Pacific Area in World War II', *Australian Outlook*, Vol.32 No.3 December 1978

LAYTON, Rear Admiral E.T., 'America Deciphered Our Code', *US Naval Institute Proceedings*, Vol.105, June 1979

MACPHERSON, B. Nelson, 'The Compromise of US Naval Cryptanalysis after the Battle of Midway', *Intelligence and National Security*, Vol.11, April 1987

MASATAKA CHIHAYA, 'The Withdrawal from Kiska', No.7 in The Japanese Navy in World War II: An anthology of articles by former officers of the Imperial Japanese Navy and Air Defense Force, originally published in the US Naval Institute Proceedings, 1969

OTHER

FRANCIS, Lt Cdr S.W., 'History of the Special Intelligence Organisation in the Far East for the Period of the War September 1939 to August 1945 (Work of the Far East Combined Bureau), May 1979

LONGRIGG, Paul, 'HMS *Anderson* & Far Eastern Direction-Finding Network in World War II', 29 December 1977

MOUNTBATTEN OF BURMA, 'Secret Supplement' to Report to the Combined Chiefs of Staff, 30 July 1947, New Delhi, 1 February 1948

ROCHEFORT, Captain Joseph J., USN, 'Oral History', from interviews of 14 August, 21 September, 5 October and 6 December 1969, in 'The Reminiscences of Captain Joseph J. Rochefort US Navy Ret'd', US Naval Institute, Annapolis, Maryland, 1983

PRO DOCUMENTS

ADM 199/426 Eastern Command, War Diaries
/549 German/Japanese Blockade Running
/643 C-in-C Eastern Fleet, War Diaries
/1090 Eastern Fleet Communications Orders
/1185 C-in-C Eastern Fleet, War Diaries
/1388 Eastern Fleet War Diaries
/1427A Admiral Layton Papers
ADM 205/42 First Sea Lord's papers, Letter of 21/6/44 from Somerville to Cunningham on Sigint
ADM 223/22 Disposition of Japanese Fleet OIC/SI/J 3-175
/23 Japanese Intelligence Summaries OIC/SIJ 176-314
/38 Operations THWART and SLEUTH
/52 Opnav Ultra Bulletins, Japanese War, 1–23 August 1945
/53 Opnav Ultra Bulletins, Japanese War, October 1943–September 1944
/54 Opnav Ultra Bulletins, Japanese War, 1 October 1944–24 September 1945
/57 Operation TRANSOM: Attack by carrier-borne aircraft on Japanese base, Surabaya, Java, May 1944
/259 Operations of Japanese fleet in the Indian Ocean, April 1942
/261 OIC Summaries
/462 Military Attaché, Chungking, Signale
WO 193/920 Director of Military Operations, Collation Files, Intelligence Organisation in the Far East, 6 January–18 January, 1941

NSA/CSS Cryptologic Documents consulted in the National Archives and Records Administration (NARA), Military Archives Division, Modern Military Headquarters Branch, Record Group 457, Washington DC:
SRH: Special Research Histories
SRMD: Discrete Records of Historical Cryptologic Import; Joint Service and /or US Government Cryptologic Agencies
SRMN: Discrete Records of Historical Cryptologic Import: US Navy
SRN: Individual Translations: Japanese Navy Messages
SRNA: Individual Translations: Japanese Naval Attaché Messages
SRNM: Miscellaneous Records: Japanese Navy Communications
SRNS: Summaries: Japanese Naval Radio Intelligence

C.I.:   Communications Intelligence
R.I.:   Radio Intelligence
SRH–011   The role of C.I. in Submarine Warfare in the Pacific, Vol.I Jan.1943–Oct.1943, Vol.VIII
SRH–012   The role of R.I. in the American–Japanese Naval War. (4 vols), Aug. 1941–Sept.1942
  Vol I Coral Sea and Midway
  Vol II Aleutians
  Vol III Guadalcanal and Savo Island
  Vol IV Eastern Solomons
SRH–019   Blockade Running between Europe and the Far East by Submarines 1942–1944
SRH–020   Narrative Combat Intelligence Center JICPOA [Joint Intelligence Centre Pacific Ocean Area]
SRH–027   MAGIC Background of Pearl Harbor
SRH–036   R.I. in WWII Tactical Operations in the Pacific, Jan. 1943
SRH–056   Preliminary Report to Pacific Order of Battle Conference, 15 Aug. 1945
SRH–059   Selected Examples of Commendations and Related Correspondence Highlighting the Achievements of Value of U.S. Signals Intelligence during World War II
SRH–063   Japanese Surface and Air Operations, 1–31 Jan. 1942
SRH–064   Japanese Submarine Operations, 23–25 Jan. 1942
SRH–065   Japanese Surface and Air Operations, 1 Feb. 1942–31 Mar.1942
SRH–066   Examples of Intelligence obtained from Cryptanalysis, 1 Aug. 1946
SRH–081   Information from Captain George W. Linn USNR Ret.
SRH–097   Proceedings of Pacific Order of Battle Conference, 3–19 Jul. 1944
SRH–098   Report of Pacific Order of Battle Conference, 15–18 Aug.1945
SRH–101   Estimated Disposition of Japanese Fleet Naval Aircraft and Merchant Shipping, 13 Aug. 1944
SRH–102   Identifications Locations and Command Functions of Significant Japanese Army Navy Personnel
SRH–103   Suicide Attack Squadron Organization, Jul.1945
SRH–104   Enemy Combat Ship Losses
SRH–105   Japanese Swept Channels and Sunken Vessels as Indicated in Ultra

232

Territory, Australia, 23 Mar. 1943–21 Sep. 45

SRH–317 Mobile Radio Intelligence Unit Pacific

SRH–324 U.S. Navy Pacific Ocean Mobile Radio Intell Units Related Correspondence

SRH–326 U.S. Naval Radio Station, Libugon, Guam, 1926–1944

SRH–352 U.S. Naval Radio Station, Dutch Harbor, Unalaska Island, Alaska

SRH–355 Naval Security Group History to World War II

SRH–403 Papers of Rear Admiral J. N. Wenger USN

SRMD–012 Enemy Combat Ship Losses, Jan. 1944–Jul. 1945

SRMD–013 Japanese Merchant Ship Losses, Dec. 1941–Apr.1944

SRMN–002 Convoy Routes of Japanese Merchant Tanker and Combatant Ships in the Pacific Area, Dec. 1943–Oct. 1944

SRMN–004 OP20G Fleet of CincPac Intelligence Bulletins, 16 Mar.–1 Jun.1942

SRMN–005 OP20G File of Memoranda and Reports relating to the Battle of Midway

SRMN–006 Summaries/Translations of Japanese Messages, Feb.–Dec. 1942

SRMN–008 CINCPAC and COMFOURTEEN CI Bulletins/Radio Digests, 1 Mar.–31 Dec. 1942

SRMN–009 CINCAP Fleet Intelligence Summaries, 22 Jun.1942–8 May 1943

SRMN–013 Commander in Chief, Pacific Intell. Bulletins Nos. 78–666, 1 Jun. 1942–23 Sep. 1945

SRMN–014 FRUPAC 'GI Manual', 3 Feb. 1944

SRMN–016 U.S. Navy COMINCH, F22 File of Intelligence & Liaison, Pacific Area (BESAW) 10 Sep.1943–21 Nov. 1945

SRMN–020 Estimate of Enemy Strength in the Carolines–Marianas and Adjacent Areas, 20 Mar.–31 Jun. 1944

SRMN–021 Estimate of Enemy Strength in the Marshalls, Gilberts and Adjacent Areas, 6 Sep.–27 Dec. 1943

SRMN–024 Enemy Reaction to Nansei Shoto and Formosa Air Strikes (Special Report), 20 Oct. 1944

SRMN–025 Post War Summaries of Status of Japanese Naval Vessels (Sunk and Afloat), Nov. 1945

SRMN–026 Estimate of Empire Approaches and Combat Air Strength, 20 Dec. 1944

SRMN–027 Estimated Disposition of Japanese Fleet, Aircraft, Merchant Shipping and Economic Notes 2 Dec.1944–3 Aug. 1945

SRMN–028   Reports of the West Coast HF/DF Strategical Net, 1 Jul.1942–13 Aug. 1943

SRMN–039   COMINCH Pacific Strategic Intelligence Section File, May 1944–Dec. 1945

SRMN–042   COMINCH File: Anti-Submarine Warfare Actions against Japanese Submarines, 12 Sep.1944–25 Oct. 1945

SRMN–044   COMINCH File: Weekly Reports of Estimated Locations of Japanese Fleet Units, 1 Sep. 1942–9 Aug. 1945

SRMN–045   COMINCH File: Estimates of Japanese Air Strength, 5 Jan.1942–31 Dec. 1945

SRMN–050   Japanese Comint Reports as noted by U.S. Navy Intercept, 21 Jan.–6 Jun. 1944 OP20GI

SRN–01/125093   Translation of Japanese Navy Messages, Japanese Naval Force

SRN–125094/129615   Japanese Navy Messages

SRN–129616/133367   Translation of Japanese Navy Messages, Japanese Naval Forces, 5 Dec. 1941–25 Mar. 1942

SRN–133368/165038   Translation of Japanese Naval Forces, WWII CincPac, 19 Dec. 1942–31 Dec. 1943

SRN–165039/290908   Translation of Japanese Naval Forces, WWII CincPac

SRNA–001/5324   Translation of Japanese Naval Attaché Messages, WWII

SRNM–001/1292   Miscellaneous Records pertaining to Japanese Naval Communications WWII, 13 Mar. 1942–4 Jun. 1942

SRNS–001/1289   Japanese Naval Radio Intelligence Summaries, 1942–1946

SRNS–1290/1458   Summaries of Japanese Warship/Fleet/Aircraft Locations and Intentions, 1942–1945

SRNS–1459/1516   Declassified Traffic Intell. Summaries of Japan Naval Forces, 1942–1946

SRNS–1517   Fleet Radio Unit Melbourne (7th Fleet) Daily Digests, 20 Mar.1942–31 Oct. 1944

SRNS–1518   Fleet Radio Unit Melbourne (7th Fleet) Out/In Messages, Mar. 1942–Mar. 1944

SRR–001–44326   Japanese Water Transport Translations

INDEX

239

240

241

242

245

247